OCEAN GLADIATOR

Battles beneath the ocean

Mark Ellyatt

Emily Eight Publications Ltd.
London

This paperback edition first published in 2005 by
Emily Eight Publications Ltd.
P.O.BOX 576
Edgware,
HA8 4DH.

A CIP catalogue record for this book is available from the
British Library

ISBN: 978-0-9551544-0-9

Printed and bound in Great Britain by
Antony Rowe Ltd., Chippenham, Wiltshire

*Dedicated to the safety divers and boat crews who gave their time to support my follies –
hoping for the best, prepared for the worst.*

The stories in this book follow actual events very closely. Some names of people and places have been altered to protect certain sensitive dispositions.

Readers new or alien to scuba diving may wish to review the glossary section at the back to learn the meaning of any slang or technical detail used.

Many of the stories use either metres or feet interchangeably for quantifying depth. This was done to allow the reader some conversion practise and gain a better overall understanding of measurement - whether they are defenders of Imperialism *or* Metrication.

There are approximately 3.3 feet to 1 metre. If you know a NASA official – pass this information on. It could save United States taxpayers a fortune.

Enjoy...

Mark Ellyatt

Journeys below the waves take many forms. For most divers Scuba Diving is simply a relaxing way to spend time on holiday. Few things are more pleasant than swimming above a tropical reef, gazing at exotic and colourful fish. The majority of divers never venture deep, just five metres below the surface, and a stones throw from a tropical resort paradise is more than enough.

For others, each journey below the surface has to be a challenge - man versus the ocean. Whether diving on mysterious shipwrecks swept with dark and icy currents, or plunging deeper than anyone has ever done before, the rewards are not financial but give a satisfaction from success that's almost tangible.

Dives beyond the accepted norms of fun or safe *recreational* diving are becoming ever more popular. Scuba diving *off-piste* like this is called Technical Diving. Mark Ellyatt has been an instructor in this exciting facet of scuba diving for almost 12 years. He feels that to be a credible trainer of such an extreme discipline of a demanding sport, technical instructors should personally attempt to push the envelope as often as possible, allowing them to teach from actual experience.

After experiencing a shaky start at the hands of the diving industry's typical *Tropical Cowboys,* Mark shares his adventures of deep diving throughout many of the planets favourite diving destinations, from Mexico to the Philippines. With a sometimes caustic humour he tries to explain the attraction of deep scuba diving by recalling some of the most challenging dives ever completed.

There are no training texts explaining how to be a successful extreme technical diver. Only time invested in building experience and continuously dissecting the exploits of others can ensure an acceptable outcome for anyone planning a duel with the deep.

Dive Safe...Dive Educated

OCEAN GLADIATOR

Battles beneath the ocean

Chapters Within:

PAGE

Chapter 1: All At Sea

I thought scuba would be exciting, but drifting in the choppy seas midway between Cancun and Cozumel was more seasick and sunburn than adrenaline packed adventure. I started my diving course just one day earlier and already I was going to end up as a shark snack. Yesterday was spent mostly filling out forms and trying on equipment to fill time while we waited for the instructor to arrive. There were six others in the group - five from the States or Canada, I guessed from the accents, plus myself. When she did turn up, Instructor Karen introduced herself and made some excuses for the delay. By way of apology she offered us the chance to complete the course in two days instead of three, getting us back on schedule. Adding there would be no need for practice sessions in a swimming pool, or time wasted in classrooms, this was going to be a fast track scuba course for quick learners. We all agreed that this sounded like us. Karen said that despite being so quick, it was perfectly safe - this was in fact the way the whole world learned to dive, apparently. Our first session began straight from the shore, with underwater skills such as clearing water from our masks and sharing our air supplies discussed via frantic shouting as we bobbed up and down in the heavy surf.

The looks on my fellow novice divers faces as we slipped beneath the ocean for the first time were mostly of agony. Karen the instructor kept touching her nose and squealing loudly through her breathing regulator as everybody headed for the bottom. Some of the group mimicked the nose pointing, I could not see how this would help. Feeling no pain, I just dropped down to the seabed and watched. I think the rest of the group were having problems clearing their ears from the effects of the pressure. The Instructor was gesturing to me frantically from above. She seemed to be actually pulling the daisy chain of divers down with her. All these grown men were even holding hands with each other. Most of the group were kicking their flippers like they were riding bicycles and using their free arm in a breast stroke swimming style. Some clearly looked as if they would rather go back up than down.

I looked up at this gaggle being dragged down towards me with amazement. It looked like some of the guys were experiencing their first day at school, they definitely didn't want to let go of mum's hand now. I remember thinking scuba diving must be like learning to use contact lenses or giving birth - it can be quite messy at the beginning and potentially embarrassing, but hopefully worth persevering with. After about ten minutes of kneeling on the sand, watching the antics above me, Instructor Karen started giving me the thumbs up sign, I felt fine and returned the same signal. This thumb's up signal was repeated many times, and I did it back as often as I could. She let the other divers go and they bobbed straight back up to the surface. Karen started to swim down towards me. Thinking it would just be the two of us going diving, I started to swim down the nearby slope. The others in the group seemed happier floundering at the surface, some looked like they were treading grapes. I kicked my flippers up and down as fast as I could. I was creating quite a dust storm behind me, clearly startling some kind of grey flat fish. Suddenly, something grabbed me from behind, stopping me in my tracks. I recognised Instructor Karen's arm as it jabbed out from behind my head and quickly started to inflate my buoyancy jacket. All the extra air affected my buoyancy and within seconds I shot to the surface resembling a swollen puffer fish. Elated that my first dive was such a success, I thanked the instructor for the experience. She seemed lost for words and just shook her head. I imagine that these special moments were just the reward she sought, seeing land lubbers like me taking their first deep breaths underwater. I mentioned that the experience left me quite speechless, Karen looked around at some of my fellow aquanauts in the group, some of which were bleeding from the nose, she just muttered in agreement "truly amazing", continuing to shake her head.

Dive two of the course would be less threatening for me than the rest, as I was the only one in our group that dived properly the day before. I prepared for the next dive with excitement and apprehension, my girlfriend Clare lent me her diving book and I studied it all that night. In the morning two of the group decided that scuba diving was not for them, the instructor heartily agreed with their wise decision. Our group of six had dwindled to four now, plus Karen, our patient mentor. The waves from yesterday had abated and we all swam out into the blue azure of the Caribbean Sea.

We swam over a reef in 20 feet of water. Everybody saw the turtle and the Barracuda reef shark. We learned that the thumbs up from the instructor meant that it was time to go back to the surface and not "I'm fine too, thanks". After 20 minutes or so we all agreed to ascend, as now two of the group were sharing air as one had run out. I had the surfacing skill practiced now and could ascend effortlessly by pressing the "up button" on my buoyancy vest. Although I had actually left the seabed last, I quickly caught up and ended up on the surface even BEFORE my instructor. I was grinning from ear to ear, as now this was all too easy. Karen reminded me to go the surface slower as this kept the group closer together. I hoped that Dive three would as good as number two.

That afternoon, we boarded a boat with at least 30 other divers. Many divers were talking about dive tables and their duels with the deep. I sat and listened to a knowledgeable looking chap who explained that this would be a drift dive and that the currents today would be very strong and exciting. This sounded excellent to me, though my Instructor Karen said that this guy was full of crap and that the current would, in fact, be quite mild. The sea was choppy and the wind was making the tops of some of the waves quite white. The two hour boat ride took its toll on many and some faces were looking as green as the sea...mine included.

About 15 minutes from the dive site I started to be sick. I was sick as secretly as possible, but after two mouthfuls of sick swallowed back down, the next one erupted like a geyser from hell. It ended up in the equipment bag of the loudmouth man, who now looked as nauseous as me. I looked up through my streaming eyes and offered a nod of reparation to the stranger. He just swallowed and closed his eyes quickly. A second later his eyes were wide like saucers and he was sick. I was getting the stare of the seasick brethren from all corners of the boat. This look is one of total abandonment and acceptance of any situation. Many would have given anything to get of this boat now. Someone upwind was sick. Luckily the sea spray in the air concealed most of it, but it was best to keep your mouth shut just in case. Nausea is the worst feeling, it's a wonder why people get on boats at all. When you get seasick it can be enough to never visit water deeper than a bathtub again. For the worst afflicted, even a trip on an escalator can trigger the telltale yawning and salivating feeling. Such people would never contemplate a trip to Venice much less a Nile cruise. Today I was one of these retching wretched, hurling up my lunch everywhere.

The captain rang a bell to tell us it was dive time. I was being sick properly now, two or three times a minute at least. Karen the consummate dive professional asked me to get ready to dive. She added that as soon as I got under the water I would feel brand new, and that the boat was the last place I needed to be. Quite compassionately Karen intimated that those who didn't dive would have to pay again to complete the diving course, as it was our own faults we were sick - she did tell us to look at the horizon after all, and the seasick tablets she was selling were only a dollar each. These soothing words were all I needed to put my equipment on.

Dropping down the seventy to eighty feet to the bottom was fairly eventful. I learnt how to puke underwater many times. All around me, yellow tailed snapper fish snapped at my breakfast. I saw my fellow adventurers cart wheeling along the seabed, and watching my somersaulting buddies turned my stomach even faster until it felt like the spinning drum of a washing machine. I heard a pinging noise and it sounded pretty frantic. Instructor Karen was using her tank banger (a large metal nut on a loop of elastic) to signal everyone. She used this lot yesterday to get people's attention. It was her signal for us to look at a fish, or just to wake up!

The current underwater was moving along at breakneck speed. The rocks and reefs below skipped past me like a set of rapids. I wanted to stop, but as I planted my flippers in the boulders I was flung over and over again. My vomiting had turned into a predictable routine, and now the potentially jamming lumps had turned into a nasty green liquid. This meant I didn't have to take my breathing regulator out in time to the retching. This skill would prove to be very useful in twelve years time.

I got a handhold eventually, and managed to stop my gymnastic twirls. I waited on the bottom watching other divers being whisked off by the current. A minute later I was alone, the distant tank banging now a memory as distracting as a watch ticking. I waited for some time, my nausea slowly lifted just as Karen had said it would. I guess Instructors had to know all this stuff.

Scuba diving was proving very challenging to say the least. I decided that I could take it or leave it really. If I wanted to feel this sick and helpless, I would rather not have to pay for the privilege. My first two training dives were lucky escapes, culminating in this very unpleasant *regurgatory purgatory* experience. Could it get any worse? I only wanted to learn to scuba dive properly because of my girlfriend Clare. She had got certified a couple of weeks prior to me - throughout the course I got a running commentary as she raved about the turtles and dolphins in crystal clear Caribbean seas. I had only seen rough seas, no dolphins, and my life flash before me several times. The only fish life I saw were the yellow snappers that voraciously pecked at my breakfast, freshly ejected from the pit of my stomach.

Prior to Mexico, we sought tuition at our local diving club in North London. We eagerly endured all the marathon swimming bouts, the constant insults from our megaphone-touting instructor who dripped with clipboards and binoculars. We mastered the club's scuba equipment, most of it clearly used during hull inspections of Noah's Ark. We relished our evenings of paddling through balls of hair and soggy sticking plasters, duelling with ravenous cracked pool tiles. Without notice, the local council ended our dream. The sports centre was closed down by health inspectors, as virtually every scuba session ended in a bout of gastroenteritis for all concerned. We decided to wait to get some training in sunnier climes from a more professional outfit. My current perilous underwater situation was the fruit spawned from that naïve decision. During the next fourteen years, and 3000 dives later, I'm reminded virtually every day that 'professional' and 'scuba instructor' are mutually exclusive terms.

Remember...I'm still underwater at this point, alone and getting low on my air supply. It was time to return to the sunlight 80 feet above me. Less than a minute later, I threw my mask off and gasped some fresh air. I was expecting to see the bucking bronco dive boat nearby. To my disbelief, the boat was nowhere to be seen and I could not see a soul anywhere. I span around a few times to see what was on the horizon. In the distance was the Cozumel coastline, I couldn't see where we had come from. But I did notice a few hundred yards away, an orange tube floating and decided to swim towards it. I remembered the orange tube from a picture in the diving manual, it looked like a divers signalling *sausage*. This orange balloon seemed to be moving away from me, but twenty minutes later I caught up with it. Thankfully I'd met up with two others that had also missed the bus home. Karen, my instructor, was one of them and the other was an inconsolable lady from Hawaii. As the hours passed, our spirits dropped. The rawness of sunburn on our faces overtook the feeling of nausea. We twisted around at every shark sighting, but it was always a false alarm. This diving course was pretty much atrocious, and now I was going to be lost at sea, this icing on the cake tasted very bitter.

I don't know how many hours we waited, but being lost at sea does teach you to be patient. The first 30 minutes are hardest, the next 2 hours seem to fly by really, it's important not to look at the time. Without a time frame, it's easy to lose track of the hours and this kept the wolf of panic further from our doors.

We didn't say too much at all to each other. Karen asked if we were okay on the hour, every hour, and the other woman just whimpered a lot. The dive boat did eventually come back. Apparently they noticed the equipment missing from the rental stock firstly, and then noticed that instructor Karen was on the earlier boat roster. Thankfully her name was not added in pencil. It was a tense three hours back to the dive centre. Again, nothing was said the whole time. It was all a bit surreal, the staff at the dive shop laughed and joked like it was just an everyday occurrence. It did occur to me that perhaps this was, just an everyday occurrence at this dive centre. We were supposed to do another dive that afternoon, to complete our training. I didn't really fancy another round and was relieved when Karen said we should postpone it as it had been a long day. The instructor never showed for work the next day. I signed some paperwork and was refunded a few dollars for the course not being finished properly. My diver's certification card was sent to me in the post, but I didn't use it again for 12 months.

A holiday in Barbados was my next chance to match my poorly applied diving instruction against the might of the ocean. I walked into a dive centre, imaginatively called *The Dive Shop*. I showed them my valid-for-life diving card. This piece of laminated cardboard allowed me to dive at any open water dive site without supervision, as long as I was accompanied by a buddy with at least similar experience - I hoped that this would not be the case today. I mentioned that my last dive was to eighty feet and that I was a bit rusty. I added that *seized* was a better description. Within an hour we were off, wedged in a small open speed boat bouncing along at 30 knots towards the wreck *Stavronikita*. The dive guide was also the boat captain. He shouted some instructions but his voice was no match for the din of the outboard motor. The wreck sat upright in one hundred and thirty feet of water. It was still intact and was apparently safe for all divers. The driver muttered that we had arrived at the position, and without another word, slipped over the side. I introduced myself to my apparent dive partner for today. She had a look resembling a rabbit caught in the headlights. It turned out that Anna hailed from Norway and had just completed her diving course, the day before. This was her first dive without an instructor. It reassured her to learn that I had finished my course the previous year. If she found that piece of information comforting, we were indeed in trouble! What reassured *me* was our proximity to shore and that the sea was calm. I neither felt seasick nor anxious, and if the dive boat mysteriously sank or was impounded by the authorities for its un-seaworthy appearance, I could easily manage the swim back to terra-firma. We helped each other on with our equipment and Anna reminded me of the equipment checks. She rolled over the side backwards. I thought that technique was a little advanced, so attempted to stand up and just leap over the side. After my ungainly entrance we were ready for action.

Dropping back down under water after so long felt very strange. But the visibility underwater went on forever and I was overwhelmed by the electrifying blue and tranquillity of it all. The grey hull of the shipwreck came into view just below the surface. The huge Greek freighter teemed with fish of all shapes and sizes. I felt weightless and without a care. The dive guide reappeared now and gestured that we should drop inside one of the holds of the ship. I swam over to this black rectangular area and the three of us dropped inside. I signalled to my buddy, she seemed to be enjoying things as much as myself. As we descended into the vast hold, it got quite dark. Our dive guide swam ahead to point out a hole in the side of the ship that led outside. The swim through was fantastic and for the first time I felt like a proper diver. Our underwater sheep dog then turned downwards to the seabed and we both followed without question. I checked my depth gauge and was amazed to see we had reached one hundred and twenty feet. I saw a shoal of big silver fish and turned around to Anna to point them out. She looked in the right direction, but at the same moment a look of horror spread across her face as the breathing regulator fell from her mouth. The soft rubber mouthpiece that you bite on to keep the equipment in your mouth was still between her teeth but the regulator and hose piece were missing. The cable tie that secured the two pieces had obviously fallen off, it was just a matter of time until a drama ensued.

Anna pounced on me like a cat on a mouse, grabbing the breathing regulator from my own mouth. I reached down and unclipped the spare regulator that dangled from my buoyancy jacket. I put the regulator in my mouth and felt relieved and pleased that we had fixed the problem ourselves. Scuba diving is apparently as dangerous as ten-pin bowling, a fact I had read several times. This little gem probably helps the insurance underwriters sleep soundly at night, but it was no consolation when a split second later my buddy and I ran out of air, one hundred feet below the surface. I learned afterwards from the comical dive guide that the diving equipment used for customer rental goes through a schedule of maintenance that should attract anyone considering suicide. Indeed 'routine' and 'servicing' are dirty words throughout much of the dive industry. Since this day I've noticed that many scuba shops simply follow the mantra 'If it ain't broke, don't try and fix it'

When you cannot breathe underwater, it's natural to think the worst. I'm fairly pragmatic, but my buddy fell into the role of headless chicken almost immediately. We started swimming up - quickly. As we got closer to the surface, we were delivered a reprieve. My diving regulator started to supply air again, although at an asthmatic rate. It was similar to sucking a cat through a drinking straw, not so noisy but with all the difficulty. However, by the time we reached 20 feet, we were back on easy street and breathing normally. We slowed down and took a minute to hit the surface. Anna looked like she had seen a ghost, but calmed down quickly once back in the boat. We had arranged for two dives, Anna said that one was enough for today. I still fancied it, and Julian our guide said he would take me in again alone. We drove some way towards home to an underwater reef called 'Pieces of Eight" in sixty feet of water. Anna asked how long we would wait before diving again. I hoped not long as the sun was scorching, I wanted to go straight away. We exchanged our empty scuba tanks for fresh ones. Julian slipped over the side again without warning. I tried the backward roll entry technique, which I had seen earlier. Doing a little somersault, although fun, was slightly disorientating. I got my bearings and headed down. Julian was there, near the bottom. There was a giant fishing net stretched right out in front of him. My dive buddy was pulling fish from the net and letting them go. This was fun and we spent the next thirty minutes liberating small reef fish. We did struggle for a while as we tried to break the netting - I had to rest to get my breath back several times. This dive lasted close to forty minutes, we saw everything. Lion fish, turtles and a myriad of colourful reef dwellers. With all the distractions, it would be easy to miss monitoring my air pressure. Julian kept a watch out and he signalled that we should ascend when it was time. On the way up, his wrist computer started beeping. He wanted to stop for a bit just below the surface. I tried to stop too but the air in my buoyancy jacket had expanded too much and I sped past him. Julian beckoned me back down. I couldn't get the air from my jacket and was stuck at the surface floundering. Anna shouted over asking if we had a good dive, I headed over to the boat to tell her everything. Ten minutes later, Julian surfaced also. It had been a great day. In no time we were back to the dive centre and booked another dive trip for tomorrow. We explained about the running out of air episode to the boss. The shop manager explained that we should take more responsibility for our own safety and to check the equipment before use. He pointed to some little filter embedded inside my rental regulator. It was as green as the grass outside. He advised that it should be grey or silver and my instructor should have told me how to check this. Green meant it was almost completely blocked and would only give enough air for one person. He continued that there were many sets of regulators and that he alone could not be accountable for ensuring that they all worked. He blamed people like us for rinsing the regulators in the fresh water without the dust cap in place. I felt very tired all of a sudden and headed back to the hotel. I started to feel a pain in my legs about half an hour later.

Stopping at a fried chicken vendor, I sipped a juice and took a painkiller washed down with a side of B-B-Q ribs. My head started to throb and my legs were becoming weaker. I phoned the dive centre for advice, they suggested that I was experiencing heat exhaustion and was obviously dehydrated. I returned to the hotel for a lie down. A few minutes later I must have dozed off, but I woke with a start to the feeling of ants running all over my chest. Turning the light on and stumbling to the shower, I turned the water on. There were no ants, but instead a purple rash had covered my chest and arms. Maybe it was ants, but if so they had strangely gone now leaving no trace. I rubbed some E45 anti-aging cream into my chest and lay down again. That was two in the afternoon.

The next day at seven in the evening, I woke up to knocking on my door. I had forgotten I'd arranged to go to a cabaret show at a plantation museum with friends. I could just about summon the energy to shout a response to the caller. My knees were very painful and I struggled to put my legs on the floor. It felt like I had run a marathon in my sleep and then fought in a bar fight. I focussed and got up, all the recent excitement and my fast approaching twenty four years old must be catching up with me, I thought. Jenny my niece came into my room, she mentioned that a dive centre had come calling for me earlier in the day, but I didn't hear them banging. I felt very weak and very rough. I needed food and drink and some distraction. Several rum punches and some sustenance later, I felt myself a little more. At eleven thirty in the evening, I had been entered into a limbo dancing competition. I stood swaying before the waist height bar, which was now doused with Sambuca and burning merrily. My knees were on fire also - if I made it under this bar it would be a flaming miracle indeed! Moving forward under the bar meant arching my back and bending my knees. I had as much flexibility as the Leaning Tower of Pisa now. I collapsed on the floor to drunken applause and was helped from the stage. The pain stayed in my legs for ages after. Flying home, I went to the doctors for relief. The doc asked what I had been doing before the pain started. I told him "nothing really, except for some scuba diving". When I told him more about the diving drama, he consulted a dusty medical journal about Caisson's disease. The symptoms I presented were those of residual decompression sickness, otherwise known as the bends. I had heard of the bends from the movies, you got them if you wore the big brass helmets and came to the surface too fast. My whirlwind diver training made no mention of decompression illness. The rapid ascent with Anna had probably caused bubbles in my body. This explained a lot. I should have gone directly to a diver's recompression chamber in Barbados and got treated immediately. The dive shop guy had said I was just hungry and thirsty. The pain in my legs slowly resolved over the weeks but was quickly replaced with a more throbbing pain in the arse, my job.

I wanted a change from my current career of ducking and diving in the second hand car trade to something a bit less cut throat. I considered all manner of adventurous careers, including helicopter pilot and even North Sea commercial diver. I went out and bought a glossy diving magazine for more ideas. The glamorous and seemingly amorous lifestyle of the diving professional drew me like a fly to a windscreen. Within a fortnight I had enrolled in a zero-to-hero dive training special. Looking at my certification card, the dive shop guy noticed I had already been diving three years - that apparently made me an experienced diver! My new diving Instructor had been diving only six months himself, and he added (worryingly) that *I* could probably teach *him* a thing or two. These next few weeks would see me enrolled in the largest diver training school in England. It was February or March so it made for a winter training discount. I moved from my townhouse in a salubrious north London suburb, to a dilapidated caravan adjacent to the opaquely turquoise waters of a gravel pit.

How the on-site accommodation was advertised would stretch the most elastic imagination. The interior photographs had faded a lot in the sunshine, or came from an era before coloured ink. I endured a week staying in this damp freezing poverty, sharing with one guy whose snoring could keep a deaf person awake. My other 'cellmate' was the instructor, who had a serious night time teeth-grinding habit. I was surprised every morning that he had any teeth left. The bottled gas fire that smoked like burning car tyres had to be extinguished on entry due to carbon monoxide scares. Homeless tramps with mangy dogs would never rest their heads on these mouldy damp mattresses. These quaint diver's chalets resembled cardboard slums on wheels. Although costing just five quid a night, this was still daylight robbery. The adverts said that each caravan boasted a *rustic, waters edge convenience*. In no time, I realised that convenience was meant in the urinal sense of the word. The diving company was proud to offer its sub-aqua adventures from two locations. I did my Advanced Diver course in a swamp near Birmingham, followed by Rescue training back at the murky brick quarry near Cambridgeshire

During my training, I sampled daily money-wasting and pointless antics at the hands of would-be dive professionals. On the very first day, we learnt how to deep dive safely within the strict guidelines of the training agency. However, this version of deep diving was never actually deeper than 19 metres at any time, and swimming at this depth was strictly prohibited. We simply held onto a length of chain that hung from the edge of the quarry. Our next *high-octane-adventure* would be boat diving. The dive centre boasted about its very own boat. The promotional materials showed a boat being used for rescue and safety demonstrations. The boat photos contained someone resembling Jack Cousteau wearing very vintage equipment, so was clearly taken a few years back. The boat had definitely seen better days, as now it was a dilapidated inflatable dinghy that had been nailed to some planks of wood. Its floorboards were screwed to these planks, and thus it was fixed permanently to the edge of the quarry. Only half of the boat was capable of inflation, but this allowed for easy access when wearing fins. We were to simulate (pretend) that we had travelled to the dive site by boat. On the instructors command, we were to roll over back wards into the muddy water. We could then explore some dumped cars and shopping trolleys and then return to the *dive boat*. I couldn't wait for the Drift dive experience in the quarry. I thought we would just simulate ocean currents by jumping into the water without our flippers on. The instructor scoffed at my contemptuous remarks, quoting how good *he* was and that *he* had never ever dived outside this quarry. "The sea is over-rated" he would repeat, "Everything you need is in this inland oasis". It was hard to detect sarcasm or irony in his profundity, his Birmingham accent was just too concealing. After all this in-depth training, I felt truly an advanced diver capable of rescuing any distressed damsels that swam my way.

Before diving, like I said I sold cars in London, both new and used. During this time I had business dealings with gentlemen from Yakuza families, Al-Qaeda pilots, and several members of "semi-organised" crime families. At no time however, did these men or women stoop as low with their business ethics as the staff from my 'five star' diving centre. During my dive master training course, one of my fellow dive instructor lemmings developed a burst lung, I think it was technically called a mediastinal emphysema, it still sounded nasty. This guy had apparently worked previously as a commercial diver but lost his medical clearance to dive professionally due to, strangely enough, bursting his lung. When I started on this leadership level training, this chap joked to everyone that he had burst his lung at work, and was forced to leave. His new plan was to continue working under the water as a 'mere' scuba instructor instead, this sounded reasonable to me, and it sounded reasonable to our instructor.

A couple of days later, when he was carted away in an ambulance, the owner of the dive centre came up to me minutes before the police arrived and asked if I would forget the conversation about yes's and no's that we had discussed during the completion of our diving self-medicals. Apparently life and death decisions are worth only £300 in diving, when I sold cars this level of injury usually involved much more money. Still, I was not put off my path of joining the ranks of the diving professional. I completed my dive master course, and applied for my diving Instructor training. Within a couple of weeks I was sitting on my instructor development course, albeit at a competitors dive centre. I was going to give the first dive centre another thousand pounds for this tuition, but after a near drowning (my own) due to a leaking rental drysuit compounded by hired-free flowing regulators, I decided that enough was enough.

The course you undertake to become a dive instructor is quite enjoyable, both highly sociable and fun. It involves learning to teach a contrived and minimised teaching system. But this system is quite alien to common sense. It's a bit like learning a foreign language, but with a big difference - what you say is not important, only the grammar is key. Usually when you thread a few new foreign words together, the listener overlooks improper grammar, focussing purely on the important part. Often, new instructors still do not understand the important parts themselves as they have only been diving a short time. During the instructor training, the candidate gives presentations that are graded. The instructor could tell you all sorts of potentially dangerous information, but score enough points to pass by hiding the rubbish within the guidelines of the teaching system. Foreign language instructors are often provided with non-diving translators, this complements the lottery of the grading process nicely.

Imagine saying something like "In the United Kingdom we drive on the right side of the road".

You could also say that "In the United States we drive on the right side of the road".

Both sentences are grammatically correct, but explain nothing. Unless you actually know which side of the road to drive on beforehand, you will have a head on collision in England despite driving on the right side - the left...confused? You will be. My point was that new diving instructors leaving training have only learned a framework in which to teach. If the underpinning facts are misunderstood or downright dangerous, that's the way they will stay, sadly. While underwater, the details and facts keep you alive, not the way they were presented. I don't want to go on about just how shoddy diving instructors can be, but if training agencies want to endanger lives proportionally to increasing profits, then it won't be long until major government intervention and much needed regulation.

My Instructors course started smoothly, the group numbered about seventeen and we all had a good laugh. An unexpected bonus was that if you pretended to be unemployed and did a few nights additional paperwork, you could have the course for free. This special offer came courtesy of the U.K government, as part of another new initiative to waste tax payer's money. I thought this was a good deal, so I took up the challenge, as did more than half the class. They even supplied a bus to take us down to the unemployment benefit office - we went from Social-Climbers to Social-Claimers in the same afternoon.

The next nine days were gruelling with all this additional free-course paperwork but great fun. My grasp of diving theory was as good as it needed to be and probably better than anyone else's in the room though this hardly helped at all. Other candidates, who were barely coherent without alcohol and had clearly been studying for a completely different vocation - took on board the teaching system like kids to water, or more aptly, stoners to a bong. My brain seeks explanation rather than memory games. I sat alone in the evenings adding the contrived phrases to my vocabulary and trying to integrate them into my own diving knowledge database. The courses training director made the mistake of explaining the value of these techniques at the beginning of class. He said that nobody uses these methods during real diver training, ever. You simply had to remember the patter for the exam at the end and learn to high five when appropriate. As every Englishman knows, there is never an appropriate time to high five! I realised early on that becoming a diving instructor was as challenging as filling out credit card details, by the end of the course I was a fully certified diving instructor professional guru. I graduated with about fourteen of the others. We all spoke naively about lengthy careers as diving instructors. One year later, two or three were still working *in the industry*. One was cleaning the glass inside a large aquarium in the Midlands, another had graduated to the dizzying heights of leading snorkellers on a cruise ship in the Mediterranean.

Predictably, my fellow *virtually-unemployed* course-mates were caught red handed cheating with the government paperwork. Most had borrowed my coursework and had foolishly copied it verbatim. The myopic, but clearly eagle-eyed government verifier sorted the wheat from the chaff quickly and mercilessly. He offered the choice of court room appearances or course payments in full. Credit card details appeared instantly on his table the same day, along with some muffled apologies. My own work was accepted fortunately, and I collected my winnings in the form of a free instructor course.

Because of my total disregard for academic qualifications, I have had to endure the pitfalls of being a diving instructor for the past eleven years now. Maybe I will collect the resulting sainthood for this when I parole from debtors prison...many years from now. A couple of weeks staggering around intoxicated from joining the ranks of the scuba-guru had to end. I got my first job in the industry, and a rude awakening...

Chapter 2. First Break In The Business

A diving centre in Barbados, called Shades of Blue, had agreed to employ me at exorbitant cost. For seven days work, with each day near sixteen hours duration, I could relax in the knowledge I would receive the princely sum of seventy U.S dollars. Still, my rent was cheap and we got free lunch when memory served the owners. My first day at work was my first chance to experience being underwater while unconscious. A tropical storm had lashed the west coast for a week or more. Virtually every dive boat resting at its mooring was now sleeping with the fishes. Monster winds meant biblical seas. Most of the vessels had simply filled with rain water and capsized into the abyss. The dive centre I worked at had a glass-bottom boat they used for dive trips. The boat had an automatic pump that drained the water from the sieve-like hull. After 5 days of terrible wind and rain, the battery that powered the bilge pump had failed, causing the boat to list badly. I arrived at work at 7.30 am. We looked out to the stricken dive boat through damp and misty binoculars. If we didn't get over to the boat and drain it soon, it would become a permanent fixture on local maritime charts.

The waves were angry, they crashed with a promise of pain and suffering for anyone stupid enough to try and launch a rowing boat from the shore. The constant barrage of surf and its insidious undertow had already removed the sun-bleached sand from the beach, exposing the sharp coral rocks that give Barbados its coral island status. Desperate measures were needed, the situation shouted for them. Myself and Adam, the dive shop owner, dragged a little rowing boat called "Li'l Hero" from its rack and ventured closer to the rabid, snarling jaws of the ocean.

Pushing the boat quickly into the big waves was ridiculous and foolhardy, so that was what we did. The boat was spat up into the air over ten feet, it somersaulted over our heads before returning to earth upside-down between the two of us. Uninjured and not put off, with a liberal sprinkling of stupidity we tried again and again to launch the eleven foot wooden boat. Each time, the waves easily flipped the boat and sent it crashing down, miraculously missing us (mostly). I had the inspired idea to enter the water with my flippers on while dragging a tow-rope tied to the bow of the boat. I would swim out with the rope and attempt to pull the boat, which we filled a little with water to weigh it down in an effort to prevent more gymnastics.

Theoretically brilliant, but practically flawed. The waves overturned the boat in seconds, this time the undertow sucked the boat down with it still tied to my wrist. I slipped the knot luckily, and watched the boat disappear to become another days problem, or maybe some barbecue driftwood in a week or so. We resorted to swimming out in the huge seas. The tumultuous conditions made it a struggle, but thirty minutes later we were alongside to see the dive boat almost at one with the ocean. We lamely dipped plastic buckets into the boat in an attempt to bail it out. For a while it looked promising but the waves would sometimes set us back minutes in a second. We watched with dejected disbelief as the sea took its prisoner. With a burp of foul air from some compartment, the final oily groan sent our dive boat to the bottom. Bugger!

The owners had brought a bottle of the local Mount Gay Barbados Rum, and after a horrible swim back we imbibed a little of the hard stuff as a consolation prize. I earned less in a week here than sometimes an hour in my previous job. But the feeling of life that now coursed through my veins alongside the searing heat of the refined cane sugar was worth more than any used-car sale, except selling jalopies to unlicensed taxi drivers, obviously.

It was still before 9 am. We arranged a sport fishing boat to take us to our new wreck site. To recover the boat the same day meant saving thousands of dollars in repairs to the engine and hull timbers. We drove to the Careenage, the main port in Bridgetown. The town marina, used for glitzy catamarans and Marlin sport fishers, was desolate of people but full of boats shivering in the rain with their glossy canvas sails lashed tightly down, bracing the storm.

Our captain was a diminutive but very stocky Barbados coastguard member with one foot missing! I introduced myself and learned that his name was *Shorty*…perfect. The life jacket he donned was enormous, he joked that he couldn't swim and usually never wore a life vest, as they only delayed the inevitable, many local fishermen shared this view, "let de sea take what she want…mon".

The hour of knock-down seas was hard to endure, but we made it over to the hopefully temporary grave site of our dive boat in one piece. We planned to drop down atop of the wreck and fill lifting bags with air to raise it up. I asked the boat captain for a calculator and the specifications of the submerged engine with which I would work out just how much air we should take down to complete the lift. I was keen to show the other guys my academic prowess, honed to perfection during my recent diving-instructor training. Surprisingly the skipper produced the calculator but of course not the engine's instruction book. I wedged myself in a corner of the boats' heaving and spray soaked deck, tapping away on the keys but not being able to get an answer without the displacement details for the outboard. The local divers laughed out loud when they asked what I was doing,

Shorty shouted "Just fill de bag until she rise…mon - we be here all day else-ways".

I had to acquiesce to Shorty's practical logic really, it made perfect sense. We had the idea to raise the outboard engine first, and then the boat itself second. Getting the two-stroke engine to the repair shop today would increase the chances of the outboard polluting the ocean another day. Putting on our diving equipment while slipping around the bucking deck would be the first challenge though. I picked up the spare scuba tanks for the lift bags and dropped backwards into the boiling white spray that became the sea. The drop to the sea was further than ideal, the sport fisher had a very high free board and meant almost a 2metre drop on a calm day. I timed the waves as best as possible, but hit the water disastrously.

Scuba air tanks feel almost weightless when worn underwater. The large aluminium tank weighs almost 15 kilograms at the surface, but it felt more than this as it hit me in the jaw, knocking me into unconsciousness as I hit the water. I slipped beneath the surface upside-down, the clip that secured the tank allowed it to dangle in my now mask-less face. The tanks weight and the other equipment dragged me down towards the seabed and its waiting diners...The pain in my ears, caused by the gradually increasing water pressure as I drifted downwards, threw me a lucky reprieve. My eyes opened as disorientation filled every crevice of my brain. I realised soon enough that I was dropping upside-down without a mask but with a definite throbbing in my jaw. I noticed that my breathing regulator was out of my mouth next, I quickly recovered my air supply and held my nose. If I took a breath without my mask on, while upside down, I might inhale water through my nose, adding a proper drama to my predicament.

Frantically trying to 'pop' my ears, I managed to equalise the discomfort and stop water entering at the same time. I turned the right way up and headed back to the surface. My diver's wrist computer was beeping a warning, I was ascending too quickly. I slowed down to avoid getting decompression sickness, a condition many divers call the bends...I had this malady some years before in these very waters - it was enormously painful then, so best avoided today.

Reaching the safety of the surface, I felt like I had recovered enough to head down again. The boat captain threw me another mask. Down I went, swimming down to seventy feet or so, I could see the others gathering around the dive boat. She looked to be quite relaxed in the tranquil blue, the hull resting serenely in the sand. The angry waves above did not reach far below the surface, at these depths only calm prevailed. I'm sure that if a boat could feel seasick, then this one had every reason to be, after riding the rodeo waves for the best part of a week. My dive buddies had undone the bolts that held the outboard engine to the transom plate. I handed them one of the smaller lift bags. Inflating the PVC bag with air allowed the 150 kg engine to become as weightless as a cloud for a second before rapidly ascending to the sunlight above. We tied a rope to help locate the engine should the bag leak its buoyant contents. Open-ended lift bags like ours would let the engine get an unexpected second dive at an unknown location if they emptied or leaked on arrival at the surface.

So far so good. In no time we had attached the bigger lift bags to the boats hull and inflated them, but the boat wouldn't budge. If an object is partially submerged in a soft surface like mud or sand, then it will be much heavier than if it simply rested on top. Our dive boat was stuck by a vacuum to the seabed, and refused to give up its watery resting spot. Our solution to this problem should be avoided by any readers thinking of a successful maritime salvage career.

As the boat was sitting upright, we decided to run a tow line to a metal ring in the bow and attach the other end to the fishing boat at the surface. Using the tow rope to pull the boat free, we imaginatively surmised that the boat would simply float through the water and return to the surface, using the hydrodynamics of its own hull to climb upwards. It seemed like a good idea at the time, but as soon as the boat broke free of the seabed's vice-like grip, it surged forward with all the control of a newly darted elephant. The large roof area of the boat acted like an underwater sail. With all this forward motion, the roof-turned-sail made our boat start to climb upwards to the surface. We all felt pretty cool, until the roof peeled away like the lid of a sardine can. Without the roof in place, the lift bags rushed to the surface like champagne bubbles. The hull turned over immediately and headed straight back down to be smashed to pieces on some rocks.

The dive centre rented another glass-bottom boat the following week after the weather improved. I put this one on the seabed within a fortnight. During a frolic with my girlfriend, I slipped and fell into the glass bottom viewing area and knocked the glass panels out. We both shook our heads as my career dissipation light started blinking faster than the water gushing in through the new opening in the floor. Frantically I started the engine and raced towards the shore –

it became 'too late' just an anvil throw from the beach. We did however successfully raise this one after a few days. The tow and disintegrate method we perfected a week or so earlier was not used.

This dive centre was where I nurtured my interest in deep diving. At the end of every day, three or four of the staff would head out and dive deep into the ocean's belly. The feeling of descending into the electric blue of the Caribbean is truly magic. We always breathed just regular compressed air. Air is not the ideal breathing gas much below two hundred feet depth, as it takes on anaesthetic properties. Many divers compare the effects to drinking alcohol. But instead of turning to drink, every day I would dive a couple of times to two hundred feet, or only once below three hundred, breathing normal air. As a group we would decide our maximum depth before rolling over into the sea. I generally led the dives, as I always seemed to be still in the driving seat at maximum depth. My buddies were almost always rendered paralytic, overcome by the intoxicating effects of the nitrogen in the air we breathed.

Slowly the group size dwindled, as divers reached the point where they were unable to function and would rely solely on me or luck to return them to the surface. Divers, I believe, must have some kind of natural ability in this area. It requires certain skills that can be learnt, but ultimately you need to be able to function in an automated response mode that ensures a return to the surface, also an extremely strong will to tolerate the nitrogen's anaesthetic properties. My personal metabolism seems to break down hospital or dentists anaesthetic at an unusually fast rate. But I think my personal success while duelling with depth comes down to never having touched a recreational drug and even avoiding alcohol for many years. My brain seems fairly active, even now after honing a wary relationship with gin and tonic. I have noticed a definite link with stoners (pot smokers) being very poor deep divers, what with their easy-to-subdue nature, general lack of spatial awareness and tireless excuses.

The draw of deep air diving is quite addictive. To overcome the insidious side effects of breathing oxygen and nitrogen at immense depth, and return to the surface in control is very rewarding, and often leaves ardent deep divers in a euphoric state. Descending into the oceans womb in clear warm water is extremely relaxing. My breathing rate falls to 5-6 breaths per minute, my body behaving like a fine Swiss watch mechanism, totally functional while completely at rest. Dropping down quickly, I take a long blink, exhale fully and enter a state of utter calm. My left index finger is poised to hit the inflator button of my buoyancy jacket when needed. I have trained my finger to respond automatically if necessary, should unconsciousness strike. An index finger muscle and the slow rise and fall of my diaphragm will be the only activity in my body. My fins act like rudders to keep my position stable and steer me almost like a driverless ghost train. With time trained responses all working in unison, my brain slows down and my eyes become cameras only. Images in front of me cannot be processed until the nitrogen-hit subsides during the ascent. The scenes ahead will bypass my short-term memory and skip straight into old memory limbo. I will re-live the dive afterwards, during the decompression stops.

The nitrogen content of the air I breathe is acting on my central nervous system like a powerful morphine. It slows my thoughts to a virtual standstill. The oxygen part of air that I need to fuel my body and simply stay alive on the surface is far more insidious underwater though. As the nitrogen tries hard to cause a mental traffic jam, the oxygen starts to cause massive chemical changes in my blood and brain. These changes will cause epileptic convulsions if I pass the point of no return. Unfortunately this point is variable, I'm sure its not coming soon, but wonder if I will recognise it, if I'm indeed lucky enough to get an advert of its impending arrival. Oxygen toxicity is my only real concern. My deep air mantra is "Nitrogen Narcosis is for Christmas, Oxygen Toxicity is for Life"

Dropping to extreme depth breathing air has some interesting effects. As I approach three hundred feet my hearing becomes super enhanced. I can hear my own heart beat clearly and my cycle of breathing becomes as loud as barking dogs. My eyesight seems to have improved contrast, the most subtle difference in sand contours standing out like a mountain range relief. Descending further, the water gets colder and denser. Noises of ships engines are apparent, these ships are not visible on the horizon yet, but the dulcet throb of their engines projects for many miles in the deepest parts of the ocean.

Some days, I would descend towards a sandy bottom over three hundred feet down and stay for up to fifteen minutes. My brain would enter a tranquil state devoid of all back-scatter. A place for advanced thinking, math problems solved with ease, ideas to work with later, all conjured up from the brains back waters. Deep air diving is similar to Free Diving in that higher mental processes only reveal themselves when the humdrum thoughts of modern day life are sedated by water pressure. Pure Magic.

I look at my scuba tank contents gauge and it registers two thirds full as I pass three hundred and fifty feet deep today. The nitrogen has another interesting effect that now has my full attention. Something in my brain is short circuiting in the hearing department. I hear a short verse repeating in my head, getting louder and louder. The tune is quite familiar to me. I've done this dive many times before. A sort of requiem funeral beat done on a drum machine at break neck speed. The speed of the tune and its loudness always increase with depth. Sounding like the distant memory of a heart beat at two hundred and fifty feet, it progresses to a thrash rock concert with an audience of one as I approach four hundred feet.

Other deep air divers have labelled this aural phenomenon the Wah-Wah effect. The call of the Wah-Wah is to deep air divers, what the call to prayer promises the devout Christian. It was my reason for visiting today, I've heard it and now I must leave. I have dived today with a single tank of air, its eighty cubic feet volume and single breathing regulator leave little room for problem solving or equipment dramas. Like my body and its blood chemistry, the equipment must behave flawlessly. Dives to these depths done formally would require at least four diving cylinders containing exotic trimix gas mixtures, each tailored to remove each of the excesses I seek today. Oxygen toxicity has left me alone so far, to over-stay my welcome could mean becoming a permanent fixture at the Davy Jones Bed and Breakfast.

My finger draws inwards to depress the up-button, and air rushes from my tank into the buoyancy jacket, arresting my fall. To use my legs and kick my fins would require energy that swaps oxygen for carbon dioxide. Any exercise causes a rise in carbon dioxide levels in my blood. If carbon dioxide rises, a diver will become extra vulnerable to oxygen toxicity either at depth or during the return to the surface. Ten seconds of air rushing into my buoyancy jacket is enough to arrest my free fall. I become neutrally buoyant for a few seconds, then positive. I start floating up towards the sunlight, faster and faster as my buoyancy jacket grows with the decreasing pressure of the water around me. I travel upwards faster than my own exhaled bubbles. God only knows what bubbles are forming in my bloodstream. I continue upwards until I hit the safety of two hundred feet. Seeing my depth gauge flick back to the required depth, I hit the brakes by dumping the air from my buoyancy vest.

Hanging motionless in the void, looking downwards, I feel safe again. I see the cloud of bubbles that I had exhaled a minute before. In a second I will be enveloped in a Jacuzzi effect of my own breath. The tiny balls of air tickle my face as they tumble upwards away to the surface. They bump into each other and merge, growing into larger bubbles. The diminishing pressure will make sure that every breath I exhaled at three hundred and fifty feet will have grown at least eleven times bigger as it races to join the surface atmosphere above.

Believe or not, all this is actually highly pleasurable and rewarding, albeit very dangerous and apparently hugely irresponsible. Deep air diving is probably as addictive and damaging as heroin abuse with similar catastrophic consequences if you overdose. Unlike heroin it doesn't rot your teeth. Anyway that was the entertainment available most days of the week, and it was cheaper than the cinema.

My first year in Barbados allowed me unlimited diving to the depths that interested me. I had brought over from my instructor training in England, an understanding of enriched air nitrox diving and how to blend it. I set three dive centres up with enriched air back in 1994, a first in the eastern Caribbean. My thirst for advanced diver training and information was unquenched back then. Very few facilities had sought to offer training in the emerging discipline of technical diving. I had to travel to Egypt to further my knowledge and complete training in extended range diving and Trimix diving. In 1994 and 1995 Trimix diving was still in its infancy, the only available course instructor was known to me and despite that, I flew five thousand miles to receive further *tuition*.

We met at a dive facility in Sharm El Sheik on the edge of the Sinai desert in Egypt. The centre was full to the brim with shiny chrome things and loaded with people knowing little of how to operate any of it properly. We were here to train as deep as seventy five metres using mixtures of helium, oxygen and nitrogen called Trimix. Each mixture was specially blended to avoid any nitrogen narcosis and oxygen toxicity problems for the chosen dive depth. When I came to Egypt, I had more dives below seventy-five metres than many of the group had dives in their log books.

My technical dive buddy was an ex military diver with the claim to fame of being attacked by a conger eel in a loch in Scotland. He had been drinking heavily apparently, and decided to offer a night dive experience to his pub pals in a freezing seawater lake. As you'd imagine, the whole experience capsized badly, with tales of giant angry conger eels attacking the diver and dragging him to the bottom of the loch by a loop of fishing line that was hanging from the slimy leviathan's mouth.

A sprinkling of decompression sickness and a tabloid head line titled '*one eel of a story*' set back diver training in Scotland some months. I remember reading the headline in the News of the World paper one Sunday morning. Recognising the culprit straight away, I gave him a phone call to get the whole story. He was sticking with the newspaper version however unlikely it sounded.

Three years later, I taught a group to dive on the tiny island of Herm. After one of the class sessions we retired to the only pub on this diminutive rock in the English Channel. We swapped diving stories until my ferry boat home arrived. One guy said he was the recompression chamber tender on a Scottish military base some years earlier. This chap told of a dive instructor who was bought in with suspected decompression sickness. The story in the news told of duels with giant eels. The diver was apparently found hiding in undergrowth the morning after, trying to nurse a hangover and a bout of debilitating embarrassment. The diver divulged his tail of woe to the attending doctors, who were not overly sympathetic, especially when they smelled the alcohol oozing from their charge.

This patient was asking for anonymity as he was currently absent without leave from a nearby special forces training camp. The mystery diver showed his special boat squadron sweatshirt that he was wearing under his black Avon rubber drysuit. The story was almost plausible until the shirts clothing label revealed the Top Man brand. Top Man clothing is more synonymous with teenagers with customised Ford Mondeo's than trained elite underwater demolition experts. Definitely more Special Farces than Special Forces.

Still, he was a comfortable and experienced deep diver and easily outclassed the rest of the gaggle in the class. Pre-requisites for the Trimix class included having eight hundred dives logged. I noticed that several of the group had less than fifty dives total. Technical diver 'training standards' should be a registered Oxymoron. It easily equals my favourite contradiction in terms…'Mature Student'. This lack of ethics has tarnished the technical dive industry for the last ten years and gets steadily worse. Nowadays, one training agency requires little more than two dives to 71 metres during instructor training to allow the new instructor to take 4 students to 100 metres.

After some highly lacklustre academic performances by the course instructors, we did some fun dives ending at seventy-five metres for eight minutes, including the five minutes it took to get down there. The quality of the compressor filters at the dive centre was a good reason not to dive deeper or longer. Forty minute dives breathing a cocktail of carbon monoxide and entrained engine oil was more than many could endure. A respite and recovery period during our decompression stops was thankfully supplied during the shallower portion. Just below the surface, we breathed 100% oxygen to speed up the off-gassing process. Pure oxygen came in separate bottles rented from a local gas supplier. As such it didn't need to be supplemented from the dive shop compressors toxic exhaust pipe and was therefore safe to breathe.

Egypt is a popular destination. The Red Sea is both warm and clear with some fantastic reefs and walls. However, the more easily accessed dive sites would see on average ten to fifteen boats all tied to a single mooring buoy. The boats taut bow lines resembled children's balloon vendors, with many boats sharing one buoy line. If the single mooring line broke then a dozen boats would be cast adrift like pin balls, crashing into surfacing divers and, more often than not, each other. The purpose of this was to allow the boat captains to sleep in the sun while the deck hands swapped horror stories about the latest group of customers. Shoals of novice divers from dozens of boats were thrown overboard to gaze at the often featureless and over-dived moonscapes that also lured our group of deep explorers. The large groups of novices herded about by a clueless, gap-year dive instructor, intent on getting home long before happy hour finished. During our technical deep excursions, we would swim around in a dark and gloomy area close to the wall, trying to avoid the shower of lead-filled weight belts that often fell from panicking beginner divers above. After completing the course we were told not to dive deeper than our training depth until we had built up considerable experience…unless we simply paid two hundred dollars more each and dived with the chief instructor to one hundred metres in groups of eight at a time! That sounded fantastic; to save money I dived on air. The madness could not have been more complete

Life as a diving instructor has allowed me an insight into what the public get up to when they are on holiday. When people are not delivering milk or examining tax returns, they often develop a whole new persona. The more interesting ones live on in these pages. I hope that if this book does get to print, people recognise themselves and mutter the words "Bastard…he knew all along…must have been the Special Air Service speedo's I was wearing".

If my customers are to be believed, in the last ten years of recreational diver training I have apparently trained more Special Forces soldiers and spies than normal members of the public to dive. If scuba diving attracts such an odd bunch, technical diving must be the Promised Land for ex secret agents and Walter Mittys everywhere. The Special Forces must be the largest regiment in the world and easily out number the regular army if this many of their number seek scuba diver training!

This book is not trying to focus purely on the negative side of scuba diving with all its bullshitters. It's just painting an alternative picture of diving to contrast the smiling faces and pristine reefs that fill travel brochures. If even a handful of readers learn that all is not happy beneath the waves, both with the quality of the diver trainers and the aqua-scapes you train to visit, then, I will be happy. Divers should be able to make informed decisions and recognise nonsense, rather than naively support the industry cowboys that are ruining everything. Diving is very rewarding even if it has a dark side; to recognise it and shun it will be more beneficial to everybody. All I'm trying to do is shine some light onto the dark…(long sigh)

Returning to Barbados was a relief, as I had grown quite familiar with the daily script there. Teaching diving in the day and then touring bars with the customers at night was very congenial. The dive centre had taken on a new staff member while I was in Egypt, Kevin from the UK. What he lacked in diving qualifications he made up for in humorous stories. We got him up to speed with the diving certifications and in exchange he told us funny tales of his brushes with various authorities while pursuing his career as small time drugs dealer. One morning we had picked up a large group of ladies from a visiting cruise ship. What had promised to be a possibly interesting flirtatious few days of dive guiding went aground as soon as we saw the cruise ship was chartered by a gay's-only tour operator.

Kevin and I sauntered over to the meeting area facing a barrage of cat calls from moustached men and village people look-a-likes. I gave the dive shop sign that read "Go down with the experts" to Kevin to deflect most of the verbal shrapnel towards him. Some ladies with short hair and serious expressions came over and we made our introductions. The mini-bus journey took 45 minutes and we all chatted about what we could see underwater over the next few days. Some of the group had bought waterproof cameras and they dictated to the others that fish and coral were what they sought as opposed to shipwrecks.

It was my turn to lead this group today as we headed for an area called Dottins reef. Kevin the dive guide was not actually certified for leading anyone except for his friends, but he came along to assist me as the group was nearly 14 people.

I brought my new girlfriend Avril, as she had just finished her diving course, and Kevin carried along his trusty spear gun. I told him to keep it well hidden as most of the group sounded a bit environmentalist, the last thing they wanted to see was someone shooting small reef fish in the name of target practice. Kevin would have to dive with Jesus (alone) and stay well away from the group.

The group put on their diving equipment after I had given them the usual briefing as to what to expect and how to behave. They all could set up their own equipment themselves, which was highly unusual, most of the time we had to remind the customers which way around their own wetsuits went. Over the side of the boat we went, as a group, dropping down the 30 feet or so to the reef top below. I'd been to this reef many times before, so started to lead the group around the rocks and coral to look for the reef dwellers that the dive shop had promised would be in plentiful supply. Looking behind me I could see some of the group impaled in the reef much like usual. I headed into deeper water to where the seabed is mostly sand so as to give the reef mattress a well deserved rest. Divers who haven't been underwater since their last holiday tend to virtually walk across the bottom for the first twenty minutes, until they get some practise with their buoyancy control.

Most dive centres dream up very misleading names for the reefs that often included highly exotic marine life varieties. We had dive sites called 'Stingray Landing', 'Shark Alley', and 'Manta Station' plus scores of other destinations where you could virtually guarantee not seeing any of the species in the name. But you *could* get to look at a fish book after the dive to get the Latin names of what you didn't see. My favourite "semi exotic" was the Blue Spotted Manta Ray because we could often guarantee seeing at least one, even in areas where the dynamite fishing was epidemic. I looked in all the various nooks and crannies as my gaggle of divers snapped away with their cameras, the underwater strobes leaving all manner of fish life dazed and confused, swimming away quickly like they had just been through a crazy X-ray machine. Things were going swimmingly and I'd virtually crossed off all the usual suspects from my mental 'to find' list.

Photographers are the worst offenders when it comes to smashing delicate corals, as they think that lying prone on the reef for long periods taking crap photos is the only way to interact with the shy marine life. The air supply was coming to an end for the heaviest breather of the group, so we headed for shallower water where the air lasts longer. Sometimes a customer could drain his scuba tank completely of air evan before we had reached the bottom, but these 'big breathers' were ideal customers really because it meant the dives were shorter. As we travelled up across the reef I saw two large green Moray eels sticking their heads out of a hole, this would make a cool photo opportunity so I pointed the scene out to the dozen diving paparazzi spread out behind me. I felt a little sorry for the Eels as they were in for a strobe light extravaganza, and no doubt be prodded and posed endless times until every last diver had taken every last frame of film on the rolls. The depth was about 15 feet from the surface and everybody looked like they were enjoying themselves clicking away at the stunned and dazzled marine life. In amongst the background noise of divers bubbles I heard the unmistakable twang of a spear gun being fired. Being underwater means you cannot tell where a sound comes from - as sound travels so much faster in water, you lose sense of direction. I span around looking for who was firing the spear gun and saw in the distance a diver holding a discharged gun with spear dangling several feet below on the shock cord, hopefully he was just going to the surface as its customary to unload a gun before surfacing.

I quickly swam around the dive group to check everybody's air supply again. Photographers could sometimes get so focused on their prey that they would forget to monitor their air gauge and simply run out of the breathable stuff. Some of them were getting low and I signalled them to surface. All agreed and turned back for one last click of the shutter. Suddenly, I heard an almighty crack of a spear gun firing very close to me. I turned around and saw a grinning buffoon holding the smokeless gun. I looked back to see a 2 metre Moray eel which had just been skewered through the head by the harpoon and was going absolutely bloody ballistic. Photographers sometimes take on a Nirvanic stoned look as they snap away totally relaxed and oblivious to their surroundings. This look of relaxation had permeated through my group just seconds before, but they now had looks of someone who had just had a drunk throw up on their birthday cake. The poor Moray Eel still had enormous strength and was spinning around like a whirling dervish on Ecstasy. The spear gun was easily pulled from the hands of my soon-to-be-sacked colleague. As the big fish twisted and turned with the four foot spear sticking out both side of its head, the scene just exploded. Divers were having their breathing regulators pulled from their mouths as the spear and gun caught and wrapped itself around anything nearby.

I had to swim quickly and cut the spear guns shock cord, before things went further downhill. My career dissipation light was blinking so fast and bright now, I feared an epileptic seizure. I had my knife out in a blink and swam directly into the affray. Divers were panicking but had swapped to their spare regulators as they kicked the last few feet to the fresh air with the huge Eel in tow. On breaking the surface, the air tuned blue from the swearing and the water went pink from the leaking Eel. I had to cut the spear free to release the mortally wounded animal, but one of the ladies started screaming that they wanted it on the boat for the evidence photographs! Threats of law suits faded into obscurity as US law firms came up against the impenetrable brick wall that is the Caribbean legal system.

Living in a developing country can be pretty exciting; it would be great to write more about daily life on an island with some of the most colourful characters imaginable. One day you are in shop were they are literally hanging shoplifters by their necks as a message to other would-be discount shoppers, a few days later there is a live sword fight in a crowded shopping centre with arms and other bits flying around like mosquitoes. During one government election, the opposition party tried to increase their fund raising coffers by dropping huge bundles of cocaine from an aeroplane into the sea, just off shore, near to where I stayed. Unfortunately most of the consignment fell into a fish farm and the curious tuna attacked the packages thinking it was food. As the fish floated belly up, the owners of the drugs turned up at the same time as the coast guard. A small gunfight completed the scene and some of the key players were handed 100 year prison sentences.

The main presidential candidate was offered a 50 year reduction if he offered some evidence as to who might have provided the Trinidadian marching powder, plus pay a million dollar fine. He would have been 90 years old by the time he got 'early' parole.

A memorable dive trip some weeks later had me escorting a customer into deeper water. This English guy was a fairly experienced diver with fifty or so trips already under his belt. He had been diving deep with the company dive guides for a few days who remarked that although he was very quiet he was a capable diver. The idea today was to dive to fifty or sixty metres to see some black coral. The boat ride was only twenty minutes but the lack of conversation should have rung some alarm bells with me. It didn't seem like nerves but more a preoccupation of some kind. I offered my buddy du jour a spare breathing tank but he declined it, I clipped a spare bottle to my jacket before we both went over the side of the boat. This guy never looked over at me once during the descent, I had to resort to using a tank banger to break him from his trance and return hand signals. A lot of older European divers like to solo dive in this way, if he had taken the spare breathing equipment I wouldn't have minded so much him flying solo, but now he didn't even carry a spare parachute. We hovered above the top of the finger reef in forty-five metres looking into the darker waters below. Slowly we dropped another ten metres deeper in search of the black coral trees that are ironically coloured orange. My buddy was swimming slower and slower and stopping all the time. I waited for him to catch up with me and then pointed to the big bush of coral below us that resembled a Christmas tree with orange branches. He looked okay so we swam towards the target. The weight of my spare tank clipped to my chest kept me in a face down position. If I looked up I could see the guy's fins just above me. Getting to sixty-three metres, I stopped by the rare coral bush. I looked upwards to see a weight belt falling past me into the abyss. The owner had also managed to remove his buoyancy jacket and mask and fins. Incredibly, he was also swimming away from me using a comically fast doggy-paddle stroke. I was a little surprised as you could imagine. Using my flippers at full speed, I quickly caught up with him and tried to push a breathing regulator in his mouth. He was having none of it, but was quickly finding out that drowning was not the relaxing way to go, as suggested often by Hollywood movies. I dragged him back by the arm to his equipment and clipped it back around him. I picked one of his own breathing regulators up and forced it into his mouth. His eyes remained clamped shut as he pulled the mouthpiece away again. I was a little confused at this point, this was not like any nitrogen narcosis symptoms I had seen before. This chap was going exactly the right direction if he wanted to kill himself. I decided to head towards the surface and pulled him with me. It must have been close on two minutes since I saw him without equipment and he would likely pass out soon if he didn't burst his lungs first. I tried to make sure he was breathing out as we ascended, although air bubbles seemed to be coming out of his nose anyway. En route to the top I stuffed a regulator back into his mouth once more and again he rejected it. At around thirty metres depth his eyes opened like saucers and he went from calm and serene to rabid dog. He grabbed the regulator from my mouth and breathed from it.

He started to hold on to me like a limpet now and was grabbing me so hard I couldn't find either of my own spare regulators. I got a hand free and took my regulator back so I could breathe again. I kept the mouthpiece in so my own breathing could relax, although this guy had not wanted to breathe much before, now he did, but not from his own equipment. He grabbed my regulator from me again, at the same time I found the second stage of the spare tank that was clipped to my chest. Now we could both breathe, my suicidal buddy just hung limply in the water looking downwards, still without a mask. The ascent had gone fast, then slow, then fast again and we had built up decompression stops according to my wrist dive computer. I tried to fix the ascent by adding pauses at random depths before starting the more formal deco stops in the shallows. My buddy did nothing but hang motionless as I controlled the final minutes to the surface. He had decided not to wear a wetsuit just before the dive, this helped enormously now as he had thrown his weight belt away two hundred feet deeper and this would have been disastrous now if he was clad in buoyant neoprene. It was dawning on me that this was not an advanced case of narcosis but more likely an attempt to die. I would give him the benefit of the doubt until we reached the surface. The final minutes ticked off and we hit the sunlight. Before I could even voice a "what the f#@k was all that about?" this chap was repeating "sorry…sorry…I'm so sorry". This guy had issues. While waiting to be picked up by the dive boat I listened to his story. He was a doctor who had been diagnosed with something nasty. He came away on holiday without his wife with a plan to end it all. Of course he was welcome to shuffle off this mortal coil in any way he thought fit, however I was more than a little miffed as he had tried to pull his stunt on my shift, his sob story didn't dampen my anger any. As the boat pulled up to us, he washed his face with seawater and regained his composure. The other divers asked if we saw anything cool on our deep dive, some head shaking from both of us seemed to answer their questions. Getting back to the shop, the guy wandered off up the beach while waiting for his hotel taxi to arrive. He didn't come back for his belongings and some phone calls to his hotel found he had checked out the same day. I told the other guys in the dive centre about my action-filled deep dive over some rum and cokes later. The general 'compassionate' opinion of my workmates was that it was lucky he had paid in advance and even better that I had been around to recover the shops scuba tank. We put his private regulator and buoyancy jacket into the shops rental stock. I thought about going to look for his mask and fins during my next deep air adventure.

Following this, weeks were spent looking for a container of toxic waste that was bought for disposal in deep water from Japan, the story went. The local fish life was definitely decimated as the chemical cocktail was dumped only 100 metres from shore, in a planned one mile depth of water. The project planners didn't check the local sea charts very closely as Barbados has a very shallow surrounding sea. A mile of water depth could only be found many miles off shore, but the cash was useful and the government didn't have many civil servants interested in scuba diving anyway. Eventually we found the containers that had been clearly axed open before being thrown overboard, the contents dissipated with the ocean currents. For weeks after, shoals of fish continued to be washed up dead. Mutated fish were appearing all along the west coast dive sites also, so God only knows what was actually in the drums. We all purged the chemicals we had been swimming in from our bodies through a regimented consumption of alcohol. I became a bit gun shy when customers turned up wanting specifically go 'crazy deep diving', we even had some pop stars turn up wanting to go to three hundred feet deep straight after they completed their open water courses - very rock and roll. Time and rum eventually faded my reticence to take customers tandem deep diving and soon it was business as usual. Within days, three blokes walked into the dive centre looking to go deep, I agreed to organise it. They had heard at the local Boat Yard bar that an instructor was in town that taught deep diving courses. They all introduced themselves saying that they were divers from the nuclear submarine that was visiting the island for a few days and were looking for some stunt dive action rather than any instruction. Two of the group said they were SEAL Special Forces divers and the other was a British Army diver that dealt with mine clearance. All three were probably Bakers or Window Cleaners, but I gave them the benefit of the doubt. I listened intently as they bigged themselves up with tales of underwater daring deeds .My eyes normally glaze over when I hear the war stories, but I hid it like a true veteran and we arranged a dive for the next morning. They wanted to start at 200 feet deep and only if they felt *copacetic* to continue to 300 feet as it had been some time since they had done that. I imagined that the last time these guys had dived to 300 feet was in a previous lifetime, so indeed a long time back. My constant mock yawning must have looked real enough. They said I looked tired and should get some rest.

I imagined that I would help with these three as they were all pretty big and could easily prove a handful in deep water. I phoned my girlfriend Avril, who was becoming a bit of a deep diving addict and had proved herself reliable in deeper water many times recently. She thought it would be fun and jumped at the chance of a deep dive en masse.

The boat ride out in the morning had the bullshit bravado coming thick and fast. Even my girlfriend was matching her few months of diving experience against our three James Bond candidates who were talking about scuba dives to the Titanic and beyond. All the divers were lying through their teeth right up to the point I told them the depth sounder had stopped working and we would just head out into 'proper' deep water

"How will we know how deep it is, and how will we stop?" one guy said. He was clearly expecting a seabed to use as a springboard back to the surface.

I threw him a glib answer "Look at your gauges and hit the brakes when you've had enough" this caused some Adam's apples to dance up and down like Mexican jumping beans.

"Okay…let's drop to 150 feet, group up and if you're still in the drivers seat, we can drop further" I offered to the now quiet audience.

Avril was to buddy the British mine clearance diver, and I would stay with the two Americans. Down we went.

The English guy was an older vintage to the others and a bit of *Wily Fox* and sensibly pointed to his ears at about 130 feet indicating that he couldn't go any further. The rest of the group carried on steadfast on the journey to oblivion. We stopped a little short of 200 feet with one of the navy seals pointing at his head with a spinning finger. That was his cue to stop, again a sensible response. I motioned to Avril to get closer to me, together with the other guy who was looking at little spaced out by the whole experience by 240 feet.

Dives beyond established relative safety limits are generally discouraged and shunned by the diving community. Whilst it is acceptably cool to go free climbing or base jumping, there is a palpable stigma attached to seemingly irresponsible scuba diving. The diving centre I worked at did not offer training or fun dives outside of training agency outlines. At this time, I offered a deep air certification course only to 220 feet and a trimix course to 300 feet with mandatory use of adequate helium in the breathing mixture. Deep Air dives were conducted occasionally for friends of the owner, but never for walk-in customers, regardless of their experience claims.

In the early days of technical diving, trimix use was not widespread and deeper air dives were far more common, I remember hearing many early 'pioneer' tech divers commenting the fact they didn't feel the need for trimix until they were below 300 feet. I have met maybe four divers in the last ten years with whom I would be comfortable diving to 300 feet or below breathing normal air. The rest should stay nearer 150 feet even when using trimix.

It is interesting to see how things have changed since the internet *chat room* revolution. If a diver mentions in a whisper that they dived below 100 feet breathing air, they would be banished from polite conversation. Unfortunately modern technical divers use helium often to excess as it increases perceived ability, much the same way as steroid (ab)use 'helps' bodybuilders. My point being that it is better to increase ability through repetition than by relying on temporary performance enhancers. Helium really only adds a modicum of sobriety, it does not improve buoyancy skills. Helium does not give you an ability you didn't possess before the dive. This statement will raise the blood pressure of armchair tech diving gurus everywhere.

So, back to the deep air story, As the dive shop did not endorse very deep air dives, this group had agreed to dive from a privately hired boat. We would be diving in teams of one, and I was there as a guide only, as it would be unreasonably dangerous for me to effect a rescue. All the customers were *rufty tufty* types and apparently trained to take others lives, it seemed perfectly fine for them to jeopardise their own.

Around the 240 feet the last guy was overcome by narcosis, my girlfriend was 20 feet or so deeper and spiralling around drifting slowly downwards - quite literally a passenger on a driverless ride. I felt still like I was in charge of my bus, but started to slow down my descent, as you never know what's coming round the corner. Looking up I could see the surface shimmering some 300 feet above, and between me and it were two divers decompressing in the shallows and two more divers about to decompose in the deep.

Feeling like you are in control does not mean you are, but I still felt mentally alert and capable of decision making on this dive. I decided that I had had enough and headed up to meet the others. Avril was closest to me and I approached her first, she was grinning but not responding to my hand waving. It is easiest to simply take an unresponsive diver closer to the surface and often they recover quite quickly with little memory of the current situation. I lifted Avril up some 30 feet only, before she awoke from her temporary syncope. Initially quite startled, she realised what must have happened and looked kind of angry but she would have to save the self recriminations for later and any anger felt now would likely be forgotten as adrenaline fed elation always takes over when returning to the surface after an crazy air dive. Deep air diving has been likened to legalised drug abuse many times, but it won't keep you dancing all weekend.

We both drifted up towards the next guy, he also looked frozen in time, eyes open but fast asleep. I grabbed his arm and gave a circle in the air with my index finger to Avril, this was the sign that our entertainment for today was over and unless we headed towards the surface now, the diminishing air supply in our single air tanks could spice things up really unpleasantly and soon. Our sleeping dive partner snapped out of his nitrogen induced hypnosis en route. I doubt if he would ever want a repeat performance and I'm sure he felt mortified to see a small blonde girl grinning at him as his Cinderella spell was broken. When a diver is overcome by the effects of deep diving while breathing air, they appear quite normal with eyes wide open, but I've never noticed anyone blink. The afflicted diver doesn't respond to stimulation and they have no memory of the event. The oxygen and the nitrogen gases that make up normal air cause many ill effects when used at extreme depth. In a short time, excessive oxygen toxicity causes epileptic seizures and a host of other insidious although temporary ailments to occur unfortunately without warning or mercy. The symptoms if experienced at the surface would not be life threatening, but underwater they involve drowning and the outcome of this is predictably dire. Nitrogen on the other hand gives a narcotic response similar to alcohol consumption or certain anaesthetics. Diving to 330 feet breathing air would be similar to drinking half a litre of whisky in 5 minutes and then going for tight rope walk, over a precipice. Obviously some people could practice a lot and do this everyday, like myself. But I know that one day a stumble, followed by the inevitable long fall will have my internet judge and jury laughing so much they might spill their Ritalin milkshakes! Using either gas to excess will one day cause symptoms of gas toxicity to creep up on you like a stealthy mugger or worse...the seemingly friendly accountant.

This type of diving probably sounds completely irresponsible, but no more than speeding in your car, and when diving you do not endanger anyone else's life, unless you are responsible for others of course. Until a macho type of diver finds their personal limits, they tend to feel quite invincible underwater. If you are lucky enough, you will find your limits just before incapacitation, or be lucky enough to be rescued. A deep diver who feels out of control and incapable of self rescue will not stay a diver for very long, they simply give up and take up other less adventurous sports. Technical diving doesn't have to be ridiculously deep to be over-challenging. Rebreathers, drysuit's and even hostile conditions are all more than adequate to scare an ill prepared diver into becoming a skier. Sadly too many new divers leave their scuba training without self confidence or, even worse, graduate with a false sense of security gained by having an 'easy-ride' throughout training. Traditionally, diving courses were structured to give much repetition to the more challenging skills. Bad or just 'new' scuba instructors often allow fast learners to proceed without enough practise, and this does nothing to turn a fun practise session into life saving motor skills.

Barbados was a fun place to live, and working as a scuba instructor was busy and varied. When I taught holiday makers to scuba dive we sat on the beach with a paper instructor manual and just chatted for a few hours, it was very informal. Now, in 2005, I have a laptop computer full of multi media presentations from all the popular training agencies, these new cyber manuals contain far less than 10 years ago and need updating it seems on a daily basis with an accompanying 'improvement' fee.

I started work at a new dive centre after a brief trip to England and one of my first jobs was to train the shop staff in First Aid and CPR. This should have been easy, until I was told that there was no mannequin to demonstrate chest compressions with. The shop owner suggested I use one of the new dive guides who incidentally could not swim a stroke, and always wore a life jacket even when walking on the beach! My CPR dummy was called Patrick and he said he would gladly allow us to practise chest compressions on him, who was I to argue? The weather outside was overcast and raining so I had the full company of staff to train in First Aid.

We began and the next couple of hours trickled by as I rambled on and we all had a good laugh while pushing Patrick's chest in and out and inflating his lungs for 30 minutes…looking back, this was possibly not the cleverest procedure to be practising on a currently living person, but he grinned and bared it and most importantly, didn't die. The dive shop owner had pulled out all the stops and brought his video player and television from home so we could watch the crackly and poorly acted training video that was mandatory viewing for completion of the class.

I stared out of the window during a long video segment and watched as the rain fell onto the flat sea as it lapped the shore just 50 feet away. Down the beach, I could see a crowd forming and they looked out to a restaurant that stood on a pier. I could see a large slick of red in the sea and immediately feared the worst. I shouted to the class that there was a huge amount of blood in the water and dashed outside to investigate, strangely, nobody came after me.

I asked some of the crowd what was happening, but they didn't know and were just concerned holiday makers that saw the blood. I hadn't heard of any shark attacks in the area, so jumped into the water with my diving mask and snorkel. I could hardly see anything as the visibility was terrible, but I noticed a sweet smell as I swam into the red water. I came up to get some orientation and take a breath. The water tasted like melon flavoured bubblegum and my skin was turning red. I headed back to shore and saw some of the other dive guides and instructors laughing their heads off and pointing at me. The dive centre shared a stretch of beach with a hotel and a soft drink manufacturer called Juicy Drinks. Every time it rained heavily or the high tide level occurred after sunset, they would flush the drink containers into the sea to make way for a new batch of flavours. Over the next few months I taught class in Blueberry, Melon, and even Cranberry flavoured seawater. It was quite entertaining, but hardly environmentally friendly as all the local fish life had very bad teeth from drinking fizzy drinks all day.

Most of the days of work didn't see crazy antics like this but it was never dull. One of the few perks of the job is the fact that diving Instructors seem to be objects of desire for the many single ladies that holiday alone in paradise. When I was not in any long-term (more than two weeks) relationships there were many opportunities to flirt with the customers, and this is still one of the few tangible benefits that go with the job. So that this text keeps its *family show* certificate I won't go into too much detail, but maybe the tales of *relations* with ladies while attempting the deepest shag on scuba, or being caught on camera underneath a glass bottom boat by holiday makers as they looked for unusual marine life will make it into an adult version of this publication coming soon.

Chapter 3. Deeper Interest

Work as diving instructor can be very seasonal. To stay busy you need to travel to other holiday destinations as the tourist seasons rotate. After a year in Barbados, I felt a return to the United Kingdom was on the cards. Arriving back in London gave me itchy feet almost immediately, and I phoned around for work in various holiday destinations around the British south coast even before my tan had faded. In 1995, I'd had my first laptop for over a year already, but the internet still resembled semaphore and websites where just glimmers in a 'net-nurds' eye. Job searches in the diving industry then, and even more so now were best completed in person - by actually visiting various dive shops. I had arrived in London in June when most summer dive jobs were already filled, so the job search went slowly. While away though, I stayed in contact with an instructor buddy, James. He ran a dive centre on Jersey in the Channel Islands, and often said I should visit. I gave him a call and within a couple of days was on a car ferry to St Helier, the capitol of Jersey with all my diving equipment and my newest acquisition, an underwater metal detector.

Jersey was fantastic, a bit like living in a big city but by the seaside. The dive centre was absolutely huge, with ten other instructors (who never seemed to do any work), and there was an excellent social scene. I soon was busy with work as plenty of the locals had read about technical diving in magazines and now had an instructor offering deep diver training right on their doorstep.

The Channel Islands are smack in the middle of one of the largest tidal ranges in the world. At certain times of the month, the tide could rise and fall nearly 12 metres. This created very fast moving water and amazing drift dives. Mariners too, all through the ages have found these incredible tides an unmatchable force and skeletons of shipwrecks litter the seabed. Local sea charts record somewhere over 300 foundered vessels resting in the vicinity.

The dive centre had a big customer base that went diving as often as they could, this gave me a captive audience to sell my deep diving courses to. Regularly we would organise two boats to take all the customers out to the surrounding islands of Sark and Guernsey for reef dives or, interesting Second World War shipwrecks that still produced brass treasures in abundance. The popular wreck sites were, in ascending order of difficulty; the SS. Schokland, the M343 Minesweeper and the Princess Ena. The daddy of them all was the Jean Marie, locally known as the copper wreck. There were literally dozens of other wrecks nearby, but these were the ones on many divers' must-see lists.

Technical diving courses were often attended by groups of customers that would complete the entire range of training courses together, with great enthusiasm. As a busy instructor, I still liked to fun dive, but only with people who I am comfortable with. I usually dived alone for fun, but it was always nicer to go with people who could complete dives successfully in the arduous conditions. More often than not, the only time I would dive would be during a training course, and on such dives, my attention was always focused on the job. One group of divers that I felt comfortable to dive with was three friends, Jamie (BAZ), Alison and Natalie.

The three amigos finished some recreational courses with me, and then went on to complete various levels of more advanced tech training over the summer. After three months they had graduated as Extended Range divers and were all competent to join the deeper fun dives on wrecks as deep as 200 feet. We would explore wrecks such as the Copper Wreck and the Princess Ena, bringing up ships portholes, ingots of copper and all of the other rubbish that looks like it's made of divers gold (brass) until it arrives on the boat. It takes a lot of wreck dives to develop proper 'brass vision'. Quite often the treasure becomes just smelly, rusted ferrous metal as the nitrogen narcosis wears off in the shallows - then it gets thrown back immediately. The summer season is quite short in the UK and by September, the sea temperature drops inversely to the wind speed raising. When it was too horrible to take customers diving, I would join a team of Scallop divers who went out in search of sought-after shellfish in the often unpleasant winter weather. I did enjoy searching and harvesting the seabed, but the weather was becoming more and more hostile and this meant more days out of employment. This was a sign to either hang up your flippers and mask for the winter or migrate. I decided it was about time to move back to pastures warmer.

I planned to go back to Barbados again for the Christmas season and had started seeing Natalie, one of my favourite customers. She also liked the idea of working in the Caribbean for the winter, so we flew back to Bridgetown together. Having a girlfriend who was as interested in deep diving as me was great. We would work all day, she as a Dive master leading groups of divers, and me teaching recreational scuba courses. After work we would go diving again, always deep, just for fun. In no time we had built up quite a little club of divers, mostly going straight to 240 feet or thereabouts, every afternoon looking for antique bottles. Repetitive diving to the same depths each day predictably lost its challenge and allure, so Natalie and myself planned to head deeper still. As the dive depths increased, the group split up – so no one was pressured into doing something they were not ready for. To be successful in deeper diving it's important to feel relaxed and avoid being pushed into stress inducing depths. As Natalie and I wanted to drop beyond 300 feet every day, it was seldom more than the two of us.

There was this fantastic magnetic feeling that seemed to draw us to extreme depth, like moths to a flame. The sea was always electric blue, and always welcomed us with its warm and embracing tentacles, likely similar to drug taking. We both felt a sense of complete clarity of mind and I would do some of my clearest thinking only when approaching 300 feet. This total 'meditative' state was clearly addictive, if pot smokers or heroin addicts only knew about this perfectly legal high, then scuba diving would be the most popular sport imaginable. Unfortunately the side effects of deep scuba diving are every bit as hazardous as drugs and cannot be minimised without considerable practice. Even then, oxygen toxicity is so unpredictable and unforgiving...in this case practice does not make perfect.

One afternoon we didn't join the usual dive boat out of Carlisle Bay, but made other arrangements for a 'special' dive. We headed out into the setting west coast sun on a small fibreglass boat borrowed from the maritime university. Our boat driver was Cally; he worked at the University of West Indies - next door to where I used to work the year before. Cally often drove the boat to take us deep diving back then. He often grinned and joked about how foolish we were for doing these crazy air dives.

When I told him the 'plan' for today, Cally repeated his favourite phrase - "You all is nuttier than a squirrel's breakfast", I always grinned when he said that.

The boat had no depth sounder, and none was really necessary, as we weren't looking to land on the seabed and would be disappointed if sand came into view earlier than expected. Cally just headed out, he knew of an area where it was very deep. The spot we dived was rumoured to be bottomless. Even the sea charts suggested up to two hundred fathoms, about twelve hundred feet deep, more than enough.

Natalie and I had been below 350 feet dozens of times, always breathing air in single eighty feet scuba tanks. Today we planned to go to four hundred feet. This translated to 123 metres, the Holy Grail for deep air divers. The effect of Nitrogen on this dive would have an anaesthetic effect akin to a bottle of whiskey or a pile of Ketamin consumed in one fell swoop. Ketamin is a powerful horse tranquiliser proving popular with ravers and scuba professionals alike all across Asia.

As always, the dive could be aborted if necessary. Just before the dive, Natalie said that she might stop earlier than planned, as this was a big step and we were heading into depths that would stun an elephant, never mind mentally challenged diving instructors like us. Think of deep air diving as the Rock n' Roll of scuba diving, 'classical' recreational depths may seem safer but they can definitely send you mad doing them everyday. We dived deep on air simply to stretch our legs.

Rolling backwards over the side of the boat, we floated on the surface. Staring downwards, excited, and at the same time drawn to the spider's web of the abyss below. Moments spent relaxing here would calm the back-chatter in our minds and prepare the reflexes necessary to overcome today's gauntlet. This surface wait would help physically slow our breathing and heart rates down, in a similar fashion to that employed by all deep diving mammals, before they attempted their own crazy stunt dives.

Dives like this must begin without any conflicting thoughts or even a minor sense of possible failure, indeed no sense at all can be attached to such endeavours. There was no bottom, no chance of rescue, and no descent line that could be used to halt the descent. I think we thought at the time that dives must be controlled solely by good technique, exertion avoidance and finely honed self rescue abilities. The dive begins the same way as always, we vent the air from our buoyancy jackets, invert and kick towards our goal. We would drop like greased anvils towards the bottom at nearly 200 feet per minute. In diving terms this is the speed at which a fly hits a cars windscreen. Natalie was positioned just behind me, in my slipstream, her left hand would be just on the edge of my field of vision. At anytime a simple hand signal would indicate that all was OK, or all was NOT.

The time spent descending into the darkness and time spent at maximum depth is necessarily very short. Slipping through the ocean for long periods is akin to freefall parachuting, the faster you fall the easier it is to make mistakes or miss the important. My eyes scan from side to side to give better focusing and avoid the head spin effect caused by lack of reference.

Dropping down so fast is mentally taxing, trying to steer my body into a stable position, at the same time listening for any abnormalities or change in sensation. Any strange feeling could mean that oxygen toxicity is opening its can of worms must be analysed instantly, it's the secret of success. Unfortunately Nitrogen is beginning to start banging its drum kit right in the middle of my head. I'm trying to listen for the faintest nuances of escalating impending death due to oxygen toxicity. At the same time I'm overloaded by doom radio at full volume as heavy Nitrogen Narcosis engulfs my auditory senses with its ubiquitous and deafening requiem beat. The infamous Wah Wah tune that has beckoned so many deep divers to their deaths is repeating at a fantastic speed as we pass 350 feet. I signal to Natalie if she is OK and she indicates yes. I stare at my depth gauge and the numbers climb up at a ridiculous speed, I wonder If I will notice when enough is enough. We approach 400 feet and I get the sign to stop from behind me. I start to add air to my buoyancy jacket as this will arrest the descent. I remember that I should have started doing this already and a flutter of anxiety fills me. We break apart still descending and I turn to face Natalie to see what's wrong. The water still rushes past us and I lose stability for a few seconds, this separates us further. I ask if all is Okay again. Natalie eyes are open but she unblinkingly stares past me. The depth is approaching 420 feet. We have small tanks of air that can be used in emergencies for rapidly filling or buoyancy vests. I reach behind Natalie and open this tank for her. In a second the vest is full and is burping excess air as she moves upwards away from me. I watch as she leaves me, she is inert and ascending out of control, but my mind is blank to these implications.

I reach behind me to operate my ascent bottle. I turn the valve and nothing happens, I turn the valve some more and find that I have unscrewed the small cylinder from the jacket! I bring the mini tank in front of me and open the valve again. This time all the air within just empties into the water. I realise that I am very affected by the situation. I close my eyes to think. Opening them, I look around for Natalie and she is gone, I cannot remember seeing her go anywhere anymore. I look at my depth gauge, it says 428 feet and 5 minutes elapsed time. I blink again and the gauge still reads 428 feet and elapsed time 7 minutes. I look down and see bubbles coming up from beneath me. Maybe she has passed out and gone below me, I stare below and see nothing.

I consider draining my buoyancy jacket of air and dropping down to take a quick look. I won't leave her down there, not while I can still see bubbles. I look at the elapsed time on my gauge and two more minutes have elapsed. This is no good at all, I have a single 12 litre scuba tank on my back and the tank pressure reads one third full. I will have to perform a series of decompression stops before being able to break the surface. These stops will take longer than 99 minutes according to my wrist gauge. I look below and see no more bubbles. I blink again, this time I have somehow moved a bit shallower. The depth now reads 400 feet but I feel clearer and now dread is filling me. I must save myself. The decompression sickness I will undoubtedly suffer soon will possibly give me a stay in execution from the tongue-wagger's accusations. I inflate my buoyancy jacket for the rapid ascent away from death's jaws but into a guaranteed world of pain. The jacket fills with air and I start to accelerate towards the surface. I leave my bubbles behind me as I'm propelled upwards at a ridiculous speed. Looking at my gauge, I need to know the depth to make the first of my decompression stops. I get the information from my wrist computer display. I don't have enough air, I calculate, to do all of these stops; I consider that the important ones will be all of the deeper ones starting at 80 feet. These stops will repeat every 10 feet until I get just a long arm reach from the surface. The last stop will be the longest and I know that if I cut the time short there, I will definitely get the bends, but it will likely come after I get out of the water. My breathing is a little fast, if I don't control it things will be much worse. I concentrate on relaxing, my body going completely limp, just floating, every muscle except my lungs forced to do nothing. The water temperature gets warmer as the surface looms ever closer, the pleasant water temperature reminds me of the complacency a lobster must feel during his journey to the dinner table, a seemingly pleasant ending, but I know my struggle in the final minute will be more terrifying than a lobster falling unconscious during his hot bath. The warm fluid that surrounds me is impassionate about my plight, the sea has taken its harvest no doubt many times today. A few scuba divers foolishly getting too close to the fire will fill a column in a local newspaper, and no doubt a super tanker split open like firewood for daring to match money-saving designs against stormy seas will make the television news. I know I will get to the surface one way or another. I don't think much beyond that, I try to recall if there was a spare scuba tank on the boat, it was unlikely. I can't even hear the boat engine come to think of it, this would be the final nail in the coffin, an absent dive boat. I would get to the surface alone, the decompression sickness would strike me an excruciatingly painful blow that would lead to paralysis and death within 30 minutes of surfacing. Without a boat to return me to shore, my final exit from the world will be a fairly unpleasant experience.

I will float face down for a few hours until my buoyancy jacket finally gives up its hold on the surface, then I will drift back down whence I came and take my place in the food chain. These thoughts fill my head for a few seconds, then they disappear. I thought of Natalie, how would she have managed during her unconscious ride to the surface? She could have come around and is now faced with a similar dilemma as me just a stones throw away. The minutes tick by and I complete my decompression stops like a robot. With this style of diving you cannot just decide you have had enough and go to the surface, everything needs to be endured until the end and sometimes beyond this. Extreme scuba diving has no comparisons in the world of crazy pursuits. When a base jumper hits the ground, his adventure is over, much the same as an astronaut. Divers have to wait for hours after a dive before their bodies return to normal and the celebrations begin. This dive has gone wrong and now payment is being exacted. One diver is missing and another about to go the same way. During difficult times it's easy to get philosophical in the face of hopelessness, for the same reasons the elderly turn to religion, but nothing can change the outcome. Last minute confessions reconcile nothing and certainly don't lengthen your odds with the bookmakers in the sky.

Its time to replace profound thoughts with rational thinking and problem solving abilities, this is the only process that can help overcome seemingly insurmountable challenges. My wrist computer beeps madly, dragging me from my daze, I look for the problem. The surface looks very close, less than 3 metres. The electronic depth gauge is insisting I go deeper and wait another 45 minutes. I check my air gauge, the reading is so low that it defies measurement. I congratulate myself on buying a cheap air gauge that is very inaccurate, who knows how much air I have left! Some ten minutes later my breathing regulator lets me know exactly the remaining air time...none. I have lasted over an hour with less than 20 percent of a full tank. I cannot breathe now and am forced to ascend the final furlong with over 35 minutes of decompression time remaining. This is bad because my dive computer is known for having little conservatism; I wish I had purchased a model aimed at holiday divers which reflect a trend for incredible safety and conservatism. The decompression time I am missing out on will be very real indeed, there is no padding, a bit like Dolly Parton's bra I thought surreally.

I hit the surface; I'd made it for now. The sea is totally calm, flat like glass. The sun is very low on the horizon, very scenic but it will make surface searches next to impossible. I spin around and see the boat. Cally the boatman waves and turns to pull the engine start cord. I see the boat engine cough into life.

"I thought you weren't coming back...mon" Cally said,

"Neither did I, Natalie is still down there somewhere, have you seen her marker buoy?"

"No, mon I ain't seen nuttin a tall" These words brought the memories of the last hour crashing back. I threw off my buoyancy jacket and climbed into the boat.

"I don't think she is coming back, it all went wrong down there"

Cally swallowed and went quiet. I scanned the ocean surface for Natalie's surface marker buoy and saw nothing "We should look for her Signalling balloon" I said trying to add an air of optimism.

The boat started moving. We circled around and saw nothing. Despair was setting in and pain was beginning to gnaw in my hip. I said nothing. The decompression sickness was manifesting it self in my right hip area with a level of pain which was attention-getting but manageable. I was surprised at how quickly the pain had started, but kept a focus on the search for Natalie's yellow coloured marker buoy.

We carried on looking but the low sun angle was blocking a huge part of the search area. I asked Cally to head into the sun's direction so that we could see more clearly behind us. Travelling towards the sun I looked behind the boat, the sea was basked in the yellow sunlight, Natalie's marker buoy was similarly yellow, and again we drew a blank. I thought we would have been closer together at the surface, there was no current to separate us. I imagined the worst but expected the best. The boat stopped, I looked around, and there it was. A yellow lift bag was bobbing on the surface a few hundred yards behind us. The elation for myself and Cally was incredible, we had searched for over 30 minutes with thoughts of doom and despair. The pain in my hip was like a bad toothache but It didn't matter. The boat headed over and I jumped over the side with my mask, landing almost on top of the yellow balloon. I looked below. Natalie was there and breathing and smiling. I swam down and joined her, breathing off her spare breathing regulator while she completed the rest of the decompression stops that I had been forced to cut short. We looked at each other shaking our heads and grinning. This had been a close call, with all the trimmings of having to pay the ultimate price. The only lesson to learn was not to do it again.

We surfaced together, spitting out our breathing regulators at the same time, saying "Oh my god, I thought you were dead!"

The boat trip back was frenetic and animated as we both exchanged our version of what happened. Natalie recalled that she started to pass out as we approached 400 feet and signalled me to stop. After we broke apart at 420 feet, that was her last memory. During the ascent the scuba regulator she was breathing from had fallen from her mouth. Natalie had ascended from deep water to around 200 feet without breathing. The air in her lungs had expanded and miraculously harmlessly escaped through her mouth, instead of the normal route that causes irreparable damage to scuba divers lungs due to embolism. She recalled experiencing a bright light all around as she rocketed upwards to the surface. During the ascent, Natalie was aware that the breathing regulator was not in her mouth. Though still unconscious, an automatic response kicked in that recovered the breathing regulator and inserted it back in with all the usual water clearing and choking prevention techniques. As full consciousness returned, she noticed that her ascent speed was too fast so she vented the air from her buoyancy jacket; this stopped the ascent at 190 feet. A cloud of exhaled bubbles caught up shortly afterwards.

Natalie thought that I must be either still down there or had made my own way to the surface out of view. Because of her short time at depth and rapid ascent, this left her enough air to complete far more of her decompression stops than I would manage. We got back to the dive centre just before dark. I assembled the oxygen therapy set and started to breathe deeply. The oxygen started to do its work after 30 minutes and this gave me some pain relief. I phoned the recompression chamber and they were closed. The receptionist said the doctors were resting after performing multi day treatments on a deep water Lobster diver that had spent close on 50 minutes at 200 feet before ascending rapidly. He would not walk again.

The techniques used by Caribbean Lobster divers make my deep air adventures appear positively sedentary. Imagine taking six or seven loose scuba tanks tied together with string, with one breathing regulator between all the tanks. When one tank runs out, the diver *simply* swaps the regulator to the next full tank. All this happening in deep water with no means of calculating the decompression stop timings, except traditions modified by the number of Lobsters in the area.

The next morning I managed a visit to the local navy headquarters that housed the islands recompression chamber. The diving doctor said that as it was a day after the symptoms had occurred, and more importantly the fact that I had no medical insurance, meant treatment was not necessary anymore. If my discomfort persisted I could contact him in a few days, in the meantime I should chew some pain killers. That afternoon, I took a bottle of oxygen from the dive centre and went for a shallow dive on the Berwyn wreck at just twenty feet for eighty minutes. This in-water recompression session did the trick and didn't cost anything.

Chapter 4: Clarity Beckons

I dive deep using air because it is fun, cheap and most importantly, because I can. Also, deep air diving provides a level of peace and tranquillity that only parachutists and astronauts experience. We all share a minute or two of intense action at the beginning, then towards the end, lots of time for reflection and sightseeing. I suppose Astronauts get another bout of action when they attempt re-entry, which must be similar to the fickleness of decompressing after an extreme dive. However, in contrast to divers, spacemen are not making many life and death decisions, they just ride an automated fair ground ride called a rocket.

Unlike the many mainstream spectator-orientated sports where corporations can throw countless millions at a title, experience and ability are the only currencies that count in deep water. All the cash or bravado in the world counts for nothing down in the bowels of the ocean. This is what makes it such a noble pastime. It's not tainted by the dubious commerce of athletics and there are no referees to bribe. All the steroids in the world won't help at all. It's only you and *your* body against *your* ability. However, if a sports shoe company wants me to tattoo a swoosh on my butt cheek, I'm well up for it!

I don't have many other vices, I don't smoke, hardly drink. Motorbike riding scares me to death, I even keep my hair short. I think Free-Diving or *extreme snorkelling* is unacceptably dangerous and drugs just rob people of their minds. My addiction is to scuba dive deep for entertainment and reward. After the last bout of excitement though, I thought it wise to somehow add a little reliability and a future to my deep diving escapades by squirting some Helium into the breathing mixture. These 'Trimix' breathing mixtures as they are called were becoming fashionable at the beginning of the nineties. I received certification in its use in early 1995. After the training I read the small print closely, and diving deep using helium just exchanged the fairly insidious side effects associated with air diving with a host of new and helium specific ones. Air diving beyond the realms of safety sounds quite ludicrous, but it's not as bad as smoking dope before driving, or riding a motorbike while tired. Pedestrians have never been killed by deep air divers to my knowledge.

A B-list sportsman in the UK scribbled a rant to a diving magazine saying that I was promoting a type of diving in which to fail meant certain death. In his particular two wheeled discipline, I hear that any competitor with a chance of winning a non-ferrous medal is hooked on the drug E.P.O. This powerful and popular (but illegal) performance enhancer has some particularly attractive side affects. User's report having to get up every hour throughout the night to run up and down the stairs in an effort to increase a dangerously low pulse. Should the heavy sleeper fail to hear the hourly wake up call, he (or she) can rest safe in the knowledge that their heart will likely stop dead, greatly affecting the chances of glory and medals. You don't have to get up early to go deep diving and I even actively discourage early rising. Also, crazy deep divers don't suffer from 'roid-rage', (unless they are body-builders as well), yet another plus point.

I continued to dive on air, still relatively deep but I didn't go beyond 400 feet again, mostly because Natalie didn't want to and it's not as much as fun doing it alone...What is? I received my Trimix Instructor certification late 1995 and started planning my first 500 foot dive. I had dived to near 400 feet dozens of times already just with single air tanks without drama. When you put a spurt of helium in the scuba cylinders we calculated it would take six tanks each to safely complete such a deep dive. Another major drawback when using helium is its prohibitive cost. A commercial size tank of helium which contains just 7 cubic metres cost over nine hundred Barbados dollars. That is half a year's wages for a scuba instructor. To make matters worse, Natalie wanted to come so we needed three helium tanks, but luckily I didn't have to shoulder the cost completely as she had got some work dive guiding, which on most days earned her more money than I got.

The dive centre I worked at now was Coral Island Divers based in the central town harbour area called the Careenage. Working in central Bridgetown meant easy access for cruise ship travellers and the dive centre was pretty busy most days. On afternoons when we both were not either sheep-dogging hoards of snorkellers or rescuing drunken man-over board's getting a little too merry on the glass bottom boats, we would go for a deep dive to keep practising for the upcoming super deep one. The company I worked at had a very nice dive catamaran, this would have made the perfect platform to do our deep dive from, but the thought of an accident during such a crazy dive caused the companies share holders to veto our plans for using the main vessel. This setback meant hiring another boat at short notice. Finding this boat lost a few days but there were no real time constraints, other than the thought that the helium gas in our tanks would somehow escape from our scuba tanks over time, as was the popular myth of the time.

Our bosses Ken and Chantel volunteered as support divers, Ken had organised our deep dive boat and was told that it was a purpose built dive boat based on a largish speed boat. When the boat arrived, I wondered where the four of us would sit never mind where we would put the eighteen scuba tanks and associated goodies necessary for our planned epic dive. The boat was 16 feet long at best, but it did have a non-working depth sounder! However, the boat was eventually loaded and we drove very slowly out of the Careenage on another perfect sunny day. The boat was clearly overloaded, but spirits were high.

Barbados is a coral island that sits in relatively shallow water. Neighbouring Caribbean Islands are mostly volcanic and rise sharply from abyssal depths. The most easterly of island chains, Barbados sits surrounded by shoal water and looking for deep water can be tiresome, the task today hampered by the broken depth sounder. Ken knew of an area where the depth should be close on 500 feet, but we wanted something a little more concrete than this, so Ken beckoned over a nearby sport fisher boat and asked them the depth below using their depth sounder. The skipper told us it was close to 600 feet and told us to move a few hundred yards closer in to get 500 feet. Using this very accurate depth measuring technique we dropped our descent line over the side and it did seem to touch the bottom at the expected depth. Putting on our five dive tanks in the sun got tensions rising, but this was merely stress and anxiety as our bodies rebelled against the impending madness that our egos had arranged for us.

Some of the spare scuba tanks that would be used for decompression stops later needed to be tied to the descent line at the appropriate depths and Chantel was loath to be the one responsible for the fastenings on such important tanks. I had to fasten the tanks myself while wearing my five tanks and wearing a 10mm wetsuit in the blistering sun. Natalie waited in the water cooling off and preparing for the mental gauntlet that was no doubt in store. Ken was energetically telling us to hurry up as the tidal flow was now moving and we were moving into deeper water. I hit the water hot and flustered in a tangled mass of breathing regulators and hoses. Between us we were wearing half of the dive schools rental regulators, and eighteen scuba tanks were clipped either to us or the down-line, so our bosses had a double reticence in supporting this stunt. But they were being quite cool at the moment.

I held the line and took my diving mask off whilst looking down into a very blurred abyss. The feeling of cooler water on the face triggers a reflex that is used constantly by diving mammals such as dolphins. This no-mask breathing trick would cause my heart rate to drop along with slowing my breathing. When descending deep underwater, relaxed breathing cannot be over emphasized.

A few minutes of relaxation later, we began our descent. The water was very clear and at 27 degrees Celsius, a little on the warm side with our thick wetsuits. Dropping down as if parachuting through a dark blue sky felt amazing. The visibility downwards must have approached one hundred and fifty feet. I was first on the line at the beginning, I looked behind me periodically to see Natalie grinning and clearly loving it. We had switched from air at two hundred feet to a trimix mixed from equal quantities of helium and air, this mix gave us ten percent oxygen and fifty percent helium. Dropping beyond four hundred feet we still had daylight conditions, we had read that natural light permeates beyond six hundred feet in the Caribbean Sea, though I did wonder how this was proven. The water had turned a little cooler by four hundred and fifty feet, but I can't say that it felt any deeper or scarier than other dives in the past. The tanks we had to use were without manifolds, merely independent scuba tanks used daily in the dive school. I put my own Scubapro regulator on the right hand tank, on the left was a standard Sherwood Brute from the school inventory. Natalie had her own similar high end model on one tank and an Oceanic rental model on the other. Breathing gases with high helium contents make any regulator breathe great, as the popular balloon gas is far less dense than nitrogen or oxygen and flows much more easily, in addition to its more useful property of giving the breather a funny voice.

I stopped on the line to check my pressure gauges and switch regulators. Natalie dropped below me on the line and we continued downwards. On checking my gauges, I was alarmed to see that the glass had broken on one and it had filled with water, although it still offered a reading. The other resembled a snow scene table ornament, with lots of small pieces floating in an oil and water soup. The descent speed started to slow as the plan called for hitting five hundred feet in seven minutes, at this stage we were going a little fast. This dive would literally only be a *bounce* for a couple of minutes. The breathing tanks were very small, although we regularly dived with a single tank of air to four hundred feet. Breathing helium meant ascending much slower than if we used air, so most of the gas attached to us would be used solely for the ascent.

Hitting five hundred feet for the first time was a bit of an anticlimax really. The anchor line must have moved, because looking down we could see the seabed slowly moving past some sixty feet deeper. Gripping the line, we compared our depth gauges against each others to see who had gone deeper, and exchanged some grins. The Helium content of the gas we breathed made us feel as if we were diving to two hundred and fifty feet on air, with regard to nitrogen narcosis and oxygen toxicity. Our back tanks contained 50% Helium mixed with air, this caused the oxygen and the nitrogen fractions to reduce by half also. Instead of the usual 21% oxygen and 79% nitrogen as found in surface air, our mixture was 10% oxygen and 40% nitrogen with the balance 50% helium. This allowed us a sort of equivalent narcosis depth of roughly half the actual depth we dived. Being as clear headed as this was very strange and a little disconcerting. Normally, deep diving using air would give feelings of invincibility and confidence. Today our clear heads meant the whole experience was endured with an air of sobriety. Feeling both very deep *and* sober for the first time made me feel more vulnerable than during any of our crazy air dives. We wanted to grab a pebble as a keepsake, but sadly the seabed was just too far out of reach. No heroics were planned, so all that was left was to head back up.

Some might argue that diving deep just for the sake of it seems pointless, but the feeling of extreme depth can be exhilarating and priceless. If it was easier to do, many more divers would do it. Deep divers may spend only a short time at maximum depth, but this is very similar to the limited durations planned by high altitude mountain climbers. Experiences that include the mind and body are definitely more valuable than solely exercising the senses in the brain. I certainly don't understand folk who take drugs or alcohol. Artificial highs like these only offer some escapism for a few hours. Users are still the same bores after the effects wear off, minus a few brain cells. To quote an immortal line from the movie Trainspotting, *Choose life, and* exchange your televisions, drink or drugs for twin scuba tanks. That's enough of the bar room psyche lessons for now, remember we are still five hundred feet down. We had got down here but that was only half the challenge, we had to get back up. The ascent was fairly routine, although we had to ascend much more slowly than usual. Because of the helium, you have to ascend no faster than 10 metres per minute. At this stage of a deep air dive, computer alarms would be screaming as we left our exhaled bubbles far behind. Also, breathing the balloon gas meant doing decompression stops much deeper than if we breathed normal air.

We had our first formal decompression stop around two hundred feet. I had read about deeper stops and decided that we should add an extra stop at three hundred and thirty feet. At this point I would change breathing gases to air. Natalie waited until three hundred feet to do the same. Going from trimix to air at this depth was like closing the curtains and leaving a gap in the middle. I noticed my peripheral vision drop from one hundred and eighty degrees to around forty-five in just a couple of seconds. I wrote on my dive slate *vision collapsed to grey*. It was an interesting feeling, so I tried to repeat it by going back to the trimix. Returning to the lighter gas was noticeably much easier to breathe but my vision did not open back up like I imagined it would. Natalie had a similar experience a few minutes later. Vision would not return to normal until we reached the virtual shallows of two hundred feet. Remember that Helium is not narcotic but Nitrogen is. If you suddenly stop breathing Helium and replace it with mostly Nitrogen, you will experience immediate and extreme sedation. This doesn't happen at the surface, but try it while one hundred metres underwater and if you are lucky you will see what I mean. New divers would be killed, but my junkie-like adaptation to Nitrogen gained from doing excessive Deep air dives afforded me some level of protection.

Onwards and Upwards - all the pressure gauges we had were broken and several regulators were leaking from both the high pressure and low pressure hoses. All the shallower deco stops went fine, although we had to do was swap a couple of regulators over underwater. I figured that as so much equipment had failed on this dive, it would all need stripping and servicing. A couple more pieces of kit wouldn't add much to the workload, I might even get a bulk discount on the parts required. During the deco stops around one hundred feet, we had a surprise as one of the decompression tanks came whistling past us headed for the bottom. I looked up to the surface to see Chantel holding her palms out and pointing to a now empty piece of rope. I hoped we wouldn't be needing that tank! The dive lasted a little under three hours and went largely to plan except for the broken and lost equipment. Ken and Chantel swam around us during the last deco stops, snapping away with an underwater camera. In the pictures I looked quite concerned, as I was probably totalling up the costs for today, both pre-dive and for all the lost and broken equipment.

When the dive plan was finished we bobbed up to the surface and exchanged jubilations with each other. The relief was evident on our support crews faces, Natalie and I were very happy. She had become the deepest female diver in the ocean. During the deco stops, I was already planning a thousand-foot dive in my head based on today's successes.

We told our two support divers the details of the adventure throughout the journey back. Landing on the dock outside the dive centre, it was clear I had a full evening of work in front of me. I had to fix as many broken regulators as I could because tomorrow was very busy with people booked on scuba try-dives. About nine that evening we hit the bar at the Boat Yard to celebrate, but by ten o clock, tiredness and the call of bed was impossible to ignore.

This dive was late in the Barbados holiday season so it was about time to return to England to find a job ahead of the summer. I returned back to Jersey with Natalie, she had a proper job in a promotions company. I found work at a north coast dive centre called Watersports, in Bouley Bay. The company was the oldest dive centre in the world, I think. The owner Jimmy started diving here in 1958, way before the warmer seas and other benefits associated with global warming, he told me constantly. I started running recreational and technical dive classes and built up a steady business with holiday makers and locals. Jamie, aka 'Ginger Baz' had just returned from Australia with great diving adventure stories. We planned some deeper wreck dives for the next weekend. Unfortunately the tide tables predicted one of the biggest ranges of the year, close to forty feet from high to low water. Choosing to dive the Copper Wreck at two hundred feet depth on such a tide was inappropriate with hindsight. As was very often the case, divers that had chomped at the bit at the mere mention of such a dive became reticent and un-contactable as the dive day drew nearer. A planned group of six dwindled to three by the morning as we loaded the boat. A new diving charter boat was taking us to the wreck positioned half-way between Sark and Jersey. The vessel bristled with electronic monitors and shiny stainless steel fittings, plus a cheerful skipper with a hot coffee-pot.

The weather was agreeable, but big tidal movements mean poor visibility, today the seawater was green like phlegm. Arriving at the site on time, we dropped anchor. The three divers were Ginger Baz, Natalie and myself. We wore big single tanks of air with small pony bottles of oxygen used to speed up the decompression. Planning just fifteen minutes at depth, we hoped to find the elusive copper ingots that littered the seabed around the wreck. Tidal conditions were so bad in this area that just two hundred metres from this wreck was another called the Rafio. The Rafio was a salvage barge that sank while attempting to liberate the copper ingots from today's target. Rumour had it that the barges crane-grab had overreached itself and underestimated the current speed, sending it straight to the bottom. Mariner's tales mentioned lockers full of commercial diving equipment aboard this boat. I had visited a couple of times before in search of this diver's gold, but found only bare cupboards and lots of rusty metal.

Jumping over the side of the dive boat gave us a nasty surprise. The current had changed from slack to definitely not, already. We held onto the anchor line as if our lives depended on it. To give you an idea of the strength of the water flow, imagine doing pull up exercises with a sumo wrestler holding on to both legs. The water was cold, green and horrible, visibility just a couple of feet. We pulled ourselves down the rope like we were competing in a Tug of War competition. The deeper you get, the weaker the force of the current. That's the normal maxim and it usually worked but by seventy feet down,

I was still fearful that my mask would be ripped from my face. It was a proper struggle pulling down this rope. I looked around to see Natalie shaking her head as she waved a signal of good bye and let go of the line. In one second she was swept from view. Knocking this dive on the head was definitely the best idea in the face of these appalling conditions. Baz and I continued on downwards, looking for easier conditions, failing miserably.

The current was scheduled for seven knots today; the dive boat could barely manage twelve. If we mistimed the journey back, it would take forever travelling against the tide. Sometimes it made sense to just anchor for six hours until the tide changed direction. By about one hundred and sixty five feet, I stopped and turned to face my buddy while struggling to stay holding onto to the anchor line. All the natural light was left far behind and we operated by torchlight completely at this point. Trying to explain that we should abort the dive after I recovered the boat's anchor from the wreck was next to impossible in these conditions. It was like having a sign language chat at night while fighting multiple opponents. I think Baz had a rough idea about what I had planned, but after I pulled myself the final furlong to the wreck below I was sure of the communication breakdown. The anchor line was jumping up and down frantically. One second it was tight as a piano wire, the next, lost against the rusted spars of the freighter below. The up and down movement was unusual because the seas above had been flat as we left the surface. I swam further along the rope until I reached the section of chain just ahead of the anchor at two hundred feet depth. My feet felt like I was swimming in treacle and it was getting thicker. Looking behind, I realised my lifting bag and reel had come loose, the line was wrapping around my knees and legs. Away in the murky distance my dive light picked out the yellow lifting bag spinning around acting like a sea anchor while pulling more line from my reel.

I would need two hands to fix this problem but they were both busy holding onto the anchor line rodeo. Out came my knife and I cut straight through the line, setting loose my lift bag.

Now it was free to roam the ocean, free of its master like a Romjin warrior. This selfless act would cost me forty quid. Now I was loose I could pull myself along the line towards the metal hook. Holding the line was becoming a real chore, as the anchor line tensed under the strain it would generate small bubbles from the turbulence. The ship's anchor was an expensive one and our boat captain had specifically asked me to throw it clear of the wreck at the end of the dive. I timed my efforts to coincide with the upward thrust of the anchor line. I would ascend without a reference line and complete my small amount of decompression stops just hovering at the correct depths. Releasing and throwing the anchor clear was quite easy. As the line went slack, I quickly pulled the anchor blades from the wreckage. The next wave lifted the anchor free and it was gone with the current. However, it came crashing back downwards right in front of me. The chain was draped over my neck, tank and legs. Even better, the rope after the chain had caught under some wreckage. I was properly trapped now, and with every upward thrust of the line it became tighter, crushing me further downwards against the gnarly wreckage.

As if I needed more excitement, the current started lifting my mask from my face as I looked from one side to the next. Alarm bells were ringing now - I still had half a tank of air, but the decompression time was mounting quickly and I was completely pinned down. I struggled uselessly against the current for ten more minutes, now I had just a quarter of my air supply left and thirty eight minutes of decompression stops. Removing my equipment seemed like a temporary solution, I would wriggle free of it, and then put it back on. Unclipping my buoyancy jacket was next to impossible but much easier than removing the inflator hose to my drysuit. I had been down twenty minutes now, my single tank of air was almost empty. The smaller tank of oxygen that I had slung beside it could only be breathed at twenty feet, and in any case was only half full. Things were looking grim, but I kept my focus on getting free. At twenty-three minutes elapsed time, I was out of my jacket and free of the anchor line. Dragging my equipment from under the line I put one arm through the jacket harness and pushed towards the surface. The current surged me upwards away from the wreck. I grasped the anchor line with one hand, the line burned as I let it slip through my fingers quickly. I had to get out of the deeper water quickly if I wanted to tell this story to my buddies. At one hundred and fifty feet my air tank ran empty, leaving me with almost an hour of decompression to complete and no means of doing it. My buoyancy jacket contained some expanding air, I put its deflator mechanism in my mouth and took a seawater-filled breath. Choking through the brine, I managed one inhalation, the next came a little easier. I breathed back into the jacket so that I would not lose positive buoyancy. Putting the exhaled air back in this manner would water down the oxygen concentration to dangerously hypoxic levels, but mindful of the alternative, I breathed again.

I remembered a friend in Barbados that was forced to breathe the pure carbon dioxide inflation bottle that used to be put on buoyancy jackets - he passed out in seconds, but floated to the surface. Thinking I was getting light-headed I knew that these would be my last thoughts unless I breathed from the little oxygen tank behind me. I continued swimming upwards carefully exhaling my lung contents, becoming fearful of taking another breath from the buoyancy jacket. I put the oxygen regulator in my mouth at ninety feet. Taking a breath, I did some quick math, the pressure of oxygen at this depth was 3.7 ata's, but the speed of the ascent would quickly drop this significantly. My brain was too foggy at this point to calculate just how significantly, but the oxygen would surely help this. I had considered breathing a lungful of oxygen from the small tank back into my jacket inflator while I was much deeper. I would in effect be simulating a semi circuit rebreather at one hundred and fifty feet with pure oxygen and expired air. The figures I contemplated would have made more sense scribbled on a suicide note. I saved the idea for the shallower stop depths. The decompression time was still near fifty minutes, but every breath breathing the oxygen would knock down my decompression time three times faster compared to air, definitely this was in my favour.

Normally I would last about twenty-five minutes on a little tank like this, but that was at twenty feet with a full tank. I started breathing it at ninety feet and the tank was only half full, even my foggy-headed math arrived at scenarios best left until they happened. I continued to pull up the line until fifty feet from the surface. Stopping here for a few minutes, I hung onto the line in the buffeting current. The anchor was still jammed in the wreck and I was bearing the full force of five to six knots of tide by now.

I moved up to forty feet and waited for another minute, but strangely felt the need to pop my ears. I looked at my depth gauge quickly. It is rare to have to equalise your ears while travelling upwards. Congestion in the ears could cause this problem, but I was not congested now. I checked my depth gauge again - although I was holding onto a fixed line, I was definitely getting deeper. Pulling upwards, I tried to get shallower again. As I pulled the rope, it just ran through my hands without me going towards the surface. After a further minute of pulling I could see the reason. The dive boat had gone and the captain had attached a buoy to the end of the line. With my weight on the line, combined with all the pulling, I had forced the buoy under the surface. At this point, the flexible buoy would be crushed from the water pressure and sink down. This was happening now in front of me. I had the end of the line in my hands now. With no more line to play with, the current strength started to push me downwards again. I tried to inflate my buoyancy jacket to add air and temporarily fix the problem. It worked for just a minute before the current stepped up a further gear, and I was travelling downwards yet again. Thinking quickly, I released my weight belt from around my waist. Gaining 28lbs of buoyancy helped, I was able to hang semi-comfortably at ten feet, the deflated buoy stuffed between my legs. I could not hear the boat engines so it was definitely not nearby. My dive computer still read twenty-seven minutes as my pony tank of oxygen coughed its last breath. Little would be gained by breath holding here, I let go of the line and bobbed to the surface. I had again overcome some crap odds but it was too close for comfort this time. Now, again, I was about to get the bends and this time the dive boat was nowhere to be seen…

The sea had turned rough since we left the surface. I lay backwards in reflection whilst rocking up and down in the waves. The distance from the top to the bottom of the waves was sufficient to completely obscure the land some fifteen miles away. I had no compass, and a shipping lane was near with cross channel ferries routinely travelling at forty-two knots, fantastic. The small island of Sark was about nine miles away, and the current was going in that general direction. I wondered if the bends that were coming soon would affect my ability to swim in a straight line. Floating along for about fifteen minutes, I heard a boat engine. My dive hood obscured clues as to the direction of travel, but it was definitely getting louder and therefore closer. I kicked my fins to get myself upright, I needed to see the boat so I could get out of the way and then signal for help. Relieved to see it was the dive boat, they were as surprised to see me still alive. I climbed aboard and asked immediately for the oxygen kit. Natalie and Baz were both aboard the boat, and told me that everybody had thought that I was dead. They thought I had been underwater for far too long a time with only the single tank. The dive boat captain had been a little more optimistic and started looking down tide for me, similar to where the other two had surfaced.

I think it was a bit premature to think the worst. In this case they had been right, but how many divers have perished after days afloat and lost at the surface? My experience with Caribbean boat drivers had seen lost divers in conditions a lot calmer than today. After all, the captain had spotted Natalie on the surface nearly a mile away from the down line. Baz had surfaced at a similar distance, which was no surprise given the speed of the current. Because I had been down so long, without sending up a marker buoy to mark my position, the captain assumed quite rightly that I may be down tide an unknown distance, but not likely more than five miles given the time. They had been searching the whole time, but getting less and less optimistic. They were returning to the buoy position after sixty minutes elapsed time, simply to attempt the anchor recovery with the boat winch. The cavalry would normally be called after a diver had been lost for more than two hours. I breathed the oxygen bottle on board for thirty minutes as we headed back. Quite unusually I did not get decompression sickness probably due to the elevated depths I breathed the oxygen.

Several divers have died on this wreck. The last one took eighty days of searching the vicinity before he was recovered exactly where he went in. Technical diving has the ability to throw all manner of unpredictable spanners into divers plans, far more than no decompression diving. I had the whole toolbox thrown at me today. Keeping a cool head and having strong self rescue skills helped with many of the dramas. The boat captain's skills today played a very important role in tracking the divers and the current.

However, the antics I have detailed would have been avoided with a common sense approach to the conditions; both boat captain and diver are responsible in this respect. Sadly, when egos compete with a potential loss of income, disaster can serve a bitter pill. The Copper wreck is one of my all-time favourite wreck dives. Searching for the ingots of copper that have spilled from the wreck since 1917 has been the continuing reason for me to visit the site many times since. The 65kg bars, shaped like Toblerone chocolate bars polish up fantastically. They would lead me to dive in the flooded Copper Mine at Coniston in seven years time, this gave me 1500 more dives to perfect my self rescue skills. The mine dive would take most of the few lives I had left remaining and make today's dive seem like a picnic at Never Land.

Thankfully, the next few months of diving went far smoother than this dive. New customers came and went, both at recreational and technical diver levels. A group of postmen came looking to get some trimix training as they had already been doing deeper dives with lengthy decompressions. They all had their own boats, but one had recently bought a rigid hull inflatable, or RIB, that was perfect for diving and had a huge range. The next few months were spent completing training and completing dives in the English Channel that became ever more adventurous. Natalie and I wanted to look into diving some of the wrecks that lay deep into the Hurds Deep area some sixty miles north of Jersey. *The Deep,* as we called it, was littered with wrecks all along its 45 mile length, with more interesting ones between two hundred and forty and six hundred feet. This natural depression was a tributary of the French river Seine in ancient times. Because of its extreme depth, it had hosted the dumping of all things toxic from many countries. Greenpeace had recently televised some footage showing UK government vessels throwing almost fifty thousand drums of radioactive and biohazard waste into the area. This seemed the ideal dive site. Before jumping into unknown territory, we decided on a warm-up dive to five hundred feet right onto the position shown during the environmentalist's report.

Two regular deep dive buddies, Mark and Gerry, insisted they wanted a bite of this pie. Mark had the nice RIB, Gerry was a competent deep diver. As both were over twenty one ...they were in. We planned the dive for early September 1996. Three months gives plenty of time for practice and mind changing. Fast forward to September. The cylinders for the four of us were filled a week before the dive. All the equipment would be loaded into a van and be shipped by sea to the alcoholic's island of Alderney. A couple of days before, I would fly to Alderney to assemble and test the equipment, Natalie would join me a day later. Mark, Gerry and Tim would drive the empty RIB to Alderney the day before the dive. We would only have one support diver between the four of us, he would be Tim. Although young, Tim was a switched-on deep diver and had a lot of boating experience. His experience with outboard engines was invaluable, as the RIB was quite new and as such, still suffered mechanical teething problems. The dive would only be a bounce down and up, with less than two hours decompression time. All the divers would carry all that they needed to perform the dive autonomously. The plan involved using the same descent line but diving solo, that suited Natalie and I fine. A complication was that the dive site was bang in the middle of possibly the busiest shipping lane in the world. Luckily, that was Tim's problem and at least he would not get bored, what with avoiding the super tankers and bulk carriers while tending four decompressing divers.

The ferry company phoned me to advise that the van full of equipment had arrived on schedule and I booked a flight to St Anne's, Alderney for the next day. So far so good. I left on the Thursday morning, my flight taking just thirty minutes flying north over Guernsey and onwards to Alderney. The small inter-island airscraft that ply the Channel Islands were operated by Aurigny Airlines, my plane today was called Nessie. It had a big green sea monster design painted across the engine cowling. The tiny craft had a very slim fuselage that allowed you to look out the windows both sides of your seat. The pilot simply shouted the safety procedures as we taxied for take off. Today the captain had brought a friend for some flying lessons, he continued, hoping that nobody would mind. Over the roar of the engines, I don't think the other passengers heard anything. Teaching friends to fly in a commercial airliner did cross my mind as a little unusual. Still, it probably happens all the time. The friend did look very overweight, if we crashed he would be useful to soften the landing for me and the others back in Economy class. Obese people work very similar to a driver's air bag. I always counted the air bags that filled the first class and business class seats. This was the method to my madness when I asked to sit with the smokers at the back of the plane. Letting salad dodgers fly the plane was the least of my worries. Over the weekend I planned to plunge five hundred feet onto a nuclear waste dump, in a busy shipping lane, with a skeleton support crew.

The plane flew very low, sometimes it seemed no higher than the wave tops. Although the sky was blue, the wind was strong. The plane was buffeted by cross-winds so we flew a little higher. From our elevated height it was easier to see the bigger picture. The green sea was covered in white horses, although at this height it looked quite flat. The weather forecast was not looking promising for the weekend, but recently these reports seemed as accurate as tea-leaf readings from a psychic. My flight came to an end, and we landed at Alderney's only airport that doubled as the golf course and botanical gardens. My taxi driver to town said that he was also the air traffic controller today. His wife had a bed and breakfast, this arrangement constituted a multinational company in the northern Channel Islands. The guesthouse owner gave me a great deal on a suite with three double bedrooms a separate kitchen and a garden which would suit me and Natalie fine if we argued. I arranged a cosy three bunkbed deal in a converted loft at the top of the hill for the three guys coming over tomorrow. I hired an eco-friendly electric rental car that was little more than a golf buggy and headed for the harbour. The van full of equipment was still onboard the deck of the freighter tied up beside the office in Braye Harbour. I went into the Port-a-cabin and signed some release forms. Driving the van back into town, I wanted to unload everything into my little garden and inspect everything. This job took the rest of the day and some of the evening. All the equipment seemed fine and undamaged. I phoned Natalie and the guys to give them the good news.

I had a stroll around the cobbled streets of Alderney. Finding an old pub at the top of the main street, I went in for some dinner and glass of shandy. I had my food at the bar and got talking to a brandy nosed local fisherman. He was pretty drunk and asked me If I knew what Alderneys biggest import was, I shook my head. "Alcohol" he slurred, chuckling to himself. Then he asked what Alderneys biggest export was, again I was clueless. "Empty bottles" he replied almost falling of the bar stool. I looked around the bar, his story looked close to the truth. Alderney is known for being home to two thousand alcoholics clinging to a rock. But in the local paper I read that you are likely to meet more individuals with a net worth greater than one hundred million pounds in Alderney than anywhere else in the world, such was the relaxed taxation system here. Maybe I would meet some of these people tonight and borrow some cash. I tottered down the cobbled hill back to the guesthouse for some chocolate biscuits and bed, not necessarily in that order.

I picked up Natalie from the airport early in the morning. We went for some sightseeing to kill some time. Mark, Gerry and Tim were due to arrive around one that afternoon. I didn't fancy their journey of sixty miles by sea as the wind had really picked up overnight and it was properly rough now. The harbour wall, known as the Breakwater in Alderney, is an engineering marvel. Originally almost a kilometre and half long, it was built in the middle of the last century by the British navy to protect its fleet stationed here. There are no land masses between this Breakwater and the eastern United States. Unimpeded Atlantic swells can generate enormous power, the waves could hit the wall with sufficient force to send waves and spray hundreds of feet into the air. The sea conditions in the area have a challenging reputation. Areas called The Race or The Swinge have biblical tidal streams and treacherous rocks. These combinations have ruined hundreds of mariner's plans. Our three friends in the RIB would travel through the Swinge today en route to Alderney. I hope they wore good raincoats and life jackets. After lunch we strolled down to the harbour to meet our dive boat. There had been no mobile phone contact for the last three hours. There would be no contact for another four hours. It crossed my mind that they had got into trouble during the crossing, but it was more likely that they were drunk in a pub somewhere. Natalie and I waited in a cake shop, drinking tea and reading newspapers. At four o'clock, there was still no word from our buddies. Then the phone rang and I heard Tim shouting something, but all I could hear was the screaming outboard engine. Minutes later, the orange craft came into view. It looked like there was only one person on board. Mark was driving and he slowly brought the craft alongside the pier. As we peered down from the dock, we could see the other two were lying down on the floor, huddled up. The deck looked very clear of clutter, maybe they had done some modifications before leaving port.

When the boat was all secure, the two passengers climbed the ladder up to the quayside. Nobody said a word, they looked like drowned rats. From their dampened demeanours, the seas must have been a little lively during the voyage over. I asked what time they left Jersey. Tim groaned that it had taken almost seven hours of hell to get here. I asked where all the seating had gone, and that the boat looked like it had a lot more room now and was a clear improvement. Tim became spokesman, explaining that halfway between Jersey and Guernsey the waves became very large and they motored along dead slowly, unable to make any real headway. A huge wave broke over the boat, filling it to the top of the tubes with green water. Mark kept driving forwards in an attempt to drain the boat which had become very heavy and sluggish due to the weight of water inside. A minute later, he turned around to check on the two passengers. His jaw dropped when he saw an empty boat behind him. Gerry and Tim were gone, as were the seating pods and all the belongings attached to them. The freak wave had knocked everything overboard and that's why the decks looked so tidy. A frantic five-minute search behind the boat revealed Gerry and Tim waving as if attempting to fly. They were clutching the few belongings that still floated. The seats were gone, along with the spare fuel containers. They had indeed been in quite the adventure. Their combined possessions were contained in one black plastic bag now. Mark said that most of his dive equipment had been lost over the side, so he could not dive tomorrow. Gerry had lost stuff too, but there were enough spares between us to make up a complete set of kit for him. We headed for the pub first as some sorrows needed drowning. When the shivering had stopped, we nipped back to our guest house to lend Mark a pair of Natalie's jeans. I didn't have any spare trousers, so he squeezed into Natalie's bright green jeans that were covered in red starfish patterns. They commented that the room was nice and asked where they would be sleeping. Fifteen minutes walk up the hill and after a pub stop, they were climbing the attic ladder to their bunk beds. I couldn't stop laughing when I imagined the scene.

We met by the boat at nine o'clock in the morning. Looking out to sea was disappointing, the wind had dropped slightly but it was still more suited to kite-flying than boat journeys. The forecast for the next day included force 5-6 winds and rough seas. Today we had moderate to fresh winds, and the weatherman's term for the wave height was just 'rather rough'.

It certainly looked rather rough from here, but if we didn't go today we wouldn't be going at all. We loaded the boat with just three sets of twin tanks and decompression bottles, had one last cup of tea and headed into the waves. The venue wasn't far, but the sea was not playing nicely, with the wind and swell coming directly at us from the west. The dive site was roughly nine miles from the harbour entrance, but ninety minutes later we were still plodding through the swells. Gerry kept asking what HPNS would feel like, saying that this was the only thing that concerned him. Helium tremors would be new to Gerry and Natalie was winding him up by saying that the symptoms of high pressure nervous syndrome were very nasty and he should be very worried. I added that the mixtures we were breathing today should be of more concern. We would all breathe trimix 10/50 down to five hundred feet. With the Nitrogen fraction in this mix at 40 percent compared to 79 percent in regular air, rocket scientists were not needed to calculate how we would feel. If you halve the nitrogen, you would expect to feel roughly half as deep at any given point, with regard to narcosis. Today we would experience a nitrogen narcosis level equivalent to two hundred and fifty feet breathing air. Gerry had never been deeper than two hundred and twenty feet ever. Natalie kept reminding him of this now and tensions were rising. He asked if he could dive with me, I said he could if he could keep up. The boats GPS system played a tune to advise of our arrival. Tim and Mark prepared the anchor rope and threw it over the side. We seemed to be in the middle of the shipping lane as planned. Today's stunt needed to be performed in a sea area roughly one thousand metres across. This separation lane kept the super tankers from colliding as they approached each other, often on autopilot. Tim was watchman and he reassuringly looked as if he had slept properly the night before. The three of us put on our equipment and made some last minute checks. Natalie was going first and slipped backwards into the water, clearly eager to get on with it. I went next and Gerry followed me over.

The water visibility was not great because of the rough conditions, but I could see my own fins and this was sufficient.

The deeper you descended here, the clearer the water became...normally. Natalie dropped like a stone and was soon out of sight. I waited for Gerry to get his groove on, but he seemed very preoccupied with his equipment. I gave him the down signal and he replied okay. We dropped to one hundred and fifty feet, semi together. Gerry signalled to stop and started fiddling with his tank manifold. He pointed to me and then downwards. I took this as he wanted me to carry on, so I did. In the Bahamas a few months earlier, all of my good depth gauges were stolen. The insurance company replaced them with the equivalent new models from Uwatec. At about 99 metres depth I found that they were not completely similar. The figures on the digital depth gauges simply froze. I knew I was still descending as the line slipped through my fingers and my ears still needed equalising. My back up gauge still continued to register the depth and by this time said four hundred and twenty feet. I carried on downwards looking down for signs of Natalie. Narcosis was filling my head big time. I checked the gauge once more, it still said four hundred and twenty feet, but my head suggested otherwise. I felt like I was breathing air at this depth, my mind clouding over, but I did not hear any Wah-Wah symptoms. The gauge had obviously frozen and now I had no idea what depth I was at.

The sea charts in the area showed a hole nearby with up to six hundred feet depth, maybe we were in it. Dropping further I could see the glow from Natalie's dive light. When I arrived, she was looking up and holding the line just in front of the anchor weight. The seabed shot past us like a video game filled with huge rocks appearing then disappearing into the blackness. We had made a special anchor for this dive from welded sections of angle iron wrapped in chain and dipped into a vat of molten lead to add weight. The anchor now was half its original size and completely smooth. I gave her the signal that my head was full of narcosis, she agreed. Looking at her depth gauges confirmed they were as useless as mine, not surprisingly as they were virtually identical models. Drifting along in the darkness while feeling heavy narcosis in an unknown depth lost its appeal quickly, although I had only just got there, I signalled that we should leave. The trimix gas we breathed was supposed to feel the equivalent to a two hundred and fifty feet air dive and I had comfortably dived to this depth and deeper many times. But at the moment it felt much deeper, at least half a bottle of whisky deeper. The toxic waste drums we came to visit were nowhere to be seen. Just as well really, as I was in no mood to discover anything, never mind glow in the dark chemicals at five hundred feet. Interestingly though, the government report said the area was chosen because there were no appreciable currents this deep down to disturb the containers of industrial waste. I can confirm that the depths of the Hurd Deep channel experience some of the strongest tidal speeds I have ever encountered. The drums would have been instantly swept away and the contents lost into the sea and eaten by local fish life. Cap de la Hague Nuclear reprocessing plant is also nearby. It would be hard to conclude who was contaminating the area more.

We headed back up the line together. The ascent plan was fairly easy to follow. There were only three or four deeper stops before the formal deco ceiling was met. Back then in 1996, deep decompression stops took the form of Pyle stops. Richard Pyle, a famous deep diving fish scientist had the idea of incorporating deeper than traditional stops to add a feel-good factor. The special computer software we used to calculate our stops advised that we could ascend directly to fifty metres to begin decompression. To ensure our own feel-good factor we stopped additionally at ninety metres, then seventy-five and sixty metres for one to two minutes. It must have worked because we did feel good at the moment. Once natural light appeared at 80 metres, the sea took on a fabulously eerie deep purple hue. It was a bit like a desert sunrise but underwater. The software we used to plan the dives was written apparently by experts. I did find it strange even back then that the gurus writing these software programs had not dived anywhere near these depths themselves. Because of the unknown depth we had dived to, we felt it prudent to extend the shallower deco stops. I wore

Tim met us at 30 metres, bringing ours and Gerry's spare tanks with him. Everything was going fine, and we took them from him to be used maybe later. I asked him about Gerry, scribbling the question on my dive slate. He replied that Gerry had had equipment problems and was back on the boat already. By twenty metres my super expensive dive computer started squealing like a distressed pig, the information display was now blank and orange gas was pouring from underneath the front glass. It had obviously flooded down below and now the seawater was mixing with its lithium batteries. The chemical reaction got so frantic, that within minutes the display lifted completely away and the innards continued to gush orange clouds of gas. The computer had stopped reading depth at 127 metres on the way down, but started working again for the last 100 metres until now when it gave up the ghost. My spare depth gauge still worked and we were relying on a deco plan written on our dive slates anyway, so the damaged computer was just a noisy nuisance now to be added to my museum of failed equipment. The dive plan called for a switch to fifty percent oxygen from the 22 metre depth mark and one hundred percent for the 6 and 4 metre stop depths. The time spent decompressing was comfortable, as the summer ocean temperature nudged 16 degrees Celsius, and the lively swell at the surface didn't reach past 3 metres. We broke the surface at one hundred and seventy minutes elapsed time.

Natalie and I climbed back onto the boat both in high spirits, although the conditions at the bottom were crap, it was definitely quite exciting, and nothing irreplaceable had been lost or broken. Gerry said that his regulators started free flowing when he got to sixty metres, so he sensibly aborted. Natalie said that was a good decision as he wouldn't have wanted any of what was at the end of the line, the sarcasm was dripping from her words. Mark lent Gerry his brand new £900 dive computer to use on this dive, the same model as had flooded on my wrist. When he climbed back into the boat, he was still in a bit of a strop. During some heavy handed action the computer strap snagged and broke. The luxury depth gauge skipped and bounced on the buoyancy tubes before being lost over the side. Gerry's day had been both expensive and unrewarding, but at least it hadn't been painful.

Mark and Tim asked if we heard the gigantic boats that passed over the buoy line. Our anchor line had drifted straight into the shipping lanes and vessel after vessel had run over it. They had played chicken with super tankers as we decompressed unwittingly below. I remembered that the dive was very noisy throughout, in the deeper water the distant throb of engines was clear but during the shallow stops, the propeller noise became so loud that we thought we might be getting new hair cuts if we didn't watch out. Luck had pushed the descent line out of the shipping lane towards the end of the dive, but as we languished at fifteen feet during the longest decompression stop, the passing boats still felt like they were on top of us.

The wind was still in full effect and it must have been unpleasant for the guys in the boat for the last three hours, but it was all over now with no real upsets. We headed back to St Anne's harbour to get drunk. We stumbled from pub to pub, finishing in what looked like an old church converted to hold rave parties. Teenagers jigged around completely wasted. I could only manage one drink here as the din from the sound system was just too mind numbing. Gerry was asleep in the corner having celebrated a little too much. We found him still in-situ at ten the next morning. The same trance music was still blaring out. Some true hardcore ravers were still giving it large with their frantic semaphore dance moves. This was Sunday morning worship, Alderney style.

The weather had settled and maybe it would have been better to wait, but I didn't care now, it was all over. The weather could just have easily have got worse, but Gerry was having none of it. He sat there moaning over breakfast, complaining that he didn't dive because we had insisted on going when it was rough. Natalie flipped and said that he would not have dived whatever the weather and his excuses yesterday were total crap. He was scared and just bottled it. The pin drop silence meant breakfast was over, Gerry stormed out. Finishing our bacon and eggs we checked out of the guesthouse. The boat was refuelled and left, on the now flat seas it was home in an hour. I put the van full of equipment back on the ferry and called a taxi to the airfield. I could see Nessie the 'Dinoplane' waiting as we drove into the car park. Stan the cab driver put his air traffic control hat on and bade us farewell.

Chapter 5: Overhead Ineptitude

September came, and brought with it the biblical winds that marked the end of the summer season in the United Kingdom. We had decided to give Barbados a miss as I had spent almost two years there off and on. Although it was nice to see old friends and visit the same island and watch it mature, crime was increasing to unpleasant levels. Generally the evolution in the Caribbean was one of embracing American rap culture with its symbiotic cancer of drugs and crime. Impoverished and jobless island youths seemed to readily accept a lifestyle of disorder and anarchy. When I arrived in 1994, Barbados was engulfed in a suicide epidemic. No jobs and bleak futures meant young and old turned to rat poison to achieve peace. Within two years the trend had changed, along with the music. Despite a government job-creation initiative in 1996 people still died in increasing numbers, not so much from suicide but at the hands of a rival gang member or a random street mugging. A change was as good as a rest as they say, so we looked at the Bahamas, and more specifically the island of New Providence, a dive destination famous for caves and sharks as a new place to live and work, and the grass looked much greener in the brochures also. Natalie was happy to come too, as now she had graduated as a scuba instructor and wanted to teach diving full time through the Jersey winter. We booked flights to Miami and onward journeys to the beautiful capital of Nassau.

The Bahamas reputation as a playground to wealthy Americans complimented the descriptions in the travel brochure nicely. Arriving in this paradise was a bit déjà vu, in that it looked very similar to Barbados with all the tropical greenery and blue ocean vistas. At the airport, we flicked through the glossy pamphlets at the hotel booking desk. We decided on a quaint little guesthouse in the Blue Hill area of Nassau town. We were travelling lightly as our suitcases had been lost by the airline. Our taxi driver sounded a bit like a London taxi driver when he showed reluctance to take us this far north, as it was not in the typical tourist enclaves. The countryside did get a little more derelict as we drove deeper into this obviously run down part of the old town. We arrived at our destination and the driver advised us to get inside quickly, naively we thought he was just being mindful of the brewing storm clouds. The guesthouse was a converted large farmhouse with a colonial look – rich, dark woods lined the floors and ceilings. We were shown our room and the receptionist kindly offered to chase down our lost belongings.

After a shower and a nap we both woke with the sound of fireworks outside. Natalie thought that we should go outside and see the display. I thought the noise of the bangs sounded like the final scene from the movie Scarface. I said that we should lock the door and wait for whatever it was to stop before venturing outside. A few minutes later, the noise was replaced with screaming, and Natalie thought that a firework must have gone into the crowd. Opening the bedroom door, we went to look through a window across from the landing. The scene in the street below came straight from a western flick. Several kids were shooting into the hotel lobby and there was definitely someone inside shooting back. We decided to let them finish their argument without western intervention and returned to the room. I piled some furniture up against the door and we considered some alternatives. We got to within a minute of jumping from the window into a yard full of barking dogs before there was a knock on the door. Gun-toting drug fiends wouldn't be politely rapping on the door, I thought, and the voice attached sounded reassuring, so I opened it. It was the manager, come to apologise for the disturbance; he said kids from the neighbourhood often *visited* to use the guests as cash machines. Today, as there were few holidaymakers, they tried to make off with the bicycles for hire. He assured us that nobody had been shot and that we were as safe as possible in the circumstances...how reassuring - this was our welcome to the Bahamas.

We ate at the hotel while the staff put the lobby together and the police feigned interest. Although we planned to leave at first light, the manager reassured us things were fine now. The airline phoned to say our bags had been spat from the system and would be delivered to us as soon as possible. Waiting to be reunited with our belongings meant our plans to leave were sunk. After sleeping with both eyes open, we decided to buy a car the next morning to give us some freedom of movement and help with the job search. Also, I thought that with transport we would be effectively become moving targets and therefore harder to hit, my humour missing its mark with Natalie. Leaving the hotel armed with no more than a local paper we went in search of a used car. Second-hand cars seemed ridiculously expensive, with even jalopies selling for over two thousand dollars. Wandering about in downtown Nassau getting hot and nowhere took its toll. We walked across the nearby Paradise bridge that stretched its way into civilisation and tourist Mecca. Sitting in the restaurant at the Atlantis resort sipping ten dollar coffee, last nights antics seemed a world away. Scanning through the classifieds in the paper, we phoned for further details and addresses. A taxi hailed from the resort was over double the price of a cab got from the street, so we braced ourselves for another long walk in the sun. After viewing several death traps, I arranged to see a chap who was selling a Mitsubishi Galant within our price range. The cab driver said he wouldn't drive to that run-down neighbourhood, so I had to phone the seller back and arranged to meet him on the main highway not too far away from his home. The old man on the phone sounded genuine and, sure enough, he was there with the car in all its glory on time. I sold used cars for several years and felt pretty sure I would spot a *turd* in a shiny suit from a mile away. Willie, the cars owner, was very chatty as he showed me round the vehicle. The bodywork was in reasonable shape, if a little multicoloured. Willie said that the sun fades metallic paint in unusual ways over here.

The inside upholstery was fitted with fetching *muppet* skin seat covers that I would soon remove. Popping the bonnet I was a dazzled by a shining silver engine compartment. Willie had decided to waste three cans of silver spray over everything under the hood, he added that this made the car more reliable on damp mornings. We went for a test drive. The car drove okay and stopped predictably, when commanded to. As I drove, we negotiated a price and agreed on twelve hundred dollars down from two thousand. He asked to be dropped at the burger restaurant on the other side of the road where he was meeting a friend soon. We drove into the car park and stopped the car. A burger for lunch, although probably not what the doctor ordered, suited our appetites nicely. The search for a car had proved fairly easy, and it left a few hours in the day to look for some work around the island. Back in the car, we headed to the south of the island to the biggest and most famous dive shop in the Bahamas. Waiting at traffic lights to turn left was when the honeymoon officially finished with the car, despite us owning it for less than 30 minutes. As the lights changed, I pulled away and starting turning left, but nothing. The steering wheel would go straight or to the right, but not left. Horns started blaring behind, so thinking quickly, I turned the wheel hard right and reversed a few yards. Now at least we were facing the right direction. I drove down the road and pulled over. Popping the bonnet again, I checked the steering rack to see what was preventing it from going left. I couldn't see a problem other than it didn't work, although I did notice the steering rack had a Toyota badge on it, which did strike me as strange given the car was a Mitsubishi. The journey started again, albeit at a slower pace. The steering adjustments could wait for later.

The south ocean scuba centre was an incredibly big dive centre set on its own dock, and with buildings that resembled a movie set. Literally hundreds of divers came through the centre on a daily basis, and it would be the most likely place to find work. Our luck was in, as the owner was in the office. We chatted for half an hour, and coincidentally he was looking for an instructor couple with technical diving qualifications. Finding a job so quickly overcame the disappointment and deep dislike I had developed for the charming old man who had Jedi mind-tricked me into buying his crap car. It broke down not far from our guesthouse after a very stressful hour-long drive home, the 'no left turn' feature almost starting many fights with hot-headed motorists as I kept reversing through the busy streets. We could not even leave the next day, while a mechanic fiddled with the steering and distributor cap which also came from another brand of car. I phoned the guy I bought it from, unsurprisingly the people who answered the phone had never heard of anyone called Willie. Starting work the next day meant having to stay another night at shoot-out mansion. After pulling some furniture across the door, it was possible to sleep for a few hours. The first day at work was easy, meeting all the other staff was fun and one of the girls was also looking for room mates to share a large beach front house. All our cases had been miraculously delivered by the airline that afternoon, so we moved into the big apartment that evening. After a big dinner cooked by our host, we sat around drinking with some of the other dive centre staff until late, talking about the serial killer that was currently on the loose in the Paradise Island and Cable Beach area. Getting up at seven the following morning was quite inconvenient, as it meant getting to bed by two a.m. at the latest if we wanted to be fit for anything the next day. I must have been dreaming about Father Christmas and his sleigh bells, and I remember a jingling sound quite vividly. I woke up to find Santa's nemesis in the form of burglars in the bedroom. Instead of making present deliveries, our visitors were helping themselves to our stuff. Our night-time Santa's were clad in all black and ran from the room like scolded cats. They were out of the house and up the beach in a flash and I gave chase, dressed only in my birthday suit. The novelty and excitement of chasing probably armed locals up the beach while naked, at night, wore off quite quickly. I headed back to the house to get a weapon. During the chase, I noticed the scum-bags were running empty-handed, so thought that they had not got much.

Getting back to the room it was easy to see that the burglars must have been there some time and had, in actual fact, taken everything already. Even the patio doors to the beach had been removed, thus allowing a pretty sizeable means of entering the apartment. Our luggage had been in the possession and relative safety of airport baggage handlers for the last few days. We had managed to look after it for just a few hours before some friendly types relieved us of it, no doubt it was already heading to a local dive centre for disposal. My description to the police about the intruders was as vague as the reason for staying on this wild-west island. I had to make a formal statement at the big police station the next day after work. While sitting in the station talking with an officer, I noticed other cops looking to the floor behind me but didn't think much of this. I heard a noise behind me and looked round quickly to see a skinny lawman lying on the floor trying to pull some money from my pocket. I pointed this out to Natalie and advised we were wasting more of our time with these keystone cops. We got up and left. The pride of the Bahamas kept saying how they were just playing and would have given me the money back. I thought it best to just agree, as it was very likely we would be wasting more of each others time in the near future.

Great diving made this part of the world famous, though its lawlessness is very notorious also. Settling into the fun routine of working and then going home to a newly fortified apartment and bingeing on rum was the ultimate reward for diving instructors. The wages here were high enough to keep the staff from leaving despite all the crime nonsense, and it was easy to save useful sums of money. An area called Clifton Wall was just a mile or two from the dive centre and was a very popular shore dive. After 5 minutes of swimming, with the reef dropping to seventy feet, the edge of the wall came into view. Rumour had the wall dropping down miles and miles, into the area known as the Tongue of the Ocean. I air dived down to four hundred feet a couple of times and could not see the bottom or even a step, so it must have been at least fairly deep. The men's depth record for an air dive was conducted here the year before, down to 147 metres. This record still stands, as the most recent claimant with a dive to 156 metres needed rescuing on the bottom, so that hardly counts. The wall here had a reputation for claiming the lives of many deep divers. Often they were holidaymakers drawn to extreme depth by narcosis. The bodies usually floated up a few days later and we stored the equipment in a room at the dive centre, awaiting checks and verifications from insurance company vultures. When the inspections had been made, I would be given the unpleasant job of servicing the usually blameless equipment, before putting it back into the rental department. The equipment had often stood untouched for many weeks, so my restorative skills were often put to the test. In the mornings, there could be up to six hundred divers to equip and put onto the correct boat. There were often so many dozens of hung over customers frantically asking for rental equipment, tensions were bound to rise beyond a simmer. If they had nasty attitudes, or were rude or patronising, they were rewarded with a recently fouled wetsuit pulled from a corpse, or even a diving mask and breathing regulator. It really does pay to be nice when dealing with overworked staff. Fast-food restaurants are not the only places to deal out *instant justice* to rude customers, and many a dive professional has flipped burgers at BoogerKing, so they know how to reward obnoxious behaviour.

The dive centre offered most types of scuba training, but we lacked local place to go cavern and cave diving. Many customers enquired about overhead environment diving, as the Bahamas is famous for its subterranean Blue Holes. The well known ones are located at Andros, which is some distance from New Providence. The famous British cave explorer Rob Palmer made many exploratory dives into Andros and wrote extensively about the amazing subterranean landscapes. Rob lived just ten minutes from this dive centre and frequently visited for a chat. One afternoon we asked him if he knew of any areas nearby that we could use for cavern training, and as luck would have it, he remembered somewhere. Five minutes up the road was a refinery that was sitting over a labyrinth of limestone passageways. A few years back the mazes entry point to the sea was blocked, to stop the tidal water movement and possible collapse. The refinery had moved back a few hundred yards, so we just had to remove the artificial plug of rocks and sand at low tide. The area blocked up was enormous and would need an army to shift it. Dive centres are perfect at supplying low paid labourers, this centre employed scores of workers from Haiti as well as a legion of dive professionals from all over. The Haitian's all earned more than most of the scuba staff and even had a union. They spared us only a few hard workers, so we had to supplement our ranks with some heel-dragging Instructors and Divemasters. Most of the grumbling was muffled as they knew that any slouching would mean instant dismissal. Our boss constantly reminded us that hundreds of instructors were made every month in Florida, another busload were just a phone call away.

Driving down to the refinery armed with spades and axes, we found our cavern entrance. The tide was going out on cue, so we set to work. Mountains of sand and rocks were moved and as the level dropped, gallons of stinking and stagnant water poured out of the hole. It was all quite fun, and after five or six hours toiling we started to make a sizeable dent in clearing the obstruction. Rob thought we should head into the chasm and investigate further before removing more of the rubble. We all wore just shorts and T shirts but had a scuba mask each. Although it was pitch black, we waded into the foul smelling swamp water with one dive light between the six of us. The stench of rotten eggs was nauseating. Rob shouted back that we should not breath too deeply as the air was filled with Hydrogen Sulphide gas. Swimming in black water in total darkness without breathing deeply was pretty difficult, so some of our intrepid explorers broke ranks and headed back outside for a refreshing cigarette. Sometimes the water was shallow enough to stand in, but in many places became quite deep. As I was the tallest, I was handed the dive light, realistically the previous holder just found swimming with one hand too unpleasant. He would rather keep his head out of whatever we were paddling in than see anything.

After ten minutes, Rob said that we should leave immediately as he didn't think we were swimming in water but some kind of chemical spill. The smell was causing people to get light headed and although my mouth was uncharacteristically shut most of the time, I had noticed the distinct taste of fuel. Exiting as quickly as possible, we escaped without taking heavy casualties. In the daylight it was obvious we had been swimming in oil or diesel mingled with other stuff best not imagined. The refinery had been dumping various heinous waste products into the rocks below. I doubted that even a hundred exchanges of tide would make the area habitable. A telephone call to Greenpeace was what was really necessary.

Swimming in the sea for thirty minutes afterwards still left us light headed and looking like mine workers covered in engine oil. Getting back to the dive centre, we were treated to a box of clothes-washing powder to clean ourselves up with. After a scrubbing with stiff brushes, our skin looked ashen and began to crack almost immediately. My skin took almost a month to return to pre-diesel bath condition. I returned to the refinery cavern a few weeks later and it looked no better, certainly we would not be taking fare-paying divers clad in their ubiquitous brightly coloured wetsuits anywhere near this greasy swamp.

Another encounter with an oil slick was just around the corner. An elderly customer from England had requested to do some deeper dives. I was introduced to him and we discussed what he wanted to do. This dive centre had a policy of doing recreational depths only, with a maximum depth of one hundred feet, and for good reason - holiday divers always leave their brains at the airport before travelling. This cast-iron rule was seldom deviated from, except if the boss got a few extra dollars. This customer was adamant, and would pay the extra to go deeper than two hundred feet. Money often helps in a little rule-bending. I insisted on a check out dive which he only agreed to under duress and he wouldn't be paying for it. The refresher dive would be to a wreck site that we did not normally go to. The boat was a drug-smuggling craft that was sunk by the coastguard a few years before, it sat in eighty feet of water. My new dive buddy pulled from his equipment bag a tool belt, full of hammers and chisels, insisting that he always wore it instead of a weight belt. I know the customer is seldom right, but had to give him the benefit of the doubt at this point. We agreed a loose dive plan together, and jumped into the water at the same time. Directly after us, another diving lemming threw himself off the boat as if he was on fire. Paddling frantically like a drowning cat, he mask had fallen off and all hell was breaking loose. To stop the screaming and drama, I handed over my spare mask as I was closest. My offering was immediately rejected as the one that was lost was a $250 prescription mask and now the entire holiday was ruined. I mumbled something about maybe he should consider another sport, as now he wouldn't be able to recognise me without the mask. It was time to leave all the surface shouting behind. Looking back to signal to my buddy we should descend, I saw that my guy had started without me. I dropped quickly after him. I could see that other divers had beaten me to the wreck site and had already done a marvellous job of ruining the visibility. I looked around for five minutes and could not see my buddy, but could definitely hear banging coming from inside the shipwreck. Heading inside, all I saw was a snowstorm of sand and silt, without a reel I wouldn't go in further. I headed back to the surface to wait for him and tell him smugly that his deep dive plans were finished. Getting topside, the first thing I heard was people complaining that oil was everywhere and was getting all over their suits and buoyancy jackets. I asked the captain if the bilge pumps were on accidentally, and he said they were not. The oil was drifting up from the seabed below. I put the engine room banging I'd heard earlier into perspective and knew this had got to be the work of the guy supposed to be diving with me. Swimming down headfirst I could see black balls of oil floating up all around. Curious divers were grabbing the floating balls to see what they were. Looking at their fingers turned their faces to horror, automatically they wiped their hands on their suits to add further pee on their fireworks. I followed the floating oil slick towards the engine hatch, the oil was pouring from the top of the motors. My charge had removed the oil filler caps from both engines and the black lubricating goo just poured outwards and upwards. I came out of the engine area to see two divers pointing to the distance, giving me a sign to swim in that direction. A quick burst of speed and I caught sight of the culprit leaving the scene of the crime. I grabbed his foot and pulled him towards me. The filling caps were still in his hands and I took them from him without warning or explanation.

Arriving back at the engines, I reattached the caps to stop the flow of oil. I was covered in oil now but thought it better to get some detergent from the boat rather than try to rub it off on my suit. I saw the customer's expensive mask dropped earlier still lying under the boat and scooped it up, careful not to get my oily fingerprints all over it. I could say that I spent twenty minutes looking for it and this usually resulted in a good tip. I imagined the scene on the dive boat, when I surfaced the air was blue with swearing. Some of the other customers looked like they were going to get physical with the offending diver. Luckily the pacifist vote won over, and the angry divers decided to take their angst to the company owner verbally instead. I could guarantee that that would not be the most rewarding course of action. Predictably, when the English guy surfaced he feigned ignorance and used the immortal line of Shaggy "It wozn't me" as his defence. Other guests knew better, but bit their lips. I shook my head so often while working here that it was like I had developed Parkinson's disease.

I refused to dive with this guy the next day, as did most of the customers on the boat who had received the free oil bath. He went on a different boat and apparently persuaded another diver to hit two hundred feet secretly with him. All would have been fine if they had stayed together, the diver still armed with his tool belt, dropped much deeper than his partner apparently. The deeper guy ran out of air and they both managed to get back to the surface by the skin of their teeth. The fistfight after ensured tool belt man never came diving with us again. I had a lot of work to do this night to get several rebreathers ready for tomorrow. We had six Draeger units in various stages of disarray. Of the six, only two were functional, the rest had either lost important pieces, or cockroaches had made a meal out of the breathing bags. Working alone until nine thirty at night I performed some miracles and got three units cobbled together. I would wear the most borderline of the three, having gotten used to diving with them leaking and gurgling over the months. I had actually acclimatised to getting caustic soda cocktails in my mouth, and swimming to the surface exhaling was now child's play. Driving to a party that night, the car we bought earlier overheated on the highway and all I could do was limp it to a petrol station forecourt. As the car gargled its final death rattle, a mechanic sauntered out from the station's garage. This would be the start of a relationship that caused me to pour many more hundreds of dollars into this pig of a car. The mechanic was called Joe and the friendly chap even offered me a toke on his joint, I politely refused.

After a lengthy cab ride, I arrived at the bar. Working with tourists and transient staff meant that a new party was never more than a couple of hours away. The customers would ask us to join them for a holiday drink every evening. The typical evening consisted of balancing an intake of Bacardi with the confining effects of gravity. Being repetitively given late penalties at work sometimes modified the delicate drinking balance, so at least you exited the bar under your own steam and were not carried out by others. *Bacardi vision* has its benefits - you get to laugh at jokes that lesser drunks would not find amusing, and people's attractiveness rises sharply before falling vertically. The weather forecast the next day was for decks awash with seasick, but to join the ranks of the green faced punters meant ridicule, so I headed home early from the bar. My rebreather customers were both elephantine, easily tipping the scales at four hundred pounds apiece. Both produced certification cards dated the week before, so I knew the dives today would be jam-packed with excitement. Luckily they opted for no wetsuits, I breathed a sigh of relief. If we cocooned that much luvvin' in a neoprene condom, it would take a hundred kilograms of lead to sink it. The dive centre policy of no cancellations, whatever the weather, worked in my favour today. The lively waves and the boats constant ludicrous pitching meant my team quickly lost a player to nausea. The seas were monstrous, even I had secretly taken a muppet seasickness pill. We got to the dive site after an hour, those still brave enough and well enough launched themselves into the white foaming ocean.

My guy staggered to the back of the boat and fell in head first. I had to take a huge belt full of lead weights to pack his jacket and get him to sink. I jumped in and sank like a stone, even with my buoyancy jacket fully inflated. I swam upwards like a madman and frantically stuffed the lead weight into his jacket. The customer hung on to the units breathing hoses as if his hands were super-glued to them. I motioned to descend, and to my amazement he followed. Once below the topside turbulence, everything was calm and pleasant, a stark contrast to the boat trip. We dropped down to about seventy feet and headed along the reef for some fish spotting. After just a minute, my buddy started pointing to his breathing hoses in a frantic manner. When using a rebreather it is difficult to gauge how relaxed the wearer is, as a rapid breathing rate is not as noticeable as when using normal scuba. A rebreather collects the exhaled breaths by way of the breathing hoses which are reprocessed in the box on your back. This means that one obvious stress indicator is missing. Normally, the more anxious someone becomes, the faster they breathe. The eyes are another useful indicator of stress, but this guy's mask was steamed up with condensation, so all was not good. I headed up with him back to the surface. The next problem would be getting back on the boat. It was pitching up and down so violently I would have preferred jumping onto a moving merry-go-round. I asked the customer to remove the equipment, but he said he could handle it, my insistence achieved nothing. He did manage to clamber up the ladder before collapsing on the swim platform like a beached whale. He was in a dangerous position, the motion of the boat meant one second he was six feet up in the air, and the next, submerged under the water. I climbed up alongside and tried to unclip the heavy rebreather box that was also weighed down with lead weights. When it was free, the customer managed to get to his knees. Without warning, and in a rage, he threw the rebreather into the sea, shouting that it was a piece of crap. I was sure my job hinged on recovering the unit, and got a handhold on it before it quickly sank, taking me with it. Down we went, the pressure in my ears needed equalising very quickly as I dropped like a stone holding on to sixty pounds of lead and rebreather. The boat had moved with the wind and soon I would be descending past the wall and into uncharted depths. As I dropped, I inflated my jacket and the buoyancy vest on the rebreather.

At fifty metres I had thrown enough lead from the pockets to achieve neutral buoyancy. The top of the wall at forty metres was still visible and within swimming distance, so I headed over for a rest. All the exertion had virtually exhausted my scuba tank and I knew that my return to the surface could only be guaranteed if I used the rebreather unit myself. I quickly put it on and took a breath. The high oxygen mixture inside was not suitable for this depth, so I swam upwards while breathing the last few dregs of my scuba tank. One of the dive shop photographers was nearby and managed to take several pictures of my antics. I knew the day would be action packed, but this was ridiculous. I left the customer guessing on the boat for twenty minutes more. Hopefully his attitude would be tempered with a little seasickness. In some ways, this experience taught the customer some valuable lessons. He would not go on a boat again just because the dive shop said the rough weather was still diveable, also he realised that by completing three shallow certification dives on a rebreather does not prepare anyone adequately for actually using one. The spell of bad weather lasted a few weeks. Many of the diver customers visited the island on cruise ships, so they had firsthand knowledge of just how rough the sea was. If the ocean was rougher than a creased shirt, it was enough to get a flood of cancellations. This suited the dive staff and boat crews fine, as not working was definitely preferable to cleaning up piles of seasick.

There was no such thing as a quiet day at this dive centre, if there was nothing to do the boss would just invent jobs for us. One morning when a particularly bouncy sea wrote the dive day off, we sat around washing masks and wetsuits, laughing and chewing the fat. The boss came out outside and told us to get our masks and fins. We needed them to go and look for a speedboat that had sunk over a year earlier. Some incredulous looks from a new guy were enough to get this luckless chap a day cleaning out the cesspit instead. I would much rather waste time snorkelling in the ocean than in the twenty feet deep excrement vat out back. Grabbing our goggles and flippers, we started walking up the beach. Another joker inquired what specifically it was we were looking for, and where indeed it might likely be found. Our belligerent employer asked him if he knew what a speedboat looked like - if he did, he should look out for exactly that, but underwater. He optimistically added that if we found it, we should bring the outboard engine from it back with us as he needed the spares.

I had been here a few months and realised that this exercise was probably timed with a visit from the immigration services. Staff without work permits were better suited to snorkelling off the premises for a few hours when these palm greasing meetings were scheduled. My tan would get a thorough topping up today, maybe I wouldn't need a work permit by the end of it. The immigration raids were becoming more and more frequent, and this was proving quite costly to the centre owner. All staff members were required to wear pink shirts emblazoned with the words STAFF on both the front and the back. The government officials had a pretty easy job spotting who was actually working, and a few pointed questions would establish the legalities. The Bahamas immigration department were almost a paramilitary unit, wearing ridiculous jungle camouflage uniforms and rifles. The officers even listened-in on the dive centres marine radio traffic to make sure the instructors were not engaging in a bit of shirt swapping with the customers before the boats arrived back. You could buy a yearly work permit, but nobody planned to endure a year here and the employee had to pay for the permit up front, which was not much of an incentive.

Our day spent searching the ocean in this extremely low-tech fashion quite predictably turned up nothing. The visibility in the pounding waves was bad enough that we could not even say that the boat was definitely not there. We did learn, however, that we should have brought sun-block with us. Our dehydrated and lobster-red bodies, complete with pounding headache, walked back to the dive centre at the end of the fruitless day. Thankfully it was payday, and I was going to exchange most of my hard earned cash for the repair of my money pit car. Natalie was just returning from a dive trip, the female employees often went diving to keep the male customers morale up. We bought a beer and cadged a lift to the garage where our ride was being pimped.

Joe the mechanic came out shaking his head, looking like someone had passed away. I noticed that our car was now sporting a 'no wheel' look, complete with bricks. I hoped Joe had only removed the wheels to stop them from being stolen.

Not only had the wheels been robbed, but also the battery and some of the interior. Our months of being in the Bahamas had hardened us to most situations, and I simply yawned. The mechanic was asking for another eight hundred dollars to get the car back to shipshape, it wouldn't take but a couple of days more. Adding that he had fixed the engine and steering, and it was a shame how we couldn't test it because some low life scum had stolen the wheels and battery. Although I had actually been born yesterday, it was quite late in the evening. I said I would have to come back with the money as some nuns had mugged us earlier. He had the audacity to ask for a few hundred tonight to cover his costs. Realising these costs very likely meant equipment for his hydroponics lab, I said I would come back at ten that night with more cash. I realise that sarcasm is difficult to read, but readers should throw a bucket of it over the last paragraph. All I wanted to do was throw a gallon of petrol over this car while our mechanic buddy was asleep inside it. A police car pulled into the station. The officers asked to whom the car belonged as our oily-rag friend shuffled away. I said that it belonged to a friend of ours who had been deported for having no work permit, he had asked me to try and sell it while we holidayed here. I gave him a bogus name and address for the fine to be sent to. Apparently it was against the law to leave a car in such a derelict state, especially on his friend's gas station forecourt. Of course, he asked if we could pay the fine in cash there and then. I gave him the story that we had both been pick-pocketed earlier that evening. Such a plausible excuse was highly likely in Nassau, he could do nothing but believe us. After the officer drove off, I phoned Kentucky Dave, a work colleague. He sounded drunk, nothing unusual there, he laughed out loud when I told him of our predicament. I asked him for a tow home because someone had stolen our battery. Leaving out the part where the wheels and tyres were also missing wasn't important, Dave wouldn't care. We sat in a filthy bar and had some Bacardi while waiting.

Dave turned up in his big Jeep Wrangler and a thick towing chain. He didn't even notice the lack of wheels as he never even got out of his car. Natalie sat in his car and I shouted that

I was ready to go. I could see him swigging from a bottle of Canadian bourbon, and my girlfriend just laughed hysterically. He tried to pull away, and at the beginning it was a struggle. I couldn't hear his shouting as my car had electric windows that were very reluctant to operate without a battery. Natalie must have mentioned the no wheel complication, as the laughing had clearly increased as clouds of smoke belched from the aging four wheel drive vehicle. Dave found the required low gear, had another slug of whisky and we were off. The noise was dreadful and sparks were jumping everywhere. I couldn't steer or brake, all I could do was sit there and cover my face. I opened the drivers door and looked behind me, the underneath of the car was ploughing the road surface like it was a farmers field. Natalie was taking pictures now and they were both drinking from the bourbon bottle. Smoke started filling the car and the metal floor beneath my feet was glowing red. Sparks began hitting me all over and I opened the door again to shout stop. We were just passing a bar full of drinkers who fell about laughing as I screamed. Dave just drove faster and faster like a possessed maniac. I wanted to jump free so at least I wouldn't have to pay a big fine for destroying miles of road surface. I could say that the wheels were stolen when I stopped at traffic lights, or had simply fallen off, come to think of it the car did sound noisier than usual. Amazingly, we did not see a cop the entire journey. The furrows on the road were deep enough though, that it wouldn't require the skills of Sherlock Holmes to follow the trail of destruction in the morning. We pushed the car onto the driveway of a new development of apartment's right next door to ours. A large portion of denial sealed the episode nicely.

Without the car headache, it was easier to save money now. All our belongings had already been stolen, so we were now carefree and travelling light. I paid an extra two hundred dollars to get the police reports within a month and sent them home to England to fulfil the insurance claim. The insurance company characteristically tried to wiggle out of paying by saying that they thought the Bahamas were in Europe and that the policy was in fact only valid within the EEC. The policy letter from these poorly travelled jokers clearly stated the

Bahamas as I'd requested, I suggested the company provide globes for its workers in future. It took another six weeks of telephone calls and lawyer's letters before they made good on their promises.

We had some plans for deep dives from Clifton Wall, but now we had no technical dive equipment and the dive shop owner said that we had to pay a deposit on the scuba tanks in case we died! Natalie wanted to do a six hundred feet dive as this would be the deepest woman's dive. The Bahamas is perfect for deep diving, second only to the Red Sea. The dive site pencilled for the dive was reachable with just a short surface swim and this meant no boats were even necessary. I mentioned the lack of equipment problem to Rob Palmer, who offered to lend us some double tanks and buoyancy wings. He said that he didn't fancy joining us on such a deep dive, but was willing to act as a support diver. The boss came to me with a pro-forma invoice for $8000 as deposit for all the tanks and underwater scooters. The deal seemed like a scam to me, as ninety percent of the equipment on the list would be used by the support divers, and these guys were not likely to be lost in action during the deep dive. I didn't think I could trust him even to return the money, so we planned to leave within two weeks for Florida to complete some Cave training before leaving for England.

Miami is just an hour or so by plane from Nassau. We arrived with our meagre belongings and rented a car for a month. The car rental office was covered in warning signs about the car jacking's that were reaching epidemic levels around the airport. Leaving the safety of this area, we were immediately pulled over by police, who kindly advised us that we were heading the wrong way and into the no-go area of Miami South Docks region. It made sense to leave this holiday city and head north on interstate 95, we drove until tiredness prevented further safe progress. It was Valentines Day when we landed, and the only place that had an available restaurant space was the unromantic town of Boca Raton. The hotels in the area were of course totally full this night with husbands entertaining their girlfriends, but at around two in the morning we were lying on red velvet sheets in a very dingy road side motel called the Pimps Crib or something. Surprisingly, we had a good nights sleep, totally uninterrupted by the gunfire or screaming trailer trash we had gotten quite used to during our stay in the beachfront apartment in Nassau. After a long lie-in and an unhealthy breakfast colourfully called *Springer's Heart Stopper,* the journey continued the rest of the way north to sink-hole country. Cave Mecca in the US is located at Ginnie Springs in High Springs, Florida. When we arrived, the place seemed deserted and damp. Torrential rains had swamped the area making the springs and rivers swollen and brown. The shop staff said that no diving was possible here or in the vicinity. Some local dive shops were still under twenty feet of water from the flooding. There were other alternatives, and a few phone calls and a couple of hours driving had us arriving at the Devils Den sink hole, near Williston. It was mid week, but this hole in the ground was already very busy owing to the bad conditions elsewhere. We wanted some proper instruction in cavern and cave diving and could spend as long as we needed. We were introduced to an Instructor called Ronny who lived locally in an affluent little town called Hail, although when he said with a southern drawl it sounded more like Hell. Over the next three days, Ronny went through various skills that we needed to perform in the overhead environment. Although classified as a Dome cavern, it was more like an underground lake. While we swam about practising air sharing without masks near the caverns bottom, scores of new divers completed their open water training above us, adding even more hazards to the overhead environment diving by dropping their weight belts on top of us. When we got to the dive site early enough, the cavern water was so clear it made you feel like you were floating in air. If we stayed in bed and arrived late, then it was like swimming through Tea.

The cavern course covered the history and geology of cave development and Ronny explained it all quite passionately. The latter part of the week was spent doing the Intro-to-Cave diving course which would take us to other cave systems in the area, most of which were still affected by the rain storm with bad visibility. It is easy to see how cave diving is popular in the area. The water temperature is constantly warm, the visibility underwater can reach 200 feet plus and there are absolutely no boats involved. Cave diving was probably invented by frustrated technical divers who get seasick easily or don't like tide dependant early mornings. The Cavern course had us wearing our regular scuba equipment and focused mainly on working underwater with lines, although all we did was follow previously installed lines, and we were never allowed to go beyond the natural light zone. The Intro Cave level was a bit more involved, in that we ventured into the blackness of the cave system proper. We wore larger scuba tanks with redundant breathing regulators and it all felt a little more technical, but not challenging. Inside the caves, the water was often so clear as to be mesmerising. The dive venue changed several times as the course standards mandated, with the names getting ever more exotic. Like dive sites the world over, if the description contains an animal name you can guarantee not to see that animal. We certainly never saw any Peacocks, Manatees or Peanuts during our training dives. Our first week in Florida was highly enjoyable, relaxing diving in the days and eating at Red Lobster in the evenings…Shangri-La. Full Cave training was next, but we had to wait a further couple of weeks until the flood waters subsided enough to let us to dive at Ginnie Springs. The sunshine state was still suffering from its winter hangover, the cool weather meant trips to the famous theme parks were far less hectic than normal. Queues for the attractions like Summit Plummet could last 45 minutes or more on a sunnier day. However, at this time of the year, the 58 degree air temperatures meant the biggest inconvenience was whole body goose bumps and bullet hard nipples. Five days of being off-season tourists was still very expensive, but a fun distraction from the inclement weather. The call of the ocean was beginning to beckon, we had to get wet again soon. The Bermuda Triangle touches land near Marathon on Florida's lower east coast. Instructor Ronny knew of a friendly boat captain that visited wrecks in this notorious sea area.

I was expecting to see pristine shipwrecks or aeroplanes that were mysteriously drawn to the seabed with gigantic alien magnets, but this wasn't to be. Several dives to these wrecks revealed only fire and collision damage reeking of marine insurance scams typical of aging freighter fleets worldwide. This part of the world was very pleasant and Natalie and I even looked into getting some work for a few months. The foreign instructors, we met, however were all working illegally without permits, and I for one was tired of living life on the lamb, poorly paid. Ronny kindly let us stay at his fantastic house for a few weeks and this gave us (me) some welcome financial freedom. The weather steadily improved enough so we could begin a further ten days of the full cave training course. Cave divers tend to do a lot of subtle chest beating, and our two new instructors I nicknamed Thrush and Candida, for their mannerisms being non-threatening, but often very irritating. The training agency we chose was the NSSCDS, a well-known training provider specialising in Cave courses with a reputation for integrity. The two instructors assigned to us were both knowledgeable and passionate about caves, but had the aura of being Robins to a team of local Batmen. Every class lesson followed the same "George says" script. I would rather have an experienced and confident cave mentor rather than one who constantly repeats someone else's phrases. Every lesson was a virtual script; I hoped he hadn't forgotten the important parts of it in favour of some marketing spin. Too much time was spent trying to sell us a certain brand of equipment or explain some ridiculously contrived configuration method to avoid unlikely problems. I for one was sick of listening to the *irrelevant* importance of 30" contents gauge hoses. I like my gauge where I can see it, not where weekend warriors think they are more 'streamlined'. After class, we went straight to another popular equipment manufacturer not far away and bought new buoyancy jackets, primary dive lights and cavern reels directly from them. The cave dive centre sold all these products themselves too, and our instructor was clearly on commission. When we turned up for class with our new stuff...his jaw dropped. He started to pull our stuff to pieces, both literally and verbally.

The instructor came just a few seconds away from getting an elbow to the temple when he attempted to demonstrate how easy our dive-lights would break as he bent them over his knee! I made it clear that he should get on with the job as his BS was getting way too thick. After this little verbal bun-fight the other star instructor took over and wowed me with his inability to use a drysuit properly, I said I thought he would be safer and therefore we safer, if he wore a wetsuit, after all the cave-water was 23' centigrade. He mentioned only *strokes* wore wetsuits while removing his drysuit to reveal again that his pee-valve had parted company and given his suit a smell resembling a care home's diaper room. Everything on this course was about streamlining and doing-it-right. I sparred with him about how in fact his membrane drysuit can be streamlined at all, it was clearly too big for him and the excess material rucked-up to form hundreds of ridges all over it. Our *stroke* wetsuits were much smoother, so in fact it was us doing-something-right. Around the entrance to caves were picnic tables where divers drank beer and some smoked dope openly between dives. One bearded fool asked if we could help dig up his gun store which he needed to get ready for the coming of some kind of NEW DAWN. That sounded interesting, until someone explained that the dinner of Limb Chicken he offered us was actually barbequed squirrels. He raised his offer with an evening of Picking N' A Grinning on his banjo, but we declined this generous offer also.

I quickly got the feeling that our new mentor wasn't qualified to instruct this part of the course, and after a few dives his pal Candida was back. As long as he never spoke, everything was fine - he was clearly more adept at the underwater part of the job than his padawan. The dives were very enjoyable however, the water just got clearer and clearer the further we went in. The only limit applied was a turn around point based around using a third of our air consumption. The maze like cave system was almost completely mapped out and all we had to do was follow a pre-installed guide line. If we got there early enough in the morning, we avoided the divers with scooters that would often fly past us, usually hitting the ceiling and clay floor...often at the same time. I could see why these divers needed crash helmets and the purpose of the dented metal guards around their tank valves was obvious... I wondered if this style of Pin-Ball diving was good for the caves. One exercise that is normally practised during Full Cave training is called a Lost Line Drill. It involves moving away from the safety of the guide line and trying to find it again with your eyes closed and lights off. This exercise is supposed to simulate losing sight of the line caused by a loss of visibility in the cave, due to clouds of silt suddenly obscuring the divers vision. The area chosen for the drill was quite large, approximately fifty feet across. The instructor gave us the cue to start the drill during our exit from the cave. We had spent already about 40 minutes exploring the cave, mostly deeper than one hundred feet. Natalie and I were both breathing regular air and we wore huge double 21 litre steel tanks. The instructor was breathing oxygen enriched air with 36% oxygen. Additionally he had a bottle of 100% oxygen to breathe later to speed up the decompression process.

Before we had even started looking for the line, I had close on seventy minutes of decompression stops, Natalie would have had a similar amount. This had been a fairly routine amount of stops during the course, as our low breathing rates allowed us plenty of penetration time. We spent an additional 30 minutes looking for this lost guide line. Bumping around in the darkness, fishing by hand for the 4mm diameter nylon string that led out of the cave can be very painstaking, but without any visual or time reference, the time flies. In reality, you have just the time given by your air supply to find the line. I don't remember who found the line first, but when we both had it was time to check air supplies and decompression status from our gauges. My Suunto computer showed 167 minutes of stops. I looked at the instructor's wrist gauge, and he had only 30 minutes of stops to do before reaching the surface. I showed him mine and his eyes became bigger than saucers. He wrote on a slate that he thought we were breathing the same gas mixtures as him. We had no where near enough air in our tanks to complete these nearly three hours of deco stops, and we were not even near the entrance at this point. Exiting as fast as possible, I became a little irritated by our instructor again. I imagined that his job required monitoring the entire situation, especially when doing exercises in the dark

113

with our eyes closed. If indeed a cave did silt out for real, I would swim further in against the outflow of water and along the ceiling to find clear water. Once this was found, along with the guide line, I would exit through the bad visibility section following the guide line closely. This would not take 30 minutes. I would not be turning my dive lights off in a silt-out situation. This drill was handled in a similarly synthesized way to the others, and its completion served little purpose. The instructor was inattentive throughout the session and I told him afterwards. We spent the three hours of mandatory decompression stops borrowing air from any divers that passed while we shivered in our stroke-suits. The instructor simply got out at the end of his deco stops. He graciously left the remains of his oxygen tank, which lasted one of us fifteen minutes. He did check back every thirty minutes or so by poking his head underwater and eventually passed a scuba tank of air down for us to share. That was the last dive of the course luckily.

If this was the best cave training that was on offer then it is no wonder that so many divers continue to die in caves each year. Ironically and sadly, our instructor took the life of a student cave diver shortly afterwards. The student apparently got a little behind during an exit from the cave and was found later, wedged by the outflow between two bedding plains of rock called *THE LIPS*. I believe he now instructs for the *latest, even better* cave training agency.

Exploring caves can be very relaxing and interesting, so despite our training we dived a few more weeks around the area, building almost thirty more cave dives in several different systems. Since, I have dived all around the world at various cave locations. I would say that the type of diving we learnt in Florida was fun but only, and barely, prepared us for diving in those particular caves. Instructors have an obligation to find out what breathing mixtures the students are using before a dive, and to give thorough, relevant briefings of how a new skill is to be efficiently completed - rather than attempt a shabby de-briefing chock full of 'I told you so's'.

Chapter 6. Hurds Deep- Hurts Deep

Starting another season working in Jersey was made more difficult this time by arriving back there in April, much earlier than usual. The weather was still doing its worst and scuba courses were thin on the ground. The sea temperature was hovering on 9 degrees centigrade, and this wasn't persuading many customers to spend their leisure time shivering in crap-fitting wetsuits. During the winter, the dive centre I normally worked at had been hit by a storm and became almost inaccessible. The centre was situated almost 100 metres from the shore, within a fortified Victorian seawater swimming pool. A wooden access bridge was the only means of getting to the area, unless it was low tide, then a short tramp across the beach got you in. A very rough sea, combined with a huge spring tide, had pounded the bridge and caused its collapse. The authorities were loath to spend public money any time soon on repairing the bridge during winter, so the whole facility went unused.

The dive shop owners had lost tens of thousands of pounds every year running the huge dive centre badly, so it suited them also to stay closed now and simply sell-off the stock. Jersey is quite unusual in that it had up to seven dive shops catering to a maximum of two hundred divers. Most of the dive centre owners have deep pockets from other income sources, so their scuba 'emporiums' are just hobbies. Eventually each one opens for fewer and fewer hours and then closes its doors for ever. There is seldom enough business to go satisfy the dietary requirements of even one dive shop, never mind seven, especially from September until June – the ever lengthening low-season. The only worthwhile diving work available out of season was diving for scallops, odd jobs fixing swimming pools, or clearing ropes from fishing boat propellers. I had worked before with a company offering pool repairs without removing the water first. Filling private pools was fairly expensive and if the water was removed carelessly it could collapse the pool sides. So this company used me to make the repairs on scuba. Many Jersey residents have swimming pools and over the winters they often fell into disrepair. The outdoor pools were mostly unheated outside of the summer months, so after July they went unused - excepting thirsty pets of course, and insects. Many times I had to fish a dead cat that had been swimming for several months in the deep end. If the water turned acidic and the PH rose enough, then the tiles would mysteriously fall off. I spent many days replacing the grouting between fancy pool mosaics, dissolved by the acidic green pool water. The temperatures were seldom above 7 degrees centigrade, and although thick drysuit's were mandatory, the work required gloveless fingers. I think the noxious chemicals that hardened underwater were far worse for my hands than the chilly water though. The only upside to this work was that it was well paid. The fees were swollen to cover the damage caused to the diving suits, damage quickly inflicted by the acid or alkaline pool water. Some jobs could last weeks as we tiled the pool floors of leisure centre pools where the *Marbelite* base was lifting, mostly we worked through the night.

I decided that without a dive centre to work from I would buy a boat and run a commercial boat charter business, to ensure steady work. I always attained a boat captain's license at each location I worked at while overseas and had thousands of hours at sea as captain or crew. The Jersey coastline is amongst the most treacherous in the world, and the combination of this and the extreme tides meant I had to study hard to obtain a local boat masters certificate. To make matters harder, most of the local pilotage notes are in French. I bought a twenty-three feet long rigid hull inflatable boat, otherwise known as a RIB. The hull was white and the sponson tubes red, it had a 150 hp outboard engine. I named the boat LEVIATHAN, which roughly translates to Devil of the Deep, the name was used in the Moby Dick novel for the monster whale. I also wanted to be able to run the vessel as a commercial fishing boat for scalloping, the license for this cost almost as much as the boat itself, but would pay for itself quite quickly. The boat was long and wide enough to be granted a license for ten passengers plus two crew members. Now I had my own transport, it was easier to drive to far away dive sites without too much hassle. Leviathan had a two hundred mile fuel range and top speed of 48 mph. Plans were made to visit most of the deep wrecks that littered the Channel Islands and even further up towards the English coast. Also, Natalie still wanted to complete the woman's deepest scuba dive. I had the position of a wreck in six hundred feet of water positioned north of Alderney in the Hurds Deep, very close to the centre of the shipping lane area we had dived before. Between diving for scallops and evening deep dives, I could manage 15 dives per week. Natalie worked in sports marketing full time, but dived in the evenings and afternoons if something interesting was happening. Every weekend I would organise at least one trip to a deep site like the Copper Wreck or SS Bizon. I often went diving alone to different wrecks and just used the big RIB as a large surface marker buoy. Diving this way does allow some flexibility and freedom but the consequences of missing the boat or it breaking free could be extremely unpleasant. Fisherman had recently taken under tow a dive boat they thought was derelict and a hazard to shipping. A diver was decompressing from a deep dive underneath the boat, and was dragged to the surface as the boats moved away. He got terrible decompression injuries. The lone diver said that he was displaying a dive flag and the boat should have not been approached. The fishing boat captain initially said he didn't see the dive flag, and then said the flag on display was the wrong type and irrelevant anyway.

Investigations showed the flag was the wrong type, which meant the fish captain had done nothing illegal. Dive flags are only red with a white diagonal stripe in the United States and inside diver training manuals. However, internationally, a boat with divers deployed in the water has to display rigid, white and blue divers A-Flag. If doing so, other professional boaters are obliged to keep a safe distance away, unless of course they are predatory fisherman looking to make a salvage claim. We set a date for Natalie's deep dive and organised some support divers. I wanted to video-tape the event to verify the depth and maybe make a mini documentary about it. Scanning dive magazines, it was obvious that no mainstream video equipment company sold a camera housing that would not be crushed by such a deep excursion. Eventually I found a custom manufacturer who would build a camera box to withstand two hundred metre dives. It turned up within 3 weeks and I only had to sell one kidney to pay for it. The housing was delivered in a nice box that seemed undamaged. It was constructed of thick aluminium with a thick plexi-glass dome port, and weighed over seven kilograms including the camera. It was obvious that it had recently been dropped by clumsy idiots and was covered in fingerprints. Phoning the supply company, I got the expected bullshit that as it wasn't them at fault, they didn't care who was. Unfortunately, they were five hundred miles away and I needed the camera for the deep dive in a few days time. As is always the case when planning projects to coincide with the pull of the moon, the better the tides, the worse the wind. The weekend date in the diary was postponed as gale force winds ran riot across the English Channel. The boat was loaded with all our trimix tanks and decompression gases, the support divers had taken a week off work to help out, so the wait wasn't really a train crash. A good slack tide was important during very deep dives. If divers are travelling down through six hundred feet of water dripping with scuba tanks, it makes it much easier if a large part of this water is not moving in the opposite direction.

The wind stayed constantly good for kite-flying until Monday, the forecast was to drop to force 4-5 on the Beaufort scale by Tuesday morning. Winds this strong are not ideal for sixty mile sea journeys in small boats, but you have got to be in it to win it, so off we went. Almost five hours later we arrived at the dive site, all in one piece, but shaken AND stirred. Looking for the wreck was a non-starter, the RIB was dancing up and down like a ballerina on acid. The GPS navigation equipment played its jolly tune that we had arrived, at the right place and the weighted descent line was thrown overboard on this mark. Had I known that scuba diving record categories can be just dreamt up, it would have made sense to persevere with the wreck finding. The world's deepest woman's scuba dive that also happened to be on the deepest wreck had quite a nice ring to it. Shame I wasn't a woman, because the deepest men's dive was almost four hundred feet deeper. I did have my work cut out for me though, I would be taking the worlds deepest video footage with the world's not-the-smallest of cameras. Our support divers were Andy, a friend from Scotland, and Joao, a.k.a *The Monkey Boy*. Both Natalie and I were diving completely self-sufficiently today. We carried five 12 litre tanks, two of trimix with 8% oxygen and 65% helium, the others were a trimix of 20% oxygen and 30% helium for shallower use and two decompression mixes containing 50% oxygen and 100% oxygen. The dive plan allowed for up to four minutes at the maximum depth, giving a total dive time of just over three hours. The decompression planning software was an improved version of something we had used many times. Deep stops were added at 120 metres and 90 metres, but the formal stops didn't stop until much shallower, near 66 metres. The software had been just been upgraded to allow faster ascent rates in deep water. I liked to come up at 10 metres per minute normally, but the non-diving experts suggested that ascent speeds up to 24 metres per minute were all the rage now. Again, none of these gurus had ever completed deep dives of this nature, but I guess they were knowledgeable in something, else why were they called experts?

The weather was pretty appalling really, one to two metre waves were upsetting the boat and crews equilibrium alike. Rain squalls and gusty winds completed the picture. The clouds passed so quickly that the sky was like a strobe of blue and dark grey. When stationary the boat was not too unstable, but it helped to keep moving forwards slowly to keep the waves from breaking over us. The electric bilge pumps worked constantly keeping the boat as dry as conditions would allow. Natalie was ready, and went over the side to swim towards the down line. I followed shortly afterwards when I was happy that the camera looked happy. She went first down the line a minute or so ahead of me. The angry weather didn't penetrate below the waves, and everything was calm and serene just 3 metres below the surface. Juggling the camera and five breathing regulators, I went in chase after Natalie, now only visible as a faint silhouette in the darkness. Despite the blender effect of the previous days storm, the underwater visibility was excellent. The sea temperature was a balmy 14 degrees centigrade at the top, but this would drop to 6 degrees nearer the bottom. The timing for the dive seemed fine as we were definitely in a slack tide window at this moment. Diving in the English Channel on a stormy day isn't quite the same as the Caribbean Sea, daylight ceased to exist near 60 metres and an eerie dark blue ink seemed to permeate down to 90 metres. From here on down, it was darkness above and below.

Around 160 metres, everything was going very easily until I picked up an episode of frantic hand shaking. These tremors were likely caused by an effect on our central nervous system by the helium in our breathing mixtures, exacerbated by the rapid descent rates. This malady is called HPNS, or high pressure nervous syndrome. I wasn't concerned overly until I realised I could no longer hold the camera anymore, as I kept hitting myself with it. I let the security lanyards take the weight of it while I stopped and waited for the helium tremors to subside. Natalie was on the bottom now, waiting for me to record the event, so I had to get a move on. I arrived at 180 metres still shaking violently, but knew it would pass. Using the camera was out of the question for another minute. I looked around for a sign of the nearby shipwreck, but only saw a few fish. The clarity down here was fantastic, some of the best I have seen in the Channel. Our primary dive lights illuminated the scene well, unlike my smaller video camera lights that although rated for 300 metre dives, had mostly split open from the pressure far shallower. My hands stopped shaking and I turned the camera on Natalie to record the moment. I felt like my drysuit was squeezing me a little, so I pressed the chest inflator valve to alleviate some of the pressure. As I pushed the button inwards it shot outwards, taking with it the entire valve assembly. Freezing water gushed into my suit, this was definitely not good. I showed Natalie, and gave an up signal. The water had already filled my suit but I attempted to stuff the chest valve back into the hole whence it came. The water flood could not have come at a more inopportune moment. The entire decompression stop plan would still need to be endured, but the water temp at this depth (which had now filled my suit) could have sustained ice cubes.

Initially, the shock of the cold water kept me warm, I think. But just five minutes later the first of the cold shudders started as my body prepared for the battle against hypothermia. The first deco stop at 120 metres was easy, Natalie ahead of me now, by just a few metres on the rope line. At 100 metres, she felt as if she had been hit by decompression sickness in her shoulder. So early in the ascent, this was highly unusual and quite worrying. The bends tends to come on quite slowly when in the form of pain, to feel sharp pain this deep in the water must have been something else, but I couldn't imagine what. She had spent much more time at depth than me, but still, the decompression stops were based around spending a full four minutes at depth, which she had definitely not exceeded. The extra time at the bottom would have tested the decompression stops to the full, and now a weakness was possibly revealing itself. We completed some subsequent stops and luckily Natalie's shoulder discomfort did not seem to worsen. I took some more video footage during the ascent, mostly to take my mind off the cold feeling that was firmly gripping my body now. On reaching the 60 metre deco stop, I was shivering uncontrollably.

Nothing could be done except to follow the ascent plan. I hoped that the slightly warmer water closer to the surface could bring some relief. We met support diver Joao at 30 metres, he bought some spare decompression gas tanks. Besides the suit drama and Natalie's problem shoulder, the dive went well and we had surplus breathing gas reserves in our own tanks at this point. It is good practice, however, to not drain diver worn scuba tanks unnecessarily. Near-empty tanks get more buoyant and can either upset body position or, in the worst case, actually float you to the surface. The chilling effects of the water meant my breathing rate was higher than normal; I had less remaining tank pressure than Natalie because of this. I took the spare tanks from Joao and clipped them to my buoyancy jackets harness. I showed Joao my busted drysuit valve and pointed to the seabed. I add that I was shivering now, with almost two more hours of deco stops to complete. All the head shaking in the world would not warm me up though. The fresh winds still blew their worst above us, but the rough seas didn't travel much below two to three metres down. Our plan allowed for decompressing anywhere from six to three metres below the surface for the very last stop. My body lost the battle with the cold, and energy levels dropped to the point where I could not even manage to shiver. The water temperature was not cold enough to attack my hands or feet painfully, but the time immersed in it was sufficient to rob me of critical levels of consciousness. I felt like I was falling asleep as I bobbed along under the waves. I had sent up surface marker buoys earlier and clipped the attached reels directly to me. This at least saved me from the constant effort of maintaining buoyancy control, as it meant that my depth was set and I could decompress almost automatically.

Getting cold underwater for long periods affects the circulation in the same way as it does at the surface. The body protects the core temperature by restricting blood flow to the extremities. While diving, the body absorbs certain parts (inert gases) of the gas mixtures breathed in all tissues of the body. If these inert gas components are not allowed to exit the body over time by the circulation system, they will likely cause cases of the bends. Therefore, it is important not to get too cold while diving. If a scuba diver got cold on a recreational dive, the easiest solution would be to get out of the water. Because of the depth of this dive, getting out would mean missing out time spent decompressing properly, and this virtually guarantees getting nasty types of decompression sickness. Staying underwater decompressing with hypothermia is far from ideal, but is definitely the lesser of the two evils. I would stay until I couldn't stay any longer, or started to lose consciousness. Deep diving in warm oceans certainly avoids these problems, but if everything was easy it would be less rewarding. The reward lies in the complexity of the challenge. If it was sunny blue skies and 30 degrees centigrade in the Arctic circle, there would be no reason to go there except for the snow, and people get hurt all the time going crazy skiing.

The minutes ticked down slowly, and I felt very bad. Eventually I thought I would have to shorten the dive through feeling so weak, but my lowered level of awareness had shut down all of my powers of reason, I think I was just sleeping with my eyes open. The hard part of managing difficult situations is knowing when to do the right thing before you are prevented from doing anything. I knew that 'too late' would come, but I didn't want to give up early and guarantee myself the bends. Joao signalled to me that the time was now up, and It took all my strength and concentration to press the inflator button of my buoyancy jacket. Natalie said that she would stay longer than the original plan to make use of the oxygen still left in her tanks. Time spent underwater breathing enriched air or oxygen is beneficial as it has a vacuuming effect on the inert gases still remaining in the tissues. Unfortunately, when the body and brain have had enough oxygen at high ambient pressure, the brain simply shuts down without warning, usually leading to epileptic seizures, then drowning. Joao would stay underwater with her to provide assistance if necessary. I bobbed to the surface, but remained face down - I had no energy to even turn myself over. The seas were big and grey now, with spray obscuring visibility. Several minutes passed and I started to unclip my equipment, still lying face down. My body felt like ice. I remembered some cold water testing that I had strangely *paid* to experience in 1991. I was recovered from the water after the supervisor went for a cup of tea and a phone chat. Time went quickly for him but slowly for me. Those thirteen minutes submerged in ice water then, felt much like today, although then was a bit more serious, as I far beyond delirious, by the time I was dragged out.

Today, I felt very weak and tired but had enough strength to shrug off my harness and five tanks, The warmer air temperature was enough to breathe a little energy back into me, but Andy would definitely have to help me into the boat. He came alongside and I managed to get my fins beneath me. I grabbed for the handrails of the boat and with a supreme effort and Andy's help, scrambled up, over the sponson's and into the RIB. Cold and Exhaustion meant I couldn't speak properly to explain myself, and Andy could only see I was blue and unwell. He offered me some warm coffee and it seemed like a good idea to take some. Andy tipped the cup into my mouth, but my throat seemed to reject it. Instead of taking the normal path into my stomach, the hot drink went straight down into my lungs. Now this was worse than anything I'd endured up until then. I couldn't clear the coffee as I hadn't the energy to cough properly. I turned over face down and put my legs up on the back seat of the boat. Raising my body this way let some of the coffee drain out. I lay there trying not to drown in the boat for thirty minutes, taking shallow gurgling gasps like I had tuberculosis. The ensuing constant coughing seemed to be warming me up after a while, and I started to shiver again. I wanted to stand for some reason, and attempted to get up. My life seemed to drop to down into my legs instantly, and I felt faint if I did anything more than sit up straight. My flooded drysuit was pulled off to get the damp cold undersuit away from my skin. Natalie surfaced about 45 minutes after me, her shoulder still hurting with the same intensity as at 100 metres down. The coughing was still constant, now but under control, and I was able to drink without fear of drowning myself. In any subsequent deep or long dive in cold water, I made a note to bring hot liquids in submersible containers, just in case. With all divers back on the boat, we headed slowly for Alderney. Natalie sat at the back breathing oxygen but otherwise felt well. I managed to get to my feet, but could just manage to slump against the scuba tank rack. Andy remembered the deco station made up of orange buoys etc. and was it being left behind? While picking up the divers, the boat drifted away from the descent line and now it was lost in the waves. The satellite navigation equipment had a rough idea where the boat had been though. I was feeling sufficiently okay to drop my health status to Def-con 3, and Natalie seemed happy enough that a search for, and recovery of, the down line would be manageable. All this done, we journeyed back to St Anne's harbour.

As the heat returned to me, so did my strength and by the time we passed the huge breakwater I was almost fine. Natalie was off the oxygen but still had shoulder pain. The weather was grim and no one really looked forward to sixty miles of rough seas back to Jersey. We definitely needed to refuel, as the boat engine had been running over eight hours now. Another five hours of punching into the incessant waves could mean running out of petrol and paddling the boat in the dark. Once inside the inner harbour that situated the fuel berth, the weather was shielded from us by the huge walls. Alongside the dock, I climbed the tall ladder up to terra firma. Natalie came too, the other two lads refuelled the boat. The fuel attendant asked what we had been doing in such rough weather. Natalie explained that we had been diving in the Hurd Deep area, and now were considering the journey back. The conversation continued as the guy did a bit of diving himself and noticed the boat was awash with twin tanks and deco tanks and 200 metres of anchor rope. Natalie said that we had just been down to six hundred feet and now she was the deepest woman diver in the world. The video camera came out. During the tiny TV show Natalie, was massaging her shoulder and breathing from the oxygen. The pump attendant asked if she had the bends and offered to drive her to the local health centre for a check-up before we left in the boat. After a bit of deliberation about going now or after we got a fish and chip dinner inside us first, we both ended going up to the medical centre. Once inside, we were asked to lie down on a couch and given some supplemental oxygen to breathe. The nurses gave us cups of tea and a blanket each before applying arm cuff's to measure our blood pressures.

As I lay there relaxing the exhaustion took over, and I must have dozed off before waking with the feeling that my arm had pins and needles. I tried to move my arm under the blanket but it just felt dead. Pulling back the cover, I saw that the blood pressure cuff was still on my bicep and still inflated. I ripped it away. My arm was grey and ashen - I couldn't feel it at all now. Without the cuff in place, slowly the colour returned, followed by the feeling. The nurse came back and I told her what had happened, but she didn't think it significant, I did. The health centre said they had organised an aeroplane back to Jersey for Natalie so she could get recompression treatment for her shoulder as soon as possible. I still felt a little weak, which worsened dramatically when I stood up. I spoke to Andy, who had stayed with the boat, via phone and said that we were both leaving by plane for Jersey. I didn't want them travelling with the boat back in this weather tonight and suggested they find a hotel. Andy agreed. The health centres' ambulance drivers had to be paged during their evening off. When they arrived they reeked of Indian food and alcohol, but were quite jovial despite their evening being ruined. We boarded the passenger plane and completed the thirty minutes of low altitude flying back to where we came from. The only complication was that the therapy oxygen bottle ran empty almost immediately after we boarded, but I didn't feel like I had the bends, so it didn't really matter, plus Natalie had been breathing oxygen for hours now, and her lungs would probably appreciate the rest.

At Jersey airport, an ambulance was waiting by the runway, and within twenty minutes Natalie was being evaluated before entering the recompression chamber. A doctor examined me and decided that I should be given some intravenous rehydration fluids before being free to go. Unfortunately, I wasn't really free to go anywhere. I had cleverly left my car key, house key and money with my mobile phone on the boat which was still in Alderney. I called my girlfriend, Sarah, who came to the chamber facility to collect me, still clad in my sexy hospital pyjamas. I was back in bed, feeling fine, by 10 o'clock in the evening. I slipped into a deep sleep immediately as today's adventure had just a little too much excitement for one day.

At two in the morning, I awoke with an arm possessed. I have never felt pain like it, and might even have considered cutting it off. The pain extended from the bicep area to the elbow on the same arm that the blood pressure cuff was left on earlier. My arm had developed a mind of its own and was banging itself against the bedroom wall quite hard. I had to restrain the arm with my good one. Sarah woke to ask what the commotion was, and I said I thought I needed a trip to the hospital straight away. At two thirty a.m. we were outside the hospital, and I was walking barefoot dressed in a hospital slip into the reception area. I looked like an escaped mental patient. The hospital trousers I wore were fetchingly backless, as I discovered for the first time when I sat down on a cold plastic chair in the waiting room - luckily the streets outside had been empty, so there were no takers for the peepshow. The nurse on duty read from a poster on the wall about what to do regarding divers and decompression sickness, and then phoned somebody for advice. I suggested I should be breathing oxygen via a demand valve, but she refused, adding that only a doctor can prescribe oxygen. The next thing I know, nurse Ratchet was trying to stuff a catheter somewhere I totally wasn't expecting one. As one door closed, another one slammed shut. I hope when you pay for private hospital treatment the level of care goes a lot further than what *I* was experiencing. When a nurse or doctor says that something will be uncomfortable, this is NO understatement. The freezing Gel used to ease and numb my discomfort was as effective as a cosh around the head. After I was *all plumbed in* unnecessarily, I had to wait until the next morning for the recompression chamber to be emptied out. After Natalie's treatment, the inside chamber tender himself also had to be treated for decompression sickness. Natalie said that he spent so much time trying to chat her up during her treatment that he wasn't breathing from his own oxygen mask enough during the ascent.

Lying on a hospital bed breathing oxygen as it blew in the through a nearby open window was not very effective treatment. However, the pain in my arm became a little more bearable as the hours ticked by until morning. In the Alderney health centre and then during the evening examination in Jersey, some blood oxygen monitors were put tightly on my index and forefingers. I was not surprised that by the morning I had decompression sickness in both these fingers too. By the time I was pressurised in the recompression chamber, eight hours had elapsed. I felt quite lucky - they said that ALL the stops were being pulled out for me! If a diver gets the bends, they should be put in a recompression chamber without delay. The longer the wait before treatment, the greater the chance of long term injury, with residual symptoms. Therefore, the sooner the treatment begins, a lesser number of treatments will be needed to successfully to treat the injury. Fast treatment can shrink the actual bubbles that are causing the pain or injury. If treatment comes slowly, these gas bubbles will have been absorbed by the body itself within a few hours - however, the oxygen starvation damage that was caused by the initial bubble, and the consequent body immune response mechanism, will take much longer to fix. Time is critical.

Pain relief came quickly once my chamber treatment began. The treatment scheduled was to last slightly less than five hours. During this, I lay on my back breathing oxygen from an aviator style mask and read some magazines. Drinks are passed through special airlocks, together with the odd bland snack. I didn't have the further embarrassment of peeing behind a sheet in the chamber, because I was still firmly attached to the invasive and awkward catheter arrangement. I felt fine after just 30 minutes of being in the chamber. The entire five hours treatment time is completed to ensure a slow trip back to surface pressure. This minimises the chances of the initial bend coming back, or even the possibility of symptoms caused by the treatment itself. The mixtures breathed during this treatment session were the common or garden 100% oxygen and air varieties. An occasional break of five minutes of air breathing ensured something or other didn't happen - the chamber tender tried to explain the reason, but it just sounded like he had failed to listen during his Nitrox class.

Most of the time inside the chamber is spent dry pressurised to 18 metres of depth, breathing 100 percent oxygen. If you are not too badly injured or uncomfortable the experience is quite interesting and enjoyable. As the chamber pressurises, the air inside gets noticeably warm, you feel like you are in a giant scuba tank that's being filled with air. Ears still need to be equalised, as you descend down in the same manner as if descending through water. My time in the pot was over...I gladly climbed out. The first thing on my mind was getting this infernal catheter removed. After saying I was lucky to be alive and a bit of head shaking, in a manner reminiscent of a backstreet car mechanic, the diving doctor said begrudgingly he would take the medieval instrument out himself. He had the bedside manner of the Yorkshire Ripper, but made worse with his shaking hands. At least he spared me the discomfort of the anaesthetic freezing Gel. While the enormous tube and inflatable balloon was extracted, I had a flashback to the scene in the movie Total Recall. The pain on Arnie's face as he pulls the flashing red tracking device out from his nose looked similar to what I was enduring now. I am sure the device hasn't changed since its invention during the Spanish inquisition.

It had become standard practice to spend a night under observation at the hospital after a recompression treatment. The ward I was put in was full of patients recovering from some serious operations. That afternoon when the Islands only newspaper, locally known as the Beano, was delivered to the bed-bound readership, more fun began. Some of the coffin dodgers sharing the room were angry with me for wasting taxpayers' money to pay for an aeroplane to evacuate us. My injuries had been demoted to sports injuries, and as such I should be expected to pay for treatment. The most vocal of these coffin dodgers said that taxpayers' money was better spent on treating ailments such as his lung cancer, which was apparently a proper condition. His obese pal in an adjacent bed backed him up, saying that his liver cirrhosis needed valuable funds to fix, better spent on him than me. On my side of the ward, the unfortunate man in the bed to my right had yesterday decided that drinking 2 litres of Vodka seemed like a good idea and could alleviate his problems. I started with him, as he was least able to defend himself with his kidney failure. As I seldom drink, I saw his drinking achievements as a world record of some sorts, 2 litres in one hour must get him some kind of recognition. The other selfless fools opposite had either eaten like pigs all their lives, or they had drunk or smoked to excess, knowing full well that these pastimes would likely take a heavy toll on them later. No-one, even fifty years ago, *actually* thought that cigarettes were like vitamin pills, they can say what they like in a court room of sympathisers. I don't smoke, don't drink all day, and my stomach is not hanging over my trousers. As I saw it, my situation was caused by a third party. But like most people, we share a dangerous interest in various unhealthy pastimes.

The drysuit valve had fallen out because the suit manufacturer had added a new type of rotating inlet valve. The valve did not fit the suit's sealing gasket properly and it leaked. To stop the leaking, the valve was tightened with such force that the plastic threads simply let go and the valve fell out, unfortunately at an inopportune time for me. I had overcome the subsequent hypothermia and surfaced without decompression injury. The absolutely botched medical care I received in Alderney with the pressure cuff incident ensured me a ride in the chamber. Natalie's injuries were likely caused by the use of the particular dive software, or an underlying physiological reason. The software we used was changed in its next evolution, and whether her injuries tipped this decision, the dive still helped protect others. Natalie's Deepest Woman's Dive was a success despite all this. The video evidence was irrefutable, the sea conditions were especially challenging and her *sports injury* was very typical considering a dive to this depth in 1999, when decompression software was still as useful as a cock-flavoured lollipop. Within days of our recovery, one of the recompression chamber staff tried to sell, quite professionally, his *inside story* of our treatments to a couple of Diving magazines. The editors contacted me to point this out, and unusually declined to print his version of the treatment SCOOP. I hope one day I have to remove *his* catheter, using the famous Magician's technique for yanking tablecloths faster than the eye can see, thus *minimising* any discomfort.

If a runner sprains his ankle or pulls a hamstring during a sprinting record, the record is still valid, probably even more so. If a climber or other explorer gets frostbite on his toes during some intrepid attempt, they still get positive recognition for their achievement. Scuba diving strangely attracts much more vociferous jealousy from armchair contenders than any other pursuit. Similar to sexual performance - if you say you are good in bed then you get criticised heavily by the impotent. Many men think they are good drivers and will get very boisterous when somebody doubts their vehicular virility, especially if that somebody has two sets of X chromosomes. Scuba academia is strangely similar to the scriptures, with scores of dubiously ordained experts all scrabbling for reputation. When a disciple is forced to defend an illogical belief in the improbable, it causes them to get extremely vexed or worse, the *facts* are usually irrelevant. If you disagree, or ridicule proponents from certain camps, get ready for the bombs to start flying, it all comes down to *Face* and money, much like religion. The more minor or basic the grounds for an argument, the more people think they understand it and want to offer their often contradictory advice.

Chapter 7: SMS BADEN meets the Ocean Terrorist

The wreck position that we dived on in 1999 was known by my Guernsey and Alderney fishermen contacts as the Baden, a very large German battleship. During Natalie's deep dive, we did not see any wreckage so can hardly count it as the deepest wreck dive, despite others only seeing the shoaling fish that habitat a wreck and slating it as a successful wreck dive. I'm sure I saw a fish down there. Several Baden's were constructed by the German Navy. As is often the case, Navies use previously issued names for new ships time and time again. The SMS (Seiner Majestat Schiff/His Majesty's ship) Baden that sits at the bottom of the Hurd Deep near Alderney was sunk during gunnery practice by the British Navy in August, 1921. The Baden had a sister ship called Bayern, together they were the ultimate dreadnoughts of the Imperial German High Seas Fleet, both launched during 1916 and 1917. Baden was the only Capitol ship saved from the notorious *en masse* sinking affair at Scapa Flow. The scuttling of the entire fleet would make maritime headlines when, on the 21st day of June 1919, the Flow saw some 400,000 tonnes of German battle steel descend to the seabed almost simultaneously. The Fleet Commanding officer, Rear Admiral Ludwig Von Reuter, gave the signal to scuttle in a coded message via flag to the officers in charge of the other interned hulks. The subtle flag phrase was 'Paragraph eleven, confirm', this caused sea cocks to be opened and then smashed.

German national flags were hoisted just before the defiant scuttling, orchestrated to prevent the ships falling into Allied use. The Allies were still fighting amongst themselves as to who would get what, now it was all decided for them, quite fairly. Fifty-one ships went to the bottom in all, the ones that were not salvaged over the years remain a popular diving destination. The BADEN was stripped of machinery and towed down to the English south coast. The heavy armour plating was tested and evaluated for days by continual bombardment from air and sea by the Royal Navy, before the ship succumbed to her wounds and she slipped below the surface. Sitting in six hundred feet of water, if the Baden were to be stood on end it would likely just scrape the surface at low tide, given its incredible dimensions. The wreck name didn't come up again until January 2000, when Natalie and I attended a dive show in London. A couple of deep divers intended to dive the Baden and claim the deepest wreck dive, they asked if I would video tape their attempt. When we were all down on the wreck, I had to promise not to go deeper than them! Natalie would join the trip, as she was more than capable of the dive and had dived the area several times also.

The diving comics published reports each month covering the preparations of the huge team of UK deep divers. I found it a little unusual that they were doing practice dives in a quarry in Wales. The maximum depth here was one hundred metres, just over half of the planned wreck dive depth. The area where the Baden lies is swept by some of the strongest tidal streams in the world -the quarry could not replicate this current even if they took their flippers off. As we had already dived the wrecks location, and also quite near it a couple of times recently, preparation dives were not that necessary. I continued to dive every day, either on the deeper local wrecks or scalloping, while the other guys practised in a quarry once a week. We liaised via e-mail and agreed to simply meet at the wrecks co-ordinates on the day. The planned dive day was pencilled for July 2000. This much-hyped team from all over England consisted of two deep divers and three dozen more in support roles, all arriving in a flotilla of boats. Their plan was to spend twenty-five minutes at six hundred feet depth, this length of time was a little optimistic I thought, considering both divers had not spent one minute at, or even dived once to, anywhere near this depth before. My dive plan allowed for 15 minutes at the maximum depth while I filmed the others setting their record. More than six months were needed to prepare the other team for this wreck dive. I continued to work as normal until one day, while a passenger on my own boat, I broke my arm. A chap was driving my RIB Leviathan at full speed on a flat, calm sea just outside of Jersey harbour. I sat at the back of the boat talking with his wife and daughter. Everybody was having a jolly time until the driver lost control while negotiating a wake from another boat. With the excessive speed and poor handling, the boat left the water for a few seconds and crashed back down badly in a scene resembling Donald Campbell's Blue Bird crash. I managed to get to the front during the mêlée and kill the engine. The driver was thrown to the floor, as was his family. I managed to hold on to the boats scuba tank rack during the action. As the boat settled, I noticed my wrist had become unusually floppy and blood was collecting under the skin, I had heard a crack a moment earlier, but felt no immediate pain. After all the shaking about, the drivers' family didn't want to play any more, so we returned to port. My hand had swollen like the Elephant Man's by now, and after tying the boat up, I thought a trip to the hospital was in order. I had it x-rayed, but the doctor said that nothing was broken and just to rest it. I bought an ice pack and went back to the dive centre to organise that afternoons' dive trip. The weather was still perfect and a group of 8 divers wanted to dive a wreck called the Princess Ena which lay at 48 metres depth some 18 miles from Jersey's south coast. I managed to find a relief captain and joined the dive group myself as it was such a nice day.

Putting my drysuit on over my swollen arm was painful but the pressure form the wrist seal did a lot to reduce the swelling, as did the cold seawater. With all the pulling I had to do to get down the anchor rope that led to the wreck site, the comfort lasted until I reached the seabed. It was clear that the pain was going to upset the dive, so I headed straight back up. Getting back on the boat and taking my drysuit off had my wrist complaining a lot. The rest of the week saw my arm changing through various shades of purple and getting steadily more useless and painful. I got a surprise phone call from the hospital saying that they had checked my x-rays a little closer and I should return to the hospital immediately. The doctor said now that my wrist was clearly broken at the Scaphoid bone. He recommended that if I broke something again, it would be better to avoid Sundays as they were too short staffed, or more likely hung over, to do things properly. I thought they would just bandage my arm now, and was surprised to see a bucket of plaster rolled out on top of a trolley. I would have to wear a cast for ten weeks. This would be extremely inconvenient, as work was busy and I was self employed. The doctor said they could operate to repair the bone as a last resort, but only after waiting two months.

Working in the dive business with an arm in plaster is not ideal; life still had to go on though. You can't beat a bit of self employment to stamp out malingerers, with all their bad backs and Monday colds. I ordered a waterproof seal for my arm so that I could shower, and maybe even go diving if I had to. Going underwater with a broken arm wrapped in a plastic bag was a huge mistake. I only road-tested the watertight bag during a shallow dive to 4 metres, but the pressure of the water collapsed the bag on my cast and as I couldn't equalise the effects of this pressure, the pain was only just short of excruciating. I was inundated with *I told you so's*, still, It was an interesting exercise. I managed to run the boat with just one arm but had to hire a scuba lackey to hump the heavy tanks and weight belts. A month after the cast was applied, I was servicing some breathing regulators. Some of the components were submerged in an ultrasonic acid bath. I picked a piece out of the bath and managed to tip some acid up my cast. This is NOT to be recommended. The feeling of rabid ants biting my arm focused my three brain cells very fast and I ran out of the dive centre to the harbour steps just outside. It was low tide unfortunately, so thirty slippery, seaweed-covered steps had to be negotiated before my arm was plunged into the cold seawater.

The hospital had told me not to get the arm wet, when I returned there and told them the story they were less than impressed. The old cast was due for a change anyway and they gave me a new covering, this time it was a much cooler colour. At eight weeks, I had an x-ray check up to see how the bones had fused. The bones had clearly moved much further apart, no doubt because I had continued to work, both driving the boat and carrying scuba tanks. Only surgery could fix it now. I was under the knife on the 6th of June, my birthday. I wondered if my arm would be ready for diving the deep wreck by mid July. With a wrist now full of self-tapping screws, I would follow the doctor's orders a little more closely. Work waited until the bandages were off, and scuba would wait until the scar healed properly. After five weeks, my hand was stiff but fully functional. I planned some deeper dives to get back into the swing of things. Extreme diving requires a large amount of mental preparation, this I had done. I had been to these depths before and felt completely relaxed about doing it again. An equal part of successful deep diving is equipment comfort and familiarity. The only way to be competent is through constant repetition. Divers who can only dedicate a few weekends a month to deeper exploits will, in my opinion, never build enough skill or comfort to remain successful or alive for long. Diving only on the weekends will not prepare anyone adequately for technical level diving, and definitely not for rebreather equipment. The more complicated the kit, the more intuition and reflex is needed to fly it safely. I had only two weeks to get match fit, but I could dive twice a day in that period. First I got comfortable in my drysuit, over the days, more and more cylinders were added. By the end of the first week, I was comfortable diving to seventy metres again with five tanks and my video camera. Natalie joined me for most of the dives as did Pete, Matt and Dave, the guys helping me as support divers for the deep dive. The dive date was chosen apparently for its ideal range of tides. It became clear that the boat captains from Weymouth that were bringing the UK divers over had no real idea regarding the tides in the area. I don't know what experience the dive team really had either, but the currents in this area would take no prisoners, they would be far from their Kansas-like welsh quarry if they miscalculated the tidal window.

A couple of days before the planned dive weekend, Natalie hurt herself in a triathlon race, support diver Dave broke his foot, and the weather turned ugly...fantastic. I heard from the other team that they were still filling tanks in Weymouth Harbour but would arrive on time, despite the inclement weather. Optimistically, I finished packing my RIB and Dave said that he could still join the trip in his boat. His leg plaster meant no diving, but the spare boat would be invaluable and very welcome. Clare, my Ex from London with whom I learnt to dive with in Mexico ten years earlier, came over to lend a hand also. Funnily enough, she had completed just 6 dives since we learnt, compared to my 2500 in the same time. The TV and Radio media had picked up on the story about the deepest wreck dive and came down to wave us off. The five of us left in two big colourful RIBs and headed up to Alderney in the now-gusting Force seven winds. It is a good feeling, heading off into the unknown to do something interesting as a team, especially in boats. The weather on the way up had the heavily loaded boats jumping and bouncing badly. The same journey could take seventy minutes on a flat sea, but took us near seven hours that day. Driving through the area known as the Alderney Race was especially fun, the currents were ganging up on the boats and threw all manner of standing waves in our path and faces. Pulling into the shelter of the huge breakwater was quite a relief, even though the weather was blowing directly into it. We all wore drysuit's for the journey, and I think everybody felt like they had done a crazy deep dive themselves by the end of the sixty mile rough water passage.

I phoned Martin, one of the UK dive team, to see if they had left and to advise the sea conditions. They would leave a day later, due to the weather and some other problems. Both my boat and Dave's had behaved themselves perfectly against the biblical seas, but had become quite thirsty by the end of the protracted crossing. Leviathan drank down 250 litres of overpriced petrol and Dave's similar sized RIB with the mouthful name of 'Cinque Ports Baron', knocked back a similar amount, which was a double bugger since I was paying the trip costs. Because of our late arrivals, we missed getting into the sanctity of the calmer inner harbour. We had to make do with the big boat moorings out into the main harbour entrance. I was concerned that with all the weight of the equipment in my boat and the crashing waves still ransacking the harbour confines, Leviathan would start to take on water overnight. The seven metre RIB had a very low transom anyway, and was totally over engined, it sat very low in the water at the best of times. I would have to leave the electric bail-out pumps on constantly in order to avoid an overnight swamping. No better mooring could be found, so I took my chances with the electric pumps versus the wave action. The tide would be high enough at two in the morning to move the boat into the inner harbour and after I moved it, I would be able to sleep with both eyes closed. Tomorrow was now free because the other guys were still not coming, so we went out for dinner. The way the weather forecast was heading looked like we would have a few extra days off before the seas settled enough to allow our deep dive.

During dinner, the rain lashed down, in between the strong gusty winds. Listening to the storm while watching the pub fireplace was very cosy, but I was always mindful of the boat tied up in the harbour and it sort of diminished the romance. I drank orange juice as the others knocked back their favourite tipples. Weeks, or even months before a deep dive, I always stopped drinking alcohol. Booze invariably lowers problem solving abilities and reduces the amount of stress needed to blow a fuse. Tomorrow I would definitely need some 50 amp protection to deal with all the antics thrown up during the deep wreck and video camera combo. We had a late night in the restaurant, just chatting about the dive plan and what I knew about the other two deep divers. One had attempted the deepest air dive the year before, but really, it had just turned into the deepest rescue, a fact that the diving media seemed to gloss over. The other chap was not amongst them when we originally met in London, and I didn't know much about him except that he did some 'deepish' dives in some French caves. I did find their choice of equipment configuration a little puzzling though. It resembled an old bedstead that had been piled high with large size scuba tanks before being strapped to their backs. I hoped that they had actually worn it in the sea - and not just at slack tide, rather than just in the static quarry. The currents here were very real indeed and not in any way virtual, having a pallet of diving crap bungeed to your back would not be conducive to success, no matter how cool you thought it looked at a dive show. About one in the morning, we left the pub for our beds. I wanted to check my boat in the harbour, as now the wind was strong enough to push dustbins over and window shutters had being battened down in the village. Matt joined me for the long walk to the harbour and throughout it you could hear the sea growling and hissing in the background. Walls of grey water were being forced high over the protective break water, easily over one hundred feet high with all the spray. It was a filthy, dark evening to be out. The sea was rough in the harbour and initially I couldn't see the boat at all...It was a moonless night with complete cloud cover, the only light came from the eerie glow of the orange dock lights. We walked closer to the mooring and still could see nothing. I immediately thought the boat had broken free of its moorings and was being smashed around somewhere in the extensive Alderney harbour. Next, I thought that Leviathan had been stolen, on a night like this detection would be impossible, but stealing boats in gale force conditions seemed a little unlikely. All the possibilities I conjured up didn't include the actual reason for the crafts' disappearing act. Standing on the breakwater directly opposite Leviathans mooring buoy, I could just see in the darkness a silver frame pitching back and forth through the waves.

Huge plumes of seawater rained down on top of us as the Atlantic breakers were sent skywards by the breakwater foundations. Through the gloom I could see the shape of the boat, just submerged under the waves. The buoyancy tubes were keeping her from sinking to the bottom, but for all intents and purposes she was underwater, with waves constantly running straight over the top. Although I had my clothes on, I had to get to the boat and move it before it actually sank from the continual battering, or turned over, dumping its contents into the silt and mud below. Taking my training shoes and soaked shirt off, I jumped from the breakwater into the rough sea. The wave height even in the harbour was high enough to mask all the surrounding boats, I had to look back at Matt standing high above on the dockside for directions to my boat. Ten minutes of swimming through the waves, I swam directly into Leviathan. I swam over the tubes and could feel the tank rack below me underwater. The mooring ropes must have tangled on something both back and front, and were visibly pulling into the buoyancy tubes, forcing the air from the overpressure valves. Once enough air left the sponsons then the boat would definitely capsize or sink completely. I removed an emergency knife that was taped to the A frame, I cut the stern anchor rope first then waded to the front to cut the two lines holding the bow down. Someone shouting caught my attention; it was a man in a very small dinghy who was leaving his yacht for a night on dry land. His boat was no more than five foot long, with a tiny outboard motor that sounded more like an asthmatic mosquito. He asked if I needed help. I asked if he could tow me towards the inner harbour, as now the tide was high enough to enter it. He nodded that he would try and I threw him a rope. Progress was slow as his two horse power engine attempted to pull my heavy and flooded boat against the wind and the waves across the harbour. We must have crashed into dozens of boats over the next half hour, one time Leviathan tried to duck under the hull of a huge yacht that was dancing energetically from side to side. I had to put both feet against its gleaming hull to drag my boat from underneath it. Adrenaline and the franticness of the situation must have acted as an insulator from the cold, all I was wearing was a pair of smart shorts yet I felt totally warm. Eventually the boat was pulled into the harbour, and although the interior could still be considered as choppy, it was like a snooker table compared to whence we came. I found a foot pump in a dry bag that was luckily still tied to the A frame. I pushed the bellows together with my hands to add air to the RIBs deflated buoyancy tubes.

I had a real workout by the time the boat lifted and reclaimed itself from the sea. I moved everything heavy back to the bow area in an attempt to raise the transom, and with it the engine, from below the water line. Now the tubes were inflated, I wanted to start the engine to see if would still fire up. Outboards are quite resilient and this one was hermetically sealed - in theory. Unfortunately, all the peripheral electronics were not sealed and the starter batteries were under the water and very soggy. If the boat was slightly emptier it would be higher out of the water and I could attempt a pull start, but as it was, removing the engine cover would just flood the entire engine. With hindsight, removing the specially sealed engine cover would simply have let the water out and stopped it from drowning the engine overnight. The outboard engine was stuck in the propeller-down position, and as the height of tide would drop by the morning, it meant my shiny but damp engine smashing into the seabed, compounding all the other nonsense. The electric motors needed to raise the engine up were flooded and useless. My last job before bed was to go underneath the water at the back of the boat and open the hydraulic lines to the engine. Feeling for small screws in freezing black water at night while swimming was quite tricky, but with a little patience proved do-able. The outboard became all floppy without its hydraulics, and I was able to tilt it up and into the protection of the boat. Floppy and easy usually mean the same thing, but when you consider that the engine still weighs 400 kilograms and I'm pushing with bare feet in a rough slimy sea, no part of it was easy. Happier that the boat was positioned in such a way that when the harbour dried out in the morning the water would drain from the hull also, I went to bed. Getting to the room I shared with Clare she asked why I was all wet and oily. I said I fell into the harbour and she laughed. When I added it was to rescue my boat which had sunk on its mooring, she saw the silver lining to my cloud almost immediately - she could now sunbathe and relax, as we were not going anywhere for a few days. I agreed that we were indeed not going anywhere for a while, but knew that relaxing was not on my horizon, only boat repairs and spiralling debts.

My adrenaline-ravaged brain was knocked unconscious, only to be rudely woken just two hours later by Clare saying that we should get up now to go sightseeing around the island especially, as the boat was now broken. I didn't know what she was talking about in my sleep starved delirious state, until I remembered everything from the night before. Dread filled my head now, I had to get up and inspect the damage in the daylight. We went to the harbour together to find the boat still awash with water. A plastic bag had blocked the drainage valves and kept all the water inside. I lifted the cover of the engine to make sure it was dry. As soon as the cover came off, gallons of oily water poured out…another bargain. Slightly disillusioned by it all, I thought about going back to bed and then getting a full English breakfast inside me to improve thinking.

Climbing up the pontoon ladder, still before seven in the morning, a voice in overalls said "You can't leave your boat there, you will have to move it, it's in the way, can't you see?"

My fate was set. I spent until ten that morning washing all I could with fresh water from a hosepipe. I drained everything of seawater, and even managed to fire up the little auxiliary engine that had been underwater most of the night. A friendly chat with the harbourmaster met with some unusual sympathy, and he allowed me to beach my boat on the sand at high tide to effect repairs. A telephone call from the other deep divers said that they were delayed a further two days by the weather and that someone had been hit in the face by a compressor fill-whip. The delay suited me as far as repairs went, but every day delayed meant a stronger and bigger tide to contend with during the dive. I was sure by this point that no-one on their team knew anything about tides and thought that in the middle of the sea there wasn't any current anyway.

Pete, Matt, Dave and Clare went sightseeing and had cream teas while I removed and replaced anything electronic on my boat. In two days, everything was shipshape and some things were better than before, except that I still could not move the main engine with the hydraulics. I had built up quite a little entourage of beach kids, all interested in listening to me swear and shout as I hit my fingers with tools and spent more money. A little teenager said he would even look after my boat during the night, as the French yachters were renowned for pilfering anything not nailed down. The kid didn't have the malice in his voice you get from a homeless bum who offers to watch your car when you park in London and then scratches or sets fire to it, so I gave him a fiver. When the boat was ready to be re-floated, Dave pulled me backwards into the sea using his boat and long tow ropes. We were ready again. News crews had descended on Alderney with proper television cameras and everything. The other team were still nowhere to be seen, and the enquiries at the harbour office said that they were not allowed to use the harbour anyways as there were no free moorings or berths. Eventually, I got through to someone in Weymouth and they advised that they would be on site by midday. The weather had improved miraculously to near-perfect conditions. Clare had decided that work was more important than diving near wrecks and took a flight back to London. The few days delay meant a different dive time and stronger tidal conditions, but that would only be of interest to those diving, so really, only affected me and maybe some of the other team's legion of support divers. They even had support divers supporting divers that were supporting the deep diving duo. Dave and myself prepped our boats and Matt and Pete readied all the dive equipment in between me giving interviews to the television and radio crews. It seemed the other two bottom divers had become a bit camera shy and were refusing to speak to anyone, also they were indeed not welcome in Alderney harbour so had to contend with relaxing eleven miles offshore. Some small RIBs from the main flotilla came into port to refuel and stock up on sweets etc. The main organiser from the project came over and said hello, he went on to explain what the others wanted. I think there had been some crossed lines, while I agreed to film these 'wankers', setting their little record, I did expect a little more interaction and some phone calls returned. I appreciate some people feel a bit like a Prima Donna, swaggering around like *rock-stars* when headlining a project, but if they aren't paying for anything, then they can't really expect too much either. The big chest-beating dive plan that called for twenty-five minutes on the wreck at one hundred and eighty metres depth had dwindled to somewhere between a one minute bounce and 'five or six minutes probably'. As I heard more details of the plan, it was plain that if these guys went into the water there would be at least a couple of spare packed lunches available for the journey home. Still, I gave them the benefit of the doubt and headed out at the right time.

We pottered out to the Hurds Deep area at a relatively slow speed, and even from a few miles away could see a large number of boats hanging about over the wreck site. I approached the main dive boat to have a chat with the *would-*

be record setters. The bearded boat captain said they were sleeping and didn't want to talk to anyone. Literally dozens of drysuited divers were busy doing something or other, and buzzed around in small boats talking gibberish on the marine radio channels. The skippers' next comments confirmed he couldn't read a tide table, so I informed him of the dive time. His fantasy of there being a three-quarters of an hour slack tide window was shot down when I advised him of the ten to fifteen minutes of slack I had when I dived on this very spot twice before. There had been talk of multiple descent lines, but the realities of the Channel Islands tidal streams made that a non-starter. They had already lost two anchors and lines attempting to hook into the wreck, and it was obvious I wasn't welcome to use the only one that was attached to the seabed now. If the other guys wanted filming, it would have made sense to go down the same line especially onto a wreck close on six hundred feet long. I did plan to anchor my boat today anyway, and had bought half a kilometre of anchor rope and an anchoring system so knotted and gnarly that it would stick to the wreck at any state of tide. Complicating matters was the orientation of the BADEN itself underwater, it had settled upside-down parallel to the tidal stream direction. Anchoring to a smooth hull this deep would be difficult, especially with the tide running as fast as an inner-city mugger. Still, we had a couple of hours to sort it out. I picked up the wreck image on the sounder and moved up its entire length until it didn't show on the screen anymore. We ran the boat beyond the wreck to a point roughly five hundred metres in front and drifted back to make certain of the tide direction, luckily there was no wind at all today to further complicate things.

After a couple of dry-runs we threw the anchor over, but it seemed to catch the seabed too early in my estimations. Sadly, the grapnel/double-anchor/lead-weight ensemble was never designed with pulling it back up in mind. However, support diver Pete, was a bit of a strong-man and amazingly agreed to, and then succeed in, pulling it all back into the boat. I, of course could not exert myself in any way except by giving verbal support and eating snacks - as I was diving very soon. On the second attempt of deploying the anchor, we struck gold in the form of rusty steel, with the image of wreckage clearly showing on the sonar screen underneath the boat. We were roughly one hundred metres ahead of the other dive boats. My experience of diving in the area had shown that the typical fishermans' buoys used to support the descent line would not work. The tidal streams were strong enough to sink literally dozens of them, much like the barrels in the Jaws movies. The other guys had lost some very large mooring buoys for their efforts today, as I had done when learning to anchor into wrecks around the Channel Islands years before. Today, I would use the boat itself to support the down line. I only hoped that with all the extra weight aboard today we wouldn't have the boat sucked under, leaving us paddling home. My pub beer-mat calculations allowed for a three tonne pull on the rope before we would be momentarily walking on water, the anchor rope would snap at just over two tonnes of pull. I've gone into bat at worse odds than those, but we all kept our drysuit's zipped up all the same.

Some big sports cruisers came into view en route from Alderney. First they headed over to the bigger dive boats behind us, before being waved away. The boats contained television film crews anxious for a story. We shouted across the wavelets for a while, until agreeing that they could get on my boat for an interview as long as they took their boats far away, as they were belching thick black fumes. I wasn't concerned so much about the environmental impact of the diesel smoke, but it was certainly beginning to make me feel seasick. The reporter and film crew were quite funny and said that they would sell the story to a major news company if it all went well, but if it went wrong and we died then a Japanese adventure program would definitely use anything gory. I promised to make it as profitable as I could and even do a sombre voice-over if the day went pear-shaped for anyone else. The interviewer had a huge list of questions and camera shots to make. Originally, their plan was to interview the other two, as they were the self-confessed experts and I was just the underwater cameraman apparently. When they first approached the UK team's dive boat they were greeted by a couple of very scared looking amateurs, originally they thought that the two guys they spoke with were simply the boyfriends of the two hardcore deep divers. I did have a laugh at that, and managed to give them an interview for almost an hour before the tide state said that it was time to go diving. Because of the distance between the boats, I went alongside the others in Dave's boat to see what was happening. There was lots going on but nothing being achieved, I shouted over that I would drop down my own anchor line and head back towards them on top of the wreck and we should meet in the middle, one of the dynamic duo said that I could do what I wanted. I thought that they should hurry up in getting ready, the tide waits for no-one and they definitely didn't have time to finish their open water courses now. It did look like I would be diving alone today anyway, and carried on getting ready regardless. Within twenty minutes, I was sitting ready on Leviathans tubes. Pete and Matt were happy with their roles and the timings, which were often quite critical for me. I went over the side after smiling for the camera, I probably looked pretty smug but I suppose preparation could do that for anyone. *The more I practiced the luckier I got* was a great quote from the famous golfer Arnold Palmer, it definitely applies to diving. Within minutes of the tide visibly slowing down, it stopped moving completely. By the time it took to type that last sentence, everyone's boats faced the opposite direction as the tide started again and made its way back to where it came from. I was just below the surface at this point, jigging my video camera about. After a few minutes breathing underwater without a mask to relax, I emptied my buoyancy wing and was gone.

Tidal currents start to pull from the top of the water first - although it was a bit of a struggle for the first sixty metres, the next hundred were fairly easy. The water was green but clear, and darkness overcame the light at around eighty metres. Apart from the unwieldy camera system, the descent went smoothly and the huge battleship came into view by around one hundred and forty metres. The camera lights illuminated the grey hulk covered in white and orange soft corals known as Dead Men's Fingers. At one hundred and fifty-five metres I was level with the top of the hull, positioned somewhere near the stripped-out propeller tunnels at the back. Visibility was at least five metres', I could see my anchor line snaking away out of view on the other side of the wreck. From the top of the wreck, I could see various holes in the hull that looked like they were made by explosions, the metal was splayed outwards like petals in some places and folded inwards in others. If underwater scooters could perform at this depth they would be the perfect tool to explore this enormous hulk. Swimming along with five large scuba tanks and a video camera just using fins was almost impossible, even with the still mild current. I was surprised by the lack of fish life, normally deep wrecks are plastered with fish, especially giant Conger Eels and Ling, but I could not see a single fish anywhere. The current strength stepped up a gear within a few minutes of arriving and was starting to bite while I was hovering above the wreck, so I dropped into the lee created by the huge keel. I waited here for five minutes for the other two jokers to arrive. The increased speed of the tide meant I wouldn't be going on any fifty metre swims despite my twelve minute planned stay. I put a strobe on the anchor line just in case the other two graced me with their presence. The wreck was crushed quite flat into the seabed but there were some gaps between the gunwale and seabed that looked interesting. I pulled some slack from the line as it zigzagged around various soft corals and went for a little jaunt to the seabed. I threw a little turn of the rope around my ankle to keep my hands free and still stay in contact with the up line. Swimming down over the side of the wreck to one hundred and seventy metres, I noticed the camera had shut down. I brought it closer to my eyes so I could play with the controls easier.

Bringing the heavy housing so high up seemed to change my centre of balance and I went head-down, feet-up almost immediately. With the loop of rope around my leg, my movement was severely limited. I tried pushing myself back away from the wreck and became aware that that current was either pushing me downwards or sucking me directly to the wreck. A fire-bell started ringing in my head as I realised that I was completely pinned down. My breathing rate started to climb, both with anxiety and the insidious chill of the helium in my trimix breathing gas. The situation looked very gloomy, as everything I did in an attempt to free myself was useless against the current. I was breathing out of control now, and looked at my dwindling gas supplies via my contents gauge. I had three tanks of trimix that were breathable at this depth. The main twin tanks had sixty bars pressure, which was just under one third full. A third tank mounted behind them still had 100 bars left. With the force of the current pushing me into the wreck, every time I pushed away with my arms it felt like I was doing press ups with someone on my back. I was sinking into the Dead Men's Fingers that carpeted the wreck now, as they must have been six to eight inches thick in places. I reached for the rope around my leg as now it was hurting a lot, and could feel that it was tight like piano wire. The boat was pulling on the anchor line from the surface, and the resistance of the entire length of rope which was fighting against the moving water was putting enormous pressure on my ankle. While pinned upside-down and pushed into the wreckage, my efforts to get free had ruined the visibility. All I could see were flashes of light coming from the camera lights. The camera body was definitely nearby as something big and heavy was constantly hitting me in the head, adding insult to injury.

If I didn't slow my breathing rate down it would all be over soon. I stopped pushing against the wreck and relaxed completely, closing my eyes. As the minutes ticked by, I could feel myself slowing down. If I kept exerting myself like before, carbon dioxide would build up in my blood, bringing with it masses of confusion, then I would run out of breathing gas shortly after. I lay slumped upside-down until I thought of a solution. Adding air to my buoyancy wings would add up to forty five kilograms of positive buoyancy and hopefully turn me the right way round. A minute later the extra flotation did its job and I was in a head-up position, but being buffeted by the full force of the current now. Pulling the noose from my leg was much easier this way round thankfully, as cutting it was out of the question. If the rope was severed, I would have to free-ascend while very low on gas - the chances of fixing that situation were too slim to contemplate. I still had two full bottles of decompression gases to use shallower, but I was still a long way from being shallow enough to use them within the realms of safety. With the line free I was able to ascend, my back tanks' contents gauge read thirty bars and the additional tank was now empty. The current was shaking the line badly now and this was all I could concentrate on. I was being pushed up by the force of the water as it sped along the seabed, plus the buoyancy wing was still fully inflated and would drag me upwards out of control unless I emptied it soon. Lifting my arm up to press the deflator button bought my wrist computer closer to my ears and I could hear it beeping a message to slow down. Venting the air from the big air cell behind caused me to slow my upward momentum rapidly. I was still at one hundred and forty metres depth and would have to stop to decompress after ascending a further twenty metres, for one minute. There were many stops to carry out before I could safely breathe my high oxygen decompression gases clipped to both sides. The needle on my tank contents gauge read twenty bars, this was very close to the surrounding water pressure. If the two figures got too close together I would not be able to breathe until I got much shallower. I was still surprisingly warm in my neoprene drysuit, and even my gloveless hands were not complaining about anything.

Stopping at one hundred and twenty metres to decompress gave me a minute to do a full body check. My hands were bleeding from various deep cuts, no doubt picked up while boxing with the rusty wreck. I had broken one fin strap and the video camera was dangling precariously by just one safety lanyard, the other one had been mysteriously severed. Four thousand pounds dangling from a two pound Chinese-made clip seemed more serious than my blood loss, so I rearranged some clips to protect my investment. Time to move up and complete the rest of the deep decompression stops. Feeling relaxed now at one hundred metres, I wasn't even bothered when all the deep water trimix in my tanks breathed its last breath. I had received the telltale signs that the tanks were near empty – first, a subtle increase in breathing effort then, a moment later, my lungs automatically compensated by breathing slower. The slow breathing caused carbon dioxide levels to rise to uncomfortable levels and I felt like I was being starved of oxygen. Eventually I could not breathe slowly enough to match the delivery and spat the breathing regulator out. I reached for my left side decompression cylinder and turned the valve on. I put the regulator in my mouth and sucked deeply on the trimix with twenty percent oxygen and thirty percent helium. This mixture was not ideal and theoretically could cause oxygen toxicity and heavy narcosis at this depth. Modern training texts gave limits that erred on the side of caution, but older manuals or those used in military training would say that the mixture I was breathing currently was just par for the course. Either way, I had used it scores of times previously, and sometimes much deeper, so I stayed relaxed. My only concern was that breathing it this deep would use it up faster, and I would definitely need the spare tank that Pete was bringing sooner rather than later. Hanging on the anchor rope was becoming a hassle as the current strength approached full speed. The angle of the rope was about sixty degrees and I just let my body be pushed against the rope by the force of the water. Holding onto lines using your hands invites decompression illness as the muscles stay flexed. Returning from such a deep dive needs every muscle relaxed except some mild leg movement to keep the circulation from snoozing. I thought about the other two divers and wondered if they were still on the wreck. The trip down the anchor line wearing all their ridiculous equipment would have been nigh on impossible, especially as they would have entered the water when the current was starting to jog along quite nicely. It was a shame we didn't meet up down there, as the images of them swimming along the wreckage would have made some great television.

As it was, with the current and conditions that I saw, the pictures would have just been of three divers hanging onto the anchor rope against a rusty background...that's if we had gone down the same line to begin with...and that never happened. I carried on up through the stops. Crossing from the darkness into the light at around eighty metres deep always gives me goose bumps as the light transition is visually amazing, much like an underwater Aurora Borealis sky. I could see Pete coming down the line when I was near seventy metres. He was a welcome sight as my decompression tank was getting low. I still had another one but it was better suited for breathing at ten metres depth and shallower. It would have been very foolhardy to sup this one at seventy metres. Pete had a maximum depth imposed by his breathing gases and this was sixty metres, I had decompression stops still to do before this depth so we could not hook up and swap tanks immediately. It was funny to be kept apart like this by such invisible barriers. Decompression ceilings are quite real even though you can't see them. However, if you ignore them, you will certainly feel them sooner or later. Pete's maximum depth was set by the threat of oxygen toxicity. Most divers seem to respect the limits imposed by breathing mixtures in the same way that kids play with electricity. It takes a small duel with discomfort to know not to do it again, but it's a learning process that can't be absorbed by reading and must be experienced. Small electric shocks are like small decompression violations, in that they are unlikely to kill you. Oxygen toxicity, however, could be like peeing on the live rail of the underground, and similarly is seldom experimented with.

The seconds ticked by, with Pete waiting just above me on the line, my tank lasted the few extra minutes and we met with a handshake. He asked me if I saw the wreck and I said I did, adding that I didn't see the other two at all down there. He wrote on his dive slate that they did not dive and had spat their dummies out over an hour earlier. Most of the boats in the convoy had already left the scene, with their propellers firmly between their legs. I was a little amazed to hear that neither of the double act had dived, but it wasn't completely unpredictable. We both hung onto the anchor line like flags on a windy day, the current was really going for it now and our multiple steel tanks were flapping and banging quite annoyingly. We planned to cut the anchor rope at sixty metres and simply drift along for the next four hours. The current was running south as predicted now so we were not expecting any traffic from the shipping lane to spice things up. I passed Pete on the line and carried on the decompression stops at fifty seven metres depth. The pull on the line was making it shake and judder constantly now, and at the same time small bubbles were being created by the strain on the rope. Pete pulled out an enormous rusty dive sword that looked quite intimidating, except it was very blunt. After several minutes of just wiping orange metal against the line, one of the rope strands broke free. It must have taken almost five minutes to cut through completely and most of the damage was due to friction, I think. As soon as the line broke, we separated as if attached to opposing elastic bungee cords. I sped away to the south and Pete would have been dragged to the seabed had he not let go of the rope. He joined me shortly after and began his own ascent, leaving me to complete my own deco stop schedule. Over the next few hours, I drank my rehydration drinks and munched on chewy bars. I had one third of a soggy paperback book in my drysuit pocket and thumbed a few pages to keep the boredom at bay. Matt and Pete appeared at regular intervals to bring fresh tanks as they were needed.

The next two hours flew by, with not so much as a death-defying incident to add any excitement, obviously that would change. At about twelve metres, one of the support divers appeared with a fresh tank to exchange for one of my soon-to-be empties. I was tired of having the video camera clipped to me as it was heavy, and would be gone forever if the rubbish quality lanyards broke. I motioned to my helper for them to take it up to the boat for safe-keeping. I unclipped it from me and clipped it to them. Within seconds, this support diver turned away from me and headed back up to the surface in a bit of a hurry. As soon as he turned away I started to drift up with him, the cameras extra weight was obviously helping me to stay neutrally buoyant. I shouted through my regulator for him to come back but it was too late. I let all the air I could out of my drysuit and buoyancy wing, but to no avail. I was heading to the surface with one hundred and fifty minutes of decompression stops still to do. Quickly I turned upside-down and started to frantically swim downwards to offset my buoyancy problem. I did this for almost ten minutes, getting more and more exhausted before starting to lose the fight against gravity's nemesis. I could see someone's legs and fins in the water above me but they were not looking down and this was just as frustrating. The closer I got to the surface, the harder it was to fin downwards. My neoprene drysuit was gaining thickness and gaining buoyancy as it neared the surface. Eventually, the diver above looked down and saw my predicament. Matt turned up within seconds at nine metres depth. I unclipped his weight belt and took it from him. Putting the belt around my neck fixed my problem immediately and I started to settle down. My breathing rate was very high from all the exertion caused by the mad finning downwards. I waved to Matt as he floated away back to the surface. He looked quite concerned as he bobbed back up out of control, but rather him than me, and I had two hours more of deco stops to complete whereas he didn't (and it was his fault!). That little drama was the last of the dive, I'm happy to say. The next two hours went to plan and I surfaced on time, on target.

The last ninety minutes had been in darkness as sunset caught up with the long day. I do enjoy night decompressions as long as there are no unpleasant surprises. I often turn my primary dive lights off and just float there in virtual darkness, with maybe just a strobe flashing behind my head. I surfaced and took a big lungful of fresh sea air, only contaminated by two-stroke engine fumes. I looked back downwards and stuck my fingers up at the wreck below. It had done its best to install me as a permanent feature and I had escaped almost unscathed. We had drifted over eight miles from the wreck site in the rollercoaster current by now, but it's the thought that counts. I climbed into Leviathan and slumped into the back seat. I felt pretty good considering the last couple of days' action. I was ravenously hungry though and found a Cornish pasty and some cream buns that one of the cameramen from earlier was grazing on. One of the guys drove the boat back in the dark to St Annes harbour, where hopefully we could all get a well-earned shandy. Thinking everyone had gone home, it was quite a surprise to see a crowd of drunken well-wishers in the harbour, surrounding a television film crew. We moored the boats under some harsh camera floodlights and I had to give a lengthy interview until about 10.30pm. By the time the boats were all unloaded, the pubs had shut, so the day was ruined. I did, however, have a bottle of Dom Spumante in my room, which we shared together with a packet of Bourbon biscuits. The day was a success for me, the only sour note came with the news of the tragic crash of the Concorde flight over Paris earlier the same day.

After the clink of plastic wine glasses filled with champagne, Dave, Pete and Matt explained the farcical topside antics of the other guys, they even had some hilarious video footage of them in action. When they had stopped shouting at each other long enough to put on their equipment death-packs, the two extreme aquanauts found that the back door of the boat was not wide enough to accommodate them. This problem was overcome by an insightful support diver who quickly buttered both divers' hips. Next, it was noticed that the comedy bump hats that were chock-full of dive lights sported by both had insufficient cable length to allow the wearer to look forwards - a simple oversight, but easily avoidable by wearing at least once before the big day, I thought. By this time the tide was going at full chat, and when they tumbled into the water the conditions were not as they had read about, far from it in fact. The water in the sea today was actually moving. They put on a brave face and kicked their flippers like clockwork divers to reach the dizzy depths of fourteen metres for one, and seven metres for the other. Shouting commenced again and one of the boat captains threw in the towel. This sensible skipper probably saved a couple of lives with that decision. Within an hour, the circus was packed and steaming back to Weymouth. Before the dive, an enormous floating platform was constructed in the water, being used to deploy divers and ropes from. It did look very impressive and expensive. In the final moments when tempers were probably incandescent, it was found to be too heavy to lift back on board. Apparently, a shotgun was produced by one of the firm's cowboys and then some holes were added to aid in the sinking of the platform (in an effort to hide the evidence probably). Had I seen the platform down there, I would have lifted it back up as a nice memento of the day. Over the next few weeks I received lots of congratulatory e-mails and phone calls, as well as several not-so-complimentary ones from the other team, accusing me of high-jacking their project and calling me an 'Ocean Terrorist' of all things. The head honcho even said that I had planned to dive alone all along, and had no doubt done something to make them look so crap. I told him that if I had wanted to dive alone I would have, and definitely would have chosen a better tide to do it on. I crossed him off my Christmas card list as I had definitely played no part in him being so crap!

An offer came to dive an interesting wreck called the Carpathia a few months later. The Carpathia was the Cunard passenger ship that came to the aid of the Titanic after its fateful evening of pinball in an ice-field. After Carpathias' skipper, Captain Rostron saved the day in 1912, the ship succumbed to World War 1 and was sunk by torpedo in 1918 in the Western Approaches some 150 miles west of Ireland. Carpathia was discovered by Dr. Clive Cussler and his NUMA team using submersibles in 1999. A couple of competing UK technical dive teams made plans to be the first scuba divers to revisit the heroic Carpathia. One of these dive groups contacted me and John Bennett in an effort to get a head start on the project. Months later, we did meet up, albeit with a different group of deep divers, with plans to pip the other team to the post. The dive organisers wanted to dive early in the year, ironically, to take advantage of the rough winter weather. This put us at a distinct disadvantage from the start. The new motley team of deep divers, most of whom had not dived even half as deep as planned, were joined by a large and friendly support group on a very impressive looking dive boat. Sadly, the boat was not ready for its mammoth journey and by the time it was made good, the weather window gusted past us. We did head out in earnest and completed near a hundred miles of some of the worst sea conditions many of us have had the misfortune of enduring. The boat looked very swish in the harbour, but in the proper sea its design had all the poise and balance of five fat men floating on a coconut tree. The decks were awash with seawater and vomit. It was like Vietnam afloat. I had wanted to try some new dive tables that promised radical changes to the length of decompressions. The RGBM algorithm was marketed heavily, a bit like cigarettes used to be, it promised to be a cure-all and would revolutionise technical diving. Much the same as cigarettes now carry a printed warning against injury and worse, RGBM went the same way. All its claims were based around a few individuals need for the limelight without caring who got injured on the way. My Carpathia plan was for 15 minutes at 160 metres with a decompression time of only 130 minutes. This was incredibly short when compared to the traditional time for the same profile of over five hours. Luckily, the weather prevented me from diving and dying on the Carpathia trip. The crowd who peddled this dive software to me said that it had been tried successfully by another accomplished deep diver, Jim Bowden, to the exact same depth. While one deep dive doth not an algorithm make, I was now happier to try it myself. Parts of the BADEN wreck in Alderney were shallower than 160 metres, so I decided to have a go in my own backyard and with a recompression chamber less than an hour away, if it all went wrong. Planning another deep dive like this involved simply refuelling my boat and finding a couple of support divers with a free afternoon. My scalloping buddies Rob and Ben were up for coming on a diving road-trip, so I filled the tanks and we left at midday on a Tuesday.

Conditions on the surface were perfect, the sea as flat as a witches chest. I still flinched when I remembered back to the previous BADEN journey and its seven hours gauntlet by sea. The entire fifty-five miles was covered in less than an hour and a half today. I found the 30,000 tonne hulk within fifteen minutes, and incredibly managed to drop the diving anchor right on top of it. The tidal conditions were okay-ish today, but most importantly the current stream would take us to the south, away from the shipping lane again during the decompression. I had no-one to wait for or video tape, so I got ready and in quickly. Initially the tide was quite slack and I had a pretty easy time for the first hundred metres. Unusually, the deeper I got, the stronger the tidal stream became. It was becoming very challenging, to say the least, being faced with an enormous wall of cold water. I had to slow right down by one hundred and fifty metres and could only manage a painstaking hand-over-hand pull for the last fifteen metres. Visibility was terrible and I felt like I would lose my mask if I turned my head, such was the ferocity of the current. I considered heading back up or letting go the line. When I reached the top of the wreck, I was expecting my battle with the tide to ease, but sadly it did not. The anchor weight seemed to snake away from the wreck out of sight. I wanted to get to the bottom to release the shot weight and just drift the rest of the dive painlessly. As I neared the tub of lead and anchors, it gave up its grip on the seabed and started to accelerate across the stony bottom. For a second everything was easy. Suddenly, the anchor jammed solid again and jerked me like a puppet on a string. I crawled another metre along the rope before it pulled free again. I was close enough to the shot weight now to see it dancing and jumping about like a wrecking ball. The attached anchor flukes were twisted out of shape and getting worse. The seriousness of the situation took hold and I wished I wasn't here.

If I let go now, I would have to free-ascend in the darkness, relying on the support crew seeing my surface marker buoy in time before it drifted out of sight. The boat would be kept roughly on station or moving slowly as the anchor dragged, but I would be moving near 4knots for the next twenty minutes before I was shallow enough to send up my signalling device. If I botched sending up the lifting balloon, the guys might follow the fluorescent orange bag away from my real position. By the time I was shallow enough to deploy the back-up signalling bag, I would have compromised the decompression plan and be minutes away from running out of breathing gas. I needed to unclip the shot weight from the line and drift with the boat. The closer I got to the bucket of solidified molten metal the nearer I got to being swatted in the head by it, it was impossible. I fancied my chances better trying to steal the lead from the Vatican church roof next time. Every few metres, the anchor would drag into something solid and I would be swung violently while holding on as tightly as I could, my life depended on it. My hands were weakening as the freezing cold water and exertion did their worst. It was no use, trying to reach the weight and anchor clip would be like attempting to cut the toenails of a stampeding elephant. Holding the line for much longer would be unlikely, so out came my trusty dive knife. I had reached the end of the dive time now and had to go upwards or stay here forever. This gave me an unpleasant time frame to work within, constantly stopping for thirty seconds to fulfil my decompression obligations. Because of the workings behind the RGBM algorithm, I had dozens of deep deco stops to perform, but as I got shallower the strength of the current just kept getting faster, making my job harder. Cutting the rope, which was for one second as stiff as steel and the next like hot fudge, was frustrating. I had a full minute decompression stop to perform at one hundred and thirty-five metres and this would be the best opportunity to cut the line. During this minute the anchor skipped and jammed constantly on the seabed. I only managed to cut one strand of the thick polypropylene rope in sixty seconds. If it was on the surface my razor sharp knife would slice through this rope like a light sabre, but now it was as effective as an unfrozen sausage. The one minute stop was not time enough and I headed onwards and upwards.

By one hundred and twenty metres, the anchor jammed for long enough to get the cutting done. The few moments spent accelerating with the current were enough to file my recent trials into deep memory. Now the line was cut, my troubles were easing. The rope I had purchased for today had a strand of lead running through the centre to keep it sinking. Or at least it should have done, because that is what I paid for. Unfortunately, like many things in modern life, you don't get what you pay for and the rope constantly tried to float upwards whenever I took my hands off it for a second. The below-stairs action had kept my breathing rate up and I was a little lower on gas reserves than ideal, but in the distance I saw Ben descending down the line, bringing with him the much needed extra tins of gas. He would wait at fifty metres because he was breathing nitrox with twenty-seven percent oxygen and it was not ideal to go deeper with this concentration. I completed some more deep-deco stops and eventually we met up. Ben had brought some gloves for me to wear during the rest of the dive. The neoprene glove material had shrunk to such small proportions because of the pressure that they would not have fitted dolls hands, never mind mine. I unclipped the extra tanks Ben carried and gave him my empties. As we made the trade, I noticed Ben constantly equalising his ears against the pressure. My ears are a little more automated and I didn't notice initially that we were descending. For some reason, the line we were holding was being paid out from the surface and we slipped down to sixty-seven metres before I noticed. Ben seemed oblivious and didn't check his depth gauge until we were back at fifty metres. One of the replacement decompression tanks had snagged the pull cord that lets air out of my buoyancy jacket. The lost gas meant we became heavier momentarily and headed back down for Ben to unwittingly complete his deepest ever dive.

It was time for Ben to head back while he was still ahead and I just carried on completing my deco stops. All was well until about six metres, when I felt like I was getting decompression illness during an air break. I started to get pain that came and went through every part of my body. I stopped breathing the normal air and went back to breathing the pure oxygen. The discomfort went away as quickly as it came on. Twenty minutes later I repeated the switch to air to give my lungs a rest and the same feeling returned, this time complete with some mental confusion. I switched back to the oxygen and the symptoms slowly went away again. After this event, I would make sure I stayed on oxygen for at least an hour after surfacing as I was convinced the ascent plan was far too short. With hindsight, I should have extended the decompression stops before surfacing, an ounce of prevention being better than a kilo of cure. I had a contingency plan for an in-water recompression treatment which involved going back down to twenty-one metres with twin tanks of enriched air Nitrox mixture containing sixty percent oxygen. I hit the surface feeling unusual but pain free. By the time I had taken off my diving rig I felt definitely bendy. I got back on the oxygen, which relieved my symptoms after ten minutes. During this time, Ben secured everything in the boat as Rob drove towards Guernsey. Experience and common sense told me to avoid the medical centre on Alderney, as they would have probably try to amputate something given the chance. We had drifted over nine miles in just over two hours and luckily it was in the right direction. I carried on breathing the oxygen to stave off the pain and Rob kept the boat cruising homewards at thirty-five knots. Every time I stopped breathing the oxygen, pain and confusion returned. I would not attempt any in-water recompression treatment feeling confused, as pain only was my cut-off for symptoms. An hour later I felt much better. Arriving home, the boat was emptied and after a few phone calls I wanted an early night. Hitting the pillow, I was out like a light. By nine pm the same evening I was awake, with intense pain in both arms and in my leg. The RGBM dive plan was too short obviously and could not be used again without padding the shallower decompression stops considerably. A full two hours on oxygen sitting in front of my computer eased the discomfort and exhausted my bedroom oxygen kit. I e-mailed the supplier in the US who provided me with the software, and told him of the outcome. He congratulated me for such an awesome job by surviving the dive, he added that he would tell the news to Jim Bowden, who was still thinking about trying the new decompression model. I was a little taken aback by that statement, as he had told me previously that Jim had already dived it deep, and that everything went fine. This kind of abysmal nonsense plagues the diving business, all I could do was buy a voodoo doll and pin selection. I hoped they went bankrupt and fairly soon after they actually did, so there must be a god after all.

My dive boat 'Leviathan' – The 7 metre Rigid Hull Inflatable was used for recreational diving trips, scalloping duties and trips all over the southern English Channel looking for deep wrecks to dive. Alongside, is my buddy Dave's RIB – 'The Cinque Port Baron'.

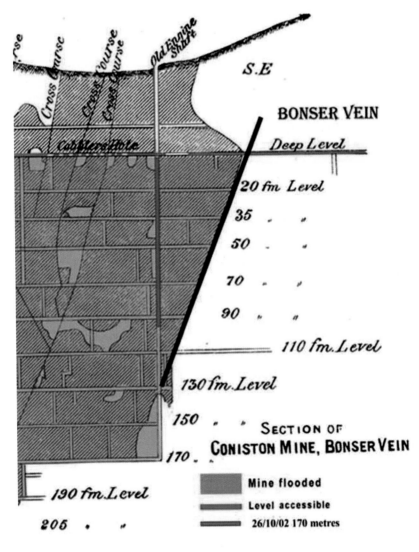

Diagram of Coniston Copper Mine layout. Red line shows deepest depth attained. Mine entrance located at extreme right of Deep Level green line.

Picture supplied by Ruskin Museum, Coniston.

Russian-Roulette?

Riding a moped on Thai roads while wearing double scuba tanks may seem dangerous. However, following the relatively innocuous dive-plan below proved far more life threatening despite being endorsed by all manner of diving *experts*. This dive-plan has too many deep stops and insufficient shallow stops – very typical of a bubble model algorithm at the time.

Depth	Time@	Leave@	o2	N2	He	Depth	Time@	Leave@	o2	N2	He
260m	10.0	18.7	5	19	76	81m	1.5	56.1	14	53	33
						78m	1	57.4	14	53	33
174m	0.5	27.8	5	19	76	75m	1.5	59.2	14	53	33
168m	0.5	28.9	5	19	76	72m	1	60.5	14	53	33
165m	0.5	29.7	5	19	76	69m	1.5	62.3	14	53	33
159m	0.5	30.8	5	19	76	66m	1.5	64.1	14	53	33
156m	0.5	31.6	5	19	76	63m	2	66.4	14	53	33
150m	0.5	32.7	5	19	76	60m	1.5	68.2	20	50	30
147m	0.5	33.5	5	19	76	57m	1.5	70	20	50	30
144m	0.5	34.3	5	19	76	54m	1.5	71.8	20	50	30
141m	0.5	35.1	5	19	76	51m	3	75.1	20	50	30
135m	1	36.7	5	19	76	48m	3	78.4	20	50	30
132m	1	38	5	19	76	45m	3.5	82.2	20	50	30
129m	1	39.3	5	19	76	42m	2.5	85	20	50	30
126m	1	40.6	5	19	76	40m	2.5	87.7	32	68	0
123m	1	41.9	5	19	76	37m	3	91	32	68	0
120m	0.5	42.7	10	40	50	34m	2.5	93.8	32	68	0
117m	0.5	43.5	10	40	50	31m	3.5	97.6	32	68	0
111m	0.5	44.6	10	40	50	28m	5	102.9	32	68	0
108m	0.5	45.4	10	40	50	25m	5	108.2	32	68	0
105m	0.5	46.2	10	40	50	22m	2	110.5	32	68	0
102m	0.5	47	10	40	50	21m	6	116.6	50	50	0
99m	0.5	47.8	10	40	50	18m	6.5	123.4	50	50	0
96m	0.5	48.6	10	40	50	15m	9	132.7	50	50	0
93m	1.5	50.4	10	40	50	12m	10	143	50	50	0
90m	1	51.7	14	53	33	9m	11	154.3	50	50	0
87m	1	53	14	53	33	6m	16	170.6	100	0	0
84m	1	54.3	14	53	33	3m	18	188.9	100	0	0
						Surface @ 190 minutes					

Suicide Note - Dive Plan for fateful 260 metre dive. Actual plan used was padded considerably from 30 metres and up. Unfortunately Decompression injuries started at 40 metres…and just got worse!
DO NOT FOLLOW THIS DIVE PLAN

Mark Ellyatt returns from 313 metres and meets Hilde Montgomery decompressing at 30 metres depth.

Mark decompressing at 50 metres depth. Rapid breathing at this point consumes underarm twin tanks after just eight minutes – keeping support divers very busy.

Photo showing dive-light batteries crushed by enormous ambient pressure at 313 metres.

The incredible sight of HMS Victoria standing vertically on its bow's since 1893. Photo shows Christian free swimming at 120 metres depth (foreground) and Paul Pitchfork at 80 metres (between starboard propeller shaft lower support) beginning his ascent to the surface.

Christian swims over to touch HMS Victoria – His long search for Admiral Tryon's enigmatic flagship finally over.

Chapter 8: A Youth-in-Asia story

Another diving season ended in Jersey, and despite scalloping and the odd diving course right into November, the winter conditions were becoming just too miserable to endure. I had spent most winters in the Caribbean up until now but had heard about Asia, and in particular Thailand, being fantastic. I booked a ticket to Bangkok for early December 2000. I was travelling alone again, or so I thought, and made no plans whatsoever. Arriving at Jersey airport to make a connecting flight to Switzerland, I met a group of guys I had worked with a couple of years before in a local dive shop. Coincidentally, they were going to Koh Samui for a month to get into as much trouble as possible. Without my own timetable I thought it would be fun to tag along with them for a week. Their pre-flight ritual today consisted of five or six pints of lager followed by a handful of anti-depressants to make the plane fly faster. This set the tone for the rest of the trip, and I had to help carry two of them off the plane when we landed at Zurich airport. Luckily we weren't sitting close together for the long-haul flight, but it would not have mattered as they were all out of the game completely for the entire nine hour flight.

There was some method to their madness though, as I was knackered after the flight but they looked brand new, in the same way as a high mileage car looks more sprightly after you turn back the odometer by 50,000 miles. Within an hour of landing in the capital, we were on a Bangkok Air flight bound for Koh Samui. Just over an hour away by air, this Jewel of an island sits in the gulf of Thailand adjacent to the mainland town of Suratthani. The views as we over flew the coast were quite amazing. Samui airport is of the boutique variety, whatever that means, but is certainly very idyllic with its thatched roofs and acres of tropical greenery. Collecting our bags, we all bundled into a min van headed towards the nightlife area of Chaweng beach. I had three big suitcases full of diving frippery, heavily contrasting with my seasoned Asian travel mates with their plastic carrier bags containing just toothbrushes, underpants, condoms and Rizla papers. Clothing brands, from Prada and Versace to Fila and Boss were being sold in virtually every shop we saw as we drove into town. John and Mutley said you get could a complete designer wardrobe for under twenty pounds and it often lasted the entire holiday - as long as you didn't put it into a washing machine of course. It was even actually cheaper to buy a new t-shirt than get a dirty one cleaned. I felt a little over-prepared with my bags of new clothes, but at least they would survive a trip to the launderette or a heavy downpour. The minibus stopped outside a bright neon-pink bar full of pot-bellied, balding, fat men in string vests, each with a local girl writhing on their laps in tune to a Skorpions classic. We alighted here and the guys all filed into the bar. Our entrance was met with high pitched screams and unintelligible shouting. I understood "where you go...sexy man" and "take me with you, I sleep cheap", but didn't find the promise of the clap (or worse) on my first night too attractive. I'd had enough of the constant pawing after thirty seconds and asked Scottish John where they were staying so that I could avoid it. He said that they always stayed at a place on the beach side of the road called the "Cock-well Inn" or something. I cringed at such a classy name.

I had read that accommodation was inexpensive in Thailand and I wasn't prepared to rough it just yet. I asked him for a hotel with as many stars as possible, and I didn't expect to be looking at them through a whole in the ceiling either. John retorted in his strong Glaswegian accent "Stop being a ponce Ellyatt, come and stay with the lads, its perfect and only a fiver a night". Put so eloquently how could I refuse? The guys drank bottles of Chang beer as if they were on fire, then we left as they needed to buy a bag of weed before it got too late. We lurched over to the accommodation which was down a very gloomy sandy track. Flickering neon tubes and barking deranged dogs outside the hostel (*hostile*, more like) chorused with the deafening chirp of Cicada beetles. I could just about hear the sound of the crashing waves in the background though, but only during the lull of cackling prostitutes. This was all totally ideal, and a bargain at only a fiver a night. Some Thai people were playing backgammon with beer bottle tops and looked over menacingly, obviously eyeing my bags as we approached. Some of my party were greeted by familiar faces and my would-be bag porters returned to playing with their Grolsch-lids. I was ready for bed now whatever it looked like. I politely declined sharing the cost of the bag of skunk with a simple "I'm brassic, mate" and a yawn. After some form filling, everybody sat down to start drinking again.

I waived my 'check-in' beer, and just asked which room was mine, a curt "you go nummer thee mister" and a pointing finger had me heading back up the lane to my cell. I opened the door and was greeted by a hot and smelly fan room that should have had a sign saying "Tenko-Mansions" hung over the entrance. The floor dipped as I shuffled across the patchwork linoleum. The romantic 15 watt bulb in the ceiling illuminated a sign saying *Farang- take shoe off, leaf outside*. I closed the door and put my cases on the foam mattress bed. Even in the dim pink room light, I could see the floor was too filthy for my bags. Apart from the bed, the room was empty. The lock on the door wouldn't need the skills of *Raffles* to bypass it, so with safety in mind I went back outside to bring the porch chair in to wedge against the door. I could hear the chaps discussing loudly the purchase of a bag of weed and how they needed a one thousand baht note from everyone - about seventeen quid each to pay for it. I went back to the reception/bar/birdcage area to get a towel, and was asked to give a hefty deposit for the loan of the tatty blue flannel. I gave them the days' wages they asked for it, taking the stained rag, plus a bar of what looked like used soap. I would only be enduring this for one night, I guaranteed myself, and went back to my room for a shower. The cold-only shower was a broken pipe that protruded from the wall. The tap next to it supplied either a jet so fierce that it gushed horizontally straight to the next damp wall, or dripped slowly down, reminiscent of the Chinese water torture method. I opted for the water-cannon approach, as I didn't have the time or patience to wash one limb at a time. Feeling slightly less grubby, I lay down on the very bobbly mattress. Despite the constant rustling and scratching noises under the bed, I fell asleep while trying to count the number of times my neon porch light buzzed and flickered. Such was my exhaustion, I fell into a dreamless sleep, oblivious even to the noisy dogs and prostitutes still barking outside. At seven the following morning, I woke up with a jump to more incandescent shouting outside. Voices of Thais and Northern Englishmen were having a loud and angry exchange in the reception-come-chickencoop area of the guesthouse.

"Go now...Farang...You go now...now" seemed to be the repetitive winning phrase, it certainly sounded menacing enough and, quite likely, good advice

A bang on my door revealed Scottish John in his boxer shorts, sporting a very dazzling *blue-vein* cheese-coloured body. I put on my sunglasses to minimise the glare from his ghost-like complexion and went outside. Over a refreshing breakfast lager, John explained that an argument was well under way over the drugs they'd bought last night. The group had arranged to purchase a kilo of holiday hash from their trusted source. Sadly the deal went sour, as the consignment weighed no more than a can of coke and was clearly more bird seed and mud than the euphoric roll-up ingredient they sought. The spokesman for the troop rightfully went to remonstrate with the Thai supplier, and was now finding the complaints department manager was less than agreeable. The dealers' only compromise was that he put his long and sharp coconut knife back under the counter, but only after he had made his *point* quite clear. My bags were already packed and my excuse worked out if I needed one...Bed Bugs. I left for a rather more upmarket spa resort for the next couple of days, before moving to pastures greener. My new room was much more like it - mini bar, satellite television, plus an air conditioning unit that could bring penguins to the Sahara. I made sure that the room was so cold that I could see my breath, before going outside for a civilised coffee. I planned to meet some scalloping pals from Jersey that were coming to Thailand, as they did every three months for some R and R. The Thai mobile number they gave me went unanswered so they had not arrived in Bangkok yet. Tom and his pals always stayed in Pattaya, a mainland town one hundred miles south east of Bangkok. I had many mental pictures of Pattaya from

Tom's many stories. The lively Koh Samui could be likened to the energetic bar scene at the beginning of *Star Wars*...Pattaya, however, epitomised the bar in the movie *From Dusk till Dawn*, definitely not a family-orientated watering hole.

I organised a flight to Pattaya for the next day and surfed the internet looking for dive sites of interest there. Before I left for Thailand, my net homework found a fascinating underwater attraction called the Vertical-Wreck. This ship was a liquefied gas transporter involved in a collision in the middle of nowhere some years before. Instead of heading directly to the seabed, it slowly settled propeller first, resting strangely vertically in sixty metres of water. The wreck site was many miles from shore and could only be reached via a three day boat trip from Pattaya. I looked forward to seeing it. The rest of my afternoon was spent touring Samui by moped. During my lap of the island I saw several huge pigs strapped onto the backs of tiny motor scooters, this explained how Thai bacon always tasted so fresh. At every road junction I was propositioned - either by a lady of the day, a lady boy, or an offer to get my picture taken while stroking a monkey baby, everything you need is available here. After all the excitement, I headed back to my icy hotel room to read a 3 day old English newspaper that cost £5 locally, purely in an effort to touch base with normality.

Koh Samui has excellent bars and dance clubs, some of the most westernised in Thailand. Entertainment for the locals and tourists elsewhere mainly consists of bad karaoke bars and cheap whisky so any place that plays a bit of BoyZone and sells UK beer can't be all bad. I stopped at the Green Mango bar for a Gin & Tonic and an early boogie before the dance-floor was hijacked by scores of manky prostitutes. Stepping one foot on the dancing linoleum saw a swarm of bar-girls descend instantly. Seeking refuge in a busy bar next door, I bumped into John and Mutley. They were a little worse-for-wear, both with sunburn and the local Sangtip whisky. One of them said they were getting married the day after, to a girl (hopefully) he'd met in a bar that very morning. I offered my congratulations to the lucky couple and hoped the twelve

English words she spoke could navigate through his thick Gorbels accent. I had heard that the whiskey in Thailand was blended with formaldehyde and amphetamine for a fuller flavour, that should at least preserve the obviously besotted soul-mates for longer and give them plenty of energy for the ensuing fight when her Thai husband showed up. I couldn't wait to leave before I was married to a lady fella, or had my organs stolen, which sounded more likely if the backpacker stories going around were to be believed. I left the bar and bought some dvd movies to watch on my laptop. I only bought a couple just in case my PC had already disappeared up the beach during the few hours I had been out of the room. I suppose I can get a little pessimistic when facing poverty. As luck would have it my room door was still on its hinges, and I fell asleep to the bad acting and zombies screaming in the movie Blade 2.

At early o'clock I headed to the airport for my flight to Pattaya. On the plane I saw a package tour from what must have been Perverts-R-Us. I have never seen so many fake tans and dyed hair. The clap clinics in Europe would have a bumper season when this lot arrived home itching and scratching. U-Tapao is the name of the airport, north of Pattaya. A US airbase in the days of Vietnam, it still has some of the longest runways in the world, and apparently hides an underground nest of interview rooms of equally vast proportions. I hopped onto the transfer bus to Pattaya proper - which was still sleeping off the previous nights' excesses at this early hour. I got out of the bus at Soi Yamato, which runs from the beach road back to the middle road. The beach was busy, the sea was inviting, and it looked like Pattaya was actually a pleasant place. Norwegians are normally not known for their raucous behaviour so I checked into the Norway Hotel, the sign outside boasted of rooms costing less than a fiver a night, even for the biggest suite. My room on the second floor promised AC, a bath and shower and even a small library. I unpacked the minimum needed before heading out into the town known as the 'Land of the Writhing Bum'.

My first port of call was a dive shop opposite the hotel, to book a trip to the Vertical wreck. The shop manager showed me lots of pictures and said that I could go to whatever depth I liked, as long as I had a dive buddy. I provisionally booked Tom a place, as he had seemed interested to dive it before. The weather was too windy for the long boat trip, and I would have to wait at least a week before this improved. I went back to the hotel to have some lunch and maybe meet some of the other inmates...err I mean residents. I had some quite tasty meatball affair washed down with a German Weis beer. My Norwegian language skills are poor to non-existent, but I could roughly understand the thread of a conversation going on around me. Several of the residents joining me for lunch were experiencing some unusual pain in their bones. The symptoms sounded like dengue, sometimes called Breakbone fever, but without the all-over rash. A petite blonde lady in a batik wrap had a small plastic bag of black beach sand in her hand. The noisy crowd said they found it unusual because yesterday the sand on the same beach had been the traditional yellow colour.

As the days progressed, the hotel residents thinned out, and soon I was the only passenger apart from the Thai and Burmese staff. I picked up a copy of the Pattaya Mail, which had become my favourite read because of its usually outrageous stories. On the front page was a photo of a beach with black sand that was a few kilometres north of Pattaya. Normally, black sand can be found in volcanic areas but Pattaya, being Pattaya, had found its very own sinister new variety. A local businessman had decided to thin out the competition for his drink supply business by poisoning their fizzy drink supplies with, and wait for it...radioactive material. He had some how laid his grubby hands on a huge bag of some hideous chemical and had introduced it into pallet-loads of soft drinks headed for his competitors bars, helping him, or so he thought, along easy street towards an early retirement. Unfortunately, the devilish plan went wrong when the man's own young son drank from the bottles and immediately fell ill. When the son died, the businessman panicked and apparently dispersed the chemicals onto the beach, which subsequently turned the sand black. The businessman then told the police he thought his son was a victim of poisoning that had been aimed at the father. Investigations found that Dad was lying, and he subsequently spilled all the beans. I don't know what happened to all my fellow hotel guests, with their radiation burns diagnosed as Dengue fever, but at least they had something exciting to talk about whilst they showed their holiday snaps. An earlier edition of the local newspaper said that Tourists should be careful regarding Dengue as it was widespread in surrounding countries, especially those frequented during visa extension trips. The hotel was a lot quieter, with fewer guests now, and quite relaxing. That changed when two highly odd European men checked into the room adjacent to mine. A stream of prostitutes, both male and female, camped on the stairs outside our rooms before they got their chance to noisily make a few dollars. The straw that broke the camels back came when some amputees were delivered to the room, strapped to sack barrows like Hannibal Lecter. Now I'm as broad minded as the next person, and everybody has to eat, but the moaning and groaning that ensued bought complaints even in Pattaya. Quite rightly the police turned up, after some shouting they carried out a collection of camcorders on tripods, followed by quite an unusual holiday movie selection recently filmed. After all this, I needed to see tropical fish and blue skies to erase the images from this evening from my tired grey hard-drive. Thankfully the big dive trip was finally happening tomorrow.

Pictures of the diving live-aboard boat looked fantastic in the shops' album, however, in the flesh, the fibreglass had seen better days, and a lot of them - it didn't even look like the same boat. When I arrived, the sea had flattened out completely and the trip was just a couple of hours from its leaving time of 9.30pm. Half the group had got stuck in traffic near Bangkok, and the captain said that the trip wouldn't leave without them as they were so anxious to see the amazing vertical wreck. They were *so* anxious though that they couldn't be bothered to drive an extra hour, and instead booked into a hotel room for the night. As I had witnessed so many times before, Thai management training doesn't cover the complaints procedure, so the few of us who stupidly turned up on time just had to sit and wait on the boats plastic garden chairs drinking warm beer. No customers meant no air conditioning or even a pump for the shower room, still, I revelled in this wilderness diving...not. The pier was so far from town that although we were free to leave for a proper bed, transport was not laid on, so we were stuck here, tied for the night to a rickety bridge near Sattahip naval base and rustic-septic fishing port. I cannot begin to describe the smell of dead fish and the constant noise from un-silenced car engines, used in both the fish delivery pick-up trucks and long-tail boats.

The worst thing about Thai beer is that the more you consume, the more restless you become, largely because of the body preserving chemicals and speed powder present. Tom, my dive buddy, had still not arrived in Pattaya, so I was the only native English speaker on the boat, and would probably be diving alone tomorrow. The three other guests on the boat had twenty-five dives between them, hardly perfect candidates for sixty-metre dive buddies, although the vertical ship wreck did have shallow areas of course. We discussed the merits of SOLO diving at length for a heated thirty minutes. One of the group was adamant that diving alone was impossible anyway because JESUS was always watching over everybody. A pretty reasonable argument considering the level of alcohol - in the morning we all rubbed our heads while repeating "Jesus...what have I done", so he must have definitely been on the boat at least.

The other punters turned up at nine in the morning looking far more fresh-faced than the rest of us insomniac early birds. My body felt like I had rowed through a Tsunami most of the night. The new guys had their drivers unload acres of brand new dive kit and cameras, plus boxes of spirits and Pringles. They had even bought some rental girlfriends for the trip, who classily and immediately started drinking Johnny Walker whisky and smoking commercially. A full ten hours behind schedule, we headed east for Cambodian waters. Breakfast came to wake me up, despite me saying earlier that I didn't want any. I nibbled at some green cake and drank some blue fizzy drink, very refreshing. Turning down a small brown bottle of Lipo 'multivitamin-tonic', I laid back down on my vinyl sponge bed / hot-plate for some more fevered discomfort as the air-con was still on the blink. Lipo is a funny drink - normally consumed by all Thai people regardless of age, it has a health warning on the label next to the advert promising to keep you awake long enough to work for twenty four hours, 'Sleep is for the poor', it translated to. I think I might still need a brain in five years time, so amphetamine concentrate was not part of my daily breakfast requirements. Arriving on-site near midnight, we were promised a night dive. However, small boats, from Cambodia maybe, crowded around the mooring buoy dropping Vietnam-era Chinese stick-grenades onto the wreck, this had a negative effect on our nocturnal fish spotting plans. I couldn't sleep anyway and just watched excitedly in case one lucky fisherman found the jackpot. The big prize would have upset many of their plans when you consider that the Vertical wreck was a liquefied gas tanker. At five-thirty a.m., the dive guide came around, hitting pots and pans to gently wake us.

The grenade fishermen had run out of ammunition and conceded to let us dive if we gave them some cash. I threw the equivalent of fifty pence into the pan and started setting up my scuba equipment. Although I didn't doubt the watchful stares of Jesus, I preferred to use the extra scuba tank worn by a buddy in case of equipment failure etc. My non-believer status probably doesn't entitle me to the full up 'free-diving Jesus-rescue' service. I had asked the group to show me their logbooks last night whilst pretending to be interested in the various diving holiday adventures. Weeding out the chaff with less than ten dives, or those with even any-amount of shore diving - only gave me two likely buddy candidates. One was still drunk, so I asked the guy with twenty-five dives if he fancied seeing the propellers today. All of a sudden it was like the conversation was about drugs or gun smuggling by the hush of the voices. I swore an oath to protect and look after him as more than just a spare air-source. Our dive-guide was happy to have one less diver to chase after and we jumped into the water ahead of the crowd. The bow was just a few metres below the surface, visibility here was absolutely fantastic, at least thirty metres. Shoals of dinner-plate sized Bat fish swarmed around, looking no worse for wear despite it raining down with thirty year old communist ordnance all last night. I saw some unexploded grenades and some improvised beer bottle fertilizer bombs lying scarily around the huge metal orbs containing liquid propane gas. I looked away quickly so my buddy didn't notice them, and we headed deeper. Going down into the abyss was fairly disappointing as there was a great deal of sediment floating in suspension. It was quite surreal though, following the hull all the way to the seabed. Passing the wheelhouse that just stared towards the surface without a crew. We wrote our names in the thick silt of the now horizontal windows. My buddy seemed to be still awake at this point, and responded that he was in good shape to proceed further. The internet pages I read about the wreck said that the propellers were deeper than seventy metres and frequented by many sharks. I touched the seabed at fifty-eight metres and saw a single propeller quite clearly, despite there being no sharks anywhere. Visibility was still okay and ambient light continued all the way down to make the dive pleasant enough.

There was no need to hang around, given our lack of back-up scuba equipment, so we started a slow ascent back up the hull after just a few minutes of arriving at the bottom. My buddy was surprised to see his dive computer still not registering this as a formal decompression dive despite the depth. As we travelled up slowly he would be less disappointed, as time would soon catch up with the depth and trigger a need for us to perform some short deco stops. Now that I had seen that there was indeed nothing to see, I didn't want to hang about with all the grenades lying around. Waiting for a scuba muppet to put an explosive device in his pocket, or simply kicking one with a flipper would have been a disappointing reason to check-out for me, and anyways I wanted an early lunch. I left my buddy to swim around with his pals under the watchful gaze of the dive guide once our few minutes of stops were finished. Our friendly fish dynamiters had returned at the thought of fleecing some divers again, and from the elevated position of our dive boat I could see that they had stocked up with fresh boxes of rusty old bombs. I hoped they'd wait for the dive group to finish up and surface, because if they hit one of the scuba tanks with a grenade then we would all be scratching our heads. I'd seen enough and started on the whisky that was being offered by one of the other divers weekend partners.

Everybody enjoyed the experience, but it was short -lived because the boat captain announced that there was no more fresh water as the water maker had packed up. I had already had a shower so wasn't too fazed by the news, I suggested that the others wash themselves in beer but it met with contempt-filled glares. With no water now and the return of the grenade flingers, we upped sticks and headed back to port at an extremely leisurely pace - apparently one engine was playing up also, but I surmised that insufficient fuel was the real reason. The sea was still as calm as it could be, so it wasn't a complete train crash, and I at least had seen what I came to. More interesting than the wreck was the sight of literally thousands of squid fishing boats on parade that night. All the vessels had dozens of bright bulbs deployed on booms low to the water. The light from the bulbs brought the squid to the surface where they were landed by net. We slowly motored through row after row of these boats that must have covered close on a hundred miles. I for one felt tired from all the lack of comfortable sleep, whereas most of the others seemed bright as buttons after consuming a bath-full of the LIPO drink. Still, I abstained from this liquid refreshment, thinking that a good nights' sleep would be less traumatic than a lengthy stay at a psychiatric hospital in the near future.

Getting back to the hotel at five in the morning saw a party going at full steam in the reception area. It was Christmas Eve morning for me, but all the Scandinavian residents were already celebrating the big day as they did traditionally, the day before the English one. I picked at some food from the buffet before heading for bed. Christmas spent in thirty-five degree sunshine feels a little strange especially without snow and Santa Claus. Over breakfast a chap showed me photos taken the night before. A line up of bar girls dressed in red outfits filled the frame. I asked him if they were in fact "Santa Whores" come to burgle tourists' rooms everywhere. He asked what I meant, so I pointed to the girls in the picture and said "Look, *Ho...Ho...Ho*". He laughed despite not having a clue what I meant. I met with my buddies from Jersey that night but they were too tired from all the travelling to want to celebrate the festive season. We arranged to meet at a Scottish restaurant on Christmas morning to have a traditional dinner, complete with all the trimmings. We all even paid thirty five pounds each for a place at the table, which is extremely expensive for Thailand. I got up on the big day and walked to the venue in the sweltering heat. Alcohol or something else must have curbed everyone's desire for the turkey dinner as I was the only one who turned up. I sat alone on a table for nine listening to Christmas hits on my CD walkman. After gorging myself for an hour, I felt more stuffed than the huge bird in the middle, and left. Slumped in bed I stared at the offerings of Thai Christmas television, but was left wholly disappointed by the MTV specials. I couldn't find the Wizard of OZ or Only Fools and Horses on any channel. I lasted another week here until New Years day, when I left for the diving island of Koh Mao which was just a speed boat ride from Koh Samui. Travelling through the islands is very pleasant, a far cry from the daily horror shows of the mainland. Approaching Koh Mao by boat bought back images of the travel brochures with emerald seas and palm tree lined white beaches. Everyone on my speed boat was from Japan and they were only snorkelling for the day. The boat crew helped me off with my three suitcases, which put me at odds instantly with all the ruck-sack toting backpackers that filled the island ferry terminal. I stood at a busy junction by Mae Had pier and took in the scene. This was Thailand as I imagined it, lots of young people colourfully dressed, complete with dread locks and knitted knapsacks. I wore jeans and a cotton long-sleeved shirt when I arrived and stood out like Nelsons column. I rummaged in my suit case for my UNICEF T-shirt to add some much needed camouflage.

Touts swarmed all over me, offering accommodation for all budgets, dive trips, massages and all in between. I saw a sign for BANANA diving which I recognised from the net and jumped into an open truck heading there. The roads were very basic, and then became invisible as we bumped over the sand in between tall coconut trees. Outside the dive centre I met a dive guide called Denis (or maybe it was Innes) and he showed me around the place. It was a huge diving resort with an on-the-beach restaurant and bungalows stretching away into sculpted gardens. They had a proper brick-built hotel part, which I checked into as I'm quite partial to air conditioning and doors that lock. This resort was like a diving factory that turned out literally thousands of divers from beginner to instructor all year long. Koh Mao has a very chilled out atmosphere, which is not surprising when you consider the number of Stoners taking diving courses - every exhaled breath adds a small amount of marijuana to the air. Those not smoking were drinking, but doing both at the same time came a close second. Evenings were spent sitting on beanbags in beach restaurants watching the latest movies as everybody tucked into Mossiman Curries or No-Name chicken. Conversations with stoner divers normally hinged around un-provoked attacks from Trigger Fish, or the stereotypical environmental topics, my favourite was the harnessing of Dolphins to generate electricity debate.

One evening, I persuaded some barefooted dimwits that tonight's movie Castaway starred Tom Hanks as the world knitting champion. At the end of the movie, my stoned acquaintances said that they did not see Tom do any knitting, so how was he the champion? Falling into this world of diving all day and getting drunk all night is fun and very addictive, but draining financially as prices on the island were very western-orientated. Backpackers often spend many months or even years on Koh Mao without working more than a couple of days a month. Despite dressing in rags, growing dreadlocks and smoking dope all day, most of these travellers are not bums at all, but instead fall into the TrustaFarian category - Rastafarian lifestyles with a Trust fund to live large on. I spent my trust fund the day I got it and would be forced to work soon, not as a child labourer or anything near as skilled, but something far worse paid with longer hours - a scuba diving instructor. There were probably a couple of thousand other destructors looking for work on the island, most settling for the sought-after unpaid positions that afforded you the *life-style*. The *life-style* is the instructors' dream, a ticket to earn a pittance yet not starve to death. Experienced diving life-stylers' are adept at eating and drinking for free at the student divers' expense by constantly recommending them to dine at the latest, rustic (lean-to) chic restaurant. Many instructors also rented motorbikes and even bungalows to naïve customers to supplement their own expensive island existences, especially with the constant ebb and flow of drug availability. There isn't much deep water around Koh Mao, but the island does have a wreck in fifty metres depth. Technical diving was in an embryonic state on the island when I got there, with only one or two shops even knowing what a wing was or where to stuff their long hoses. I bought three sets of tech equipment with me and found a place willing to hire out the doubles tanks they had. Going round the various centres to ply my wares proved disappointing, as none of them seemed interested in offering anything other than the standard PADI recreational experience.

There were two super centres on the island, BANANA Resort and Buddha-Vista, although I was staying at the formers Sairee beach resort, I rode my scooter to the south beaches to see if I could generate some work. Chalok baan Kao was the map name for this area, and it seemed to have even more dive centres than bars, although often they were one and the same. I met the dive manager there, Mike, who came from Australia, more specifically the town of Nimbin or very near it. Ironically Nimbin and Koh Mao could be twin towns as far as the inhabitants favourite pastimes go. Mike had an excellent sense of humour and possibly because of it was one of the busiest PADI Course Directors in the whole of Asia, every month, Buddha-Vista trained between twenty and thirty new diving instructors. Mike said that I could introduce myself to these guys and girls and talk about technical diving as a means to avoid become burnt-out for new instructors. This deal was excellent, most of the customers came to Koh Mao with a goal of getting as much diver training as possible before travelling around Asia and working as scuba instructors. Before giving the group a hard sell on deep diving, I helped as staff during their dive instructor training. For those wishing to keep things shallower and straightforward, they completed a Nitrox instructor rating or got certified on one of the various Rebreather units available (when the units weren't being occupied by mice). During one Nitrox class, I was midway through an academic session covering the effects of oxygen toxicity and how it can lead quickly to experiencing convulsions underwater. The group was assembled in an outside classroom set up inside a Gazebo. When we arrived in the morning, I noticed lots of dogs lying in the Gazebo looking very hot and bothered. The dogs were pushed out onto the beach and we started the class. Right on cue, one of the dogs sprang back onto the classroom floor, clearly having some kind of convulsion. I'm no vet, but I could see some blue crystals in the dogs' mouth and realised straight away - it had been poisoned. Looking around the beach, it was clear that it was mass clean-up exercise as dogs were in various states of ill-health and convulsing everywhere.

As most Buddhists will tell you, they would not actively poison any animal, as life is sacred. Putting a dozen dogs in a pen with bowls full of poisoned food however, was a whole different means to an end. After a couple of days of fasting, if the dogs chose to eat that poisoned food (as they invariably did), it was they who had decided their fate. They could have just as easily thrown the dogs out of a window, if the dogs refused to fly, then they would meet a sticky end on the pavement below. The sight of the convulsive canines upset a few fragile souls, so we had a break for lunch. I had a delicious Hot Dog as some of the sensitive others chewed into their B-B-Q flavoured Tofu and Polenta kebab. By the time we returned, the powers in charge of removing dead dogs had done their job. A tourist child asked why people had put all the sleeping dogs into the hammocks before dragging them up the beach. The eight year old said it wasn't fair, because they were only snoozing in the sun and were not bothering anyone. The only thing I could add was that he should avoid the beach barbeque for a few days. At the end of that month, I had certified over thirty new tech divers in one form or another. Even after the four-way split of the proceeds I was feeling flush, and was ready for a holiday. I flew to Manila to do a reconnaissance of some deep wreck dive sites. While back in the UK, I exchanged some e-mails with John Bennett, a well-known British deep diver based in Puerto Galera, an island famous for tech diving in the Philippines. Contrasting Bangkok, which I find quite a friendly city despite its enormous size, (it's bigger than London) Manila is a pretty lawless place. I saved a pile of cash by using the weekly Wednesday night flight provided by Egyptair.

Arriving at an ungodly hour still had all the freaks running around the airport. I headed for Robinsons Mall, like John had recommended, to have some late dinner. The menu was all in the local Tagalog language in the only place still open at that hour, so I just shut my eyes and picked something using *the Force* to guide me. A plate of chicken looking stew arrived and I was pleasantly surprised by the way it tasted. I found an English newspaper on the plane and unfolded it to read during my mystery meal. A man in an overcoat came over and asked me if I was English or American. I assured him I was the former and he showed me a police badge. In a few minutes, he explained that the New People Army were holding a march inside the mall, and they would very likely take umbrage at my being there. He continued that I should get a take-out bag and leave before any trouble started. That sounded reasonable to me, plus I would not even need to tip my casserole into a bag as I had seen some unusual shaped bones in it. I was shown an emergency exit, and was off through it like a rat up a drainpipe. The back of the shopping centre faced a medium sized hotel that had a big sign outside advertising Sundowner special rates for the rooms. The glow from my watch light confirmed it was after sunset and I went in to enquire. The clerk looked surprised that I wanted a room for the whole night, as the special rates were for people using the rooms for hourly purposes. I was very tired and not surprised when it clicked that I was about to stay in a luxury brothel. The crowd in the car-park outside looked aggrieved about something, and that made up my mind in a few seconds. The receptionist guy said he could do me a good deal on a suite as it was quiet, and if I promised to leave before the maid arrived. I caught his drift and paid him in cash. The room was great actually, decorated like a Roman villa but stylish, with mirrors everywhere. I lay back in my sultan-sized bed and relaxed to the sound of shouting outside. At eleven in the morning I was already in a taxi to the central bus station, the maid probably having slept in herself, as I never saw her. One hundred pesos brought me a ticket to Batangas Ferry Port on a public bus with air conditioning and a television. The aircon didn't work and the journey lasted eight hours instead of four. Sleep was impossible as the bus stopped every mile to pick up street vendors. Every time my eyes closed for more than two seconds, a tap on my shoulder came from someone selling water or lottery tickets. Many of other passengers were buying these small Baloot eggs that came from refrigerated polystyrene boxes. I asked what they were and wished I had not bothered almost immediately. The eggs contained small duck or chicken bodies that had been incubated and grown until just before hatching. The eggs were then frozen to kill the small bird. What was inside was then to be slurped down in one go as an aphrodisiac. The vendor cracked a small shell open and the smell of the rotten egg caught my nostrils faster than the image of the green and brown decomposed chicken inside. I retched and looked away, which I believe was the international sign *that I didn't want any*. The seller thought that my sickness was just a ploy to haggle about price, I paid him fifty pesos to go away.

I spent the rest of the journey watching a James Bond movie that had been dubbed badly into the local dialect, all the films various actors had their lines spoken bizarrely by the same male voice. Batangas port is a busy place, with long queues to enter via the metal detector search. It was early in the evening, so thankfully the sun was not in full effect anymore while I stood in line. I booked a ticket to Sabang beach from a vendor holding up a picture of a large luxury modern ferryboat. At boarding time, I went outside to board the ferry that resembled the one in the picture. As I approached the towering and gleaming vessel, my ticket was inspected and I was shown to another queue. My boat had not arrived yet and I looked over into the filthy harbour water to watch some children diving down for loose change. As I looked closer, I saw a wooden gangway being hoisted up to crowd level. The angle of the boarding ladder was almost vertical, but maybe if they waited a couple of hours the tide would rise and make it more accessible. I could hear a voice shouting from below "Meester...Meester" and then I noticed the name painted on the boat was the same as on my ticket. The skipper beckoned me and the others down the ladder to get on his tiny Banca dugout-canoe, come ferryboat. One thing you learn in Asia is patience, and that nothing is what it seems. I was travelling lighter today, with the bulk of my luggage safely checked into left baggage at Bangkok airport - this helped a lot as I negotiated the bendy plank of wood that badly impersonated the gangway. The stretch of water between Batangas and Sabang beach is in places one mile deep, the sea often claims these wooden Banca boats and the passengers that ride in them. The skipper had placed a sign next to the steering wheel of the boat that said his co-pilot was Jesus. I would have preferred a marine radio and a life raft, with in-date flares instead of a picture of the biblical hippy, but I was out of luck today.

The sea today was rough enough that everybody wore the antique life jackets. The journey today was two and a half hours of big swells and choppy seas. Within half an hour, the first of the seasickness started to flow. I had bought some pills for the occasion and gave a couple to a mother and daughter sitting near me. Instead of swallowing them down for a restful journey, the mother put them both in her shirt pocket, saying that she would rather sell them and keep the money. The rollercoaster ride came to end and I walked up the beach to the Atlantis resort. John was sitting on a stool checking his e-mails on a painfully slow internet connection, but we said hello and I checked into my room. Over a San Miguel beer or three, we discussed the deep wreck I wanted to dive and he spoke of his plans to attempt the scuba depth record. Sabang beach has some excellent deep dive sites and some often unpredictable currents to add even more spice; we planned some deeper air dives near the popular wall sites for the next few days. It was very refreshing to dive into crystal clear water which strangely got clearer the deeper you went. Thailand's gulf sea, in contrast often got very murky until visibility was almost nil beyond forty metres depth. The first dive was a simple seventy metre air dive to shake off the cobwebs, the only complication was the buoyancy wing that I had borrowed would not hold air for more than a minute. Diving here was pure luxury - you could wear a shorty wetsuit and not shiver even at one hundred metres The deeper depths that we were diving always had clear water, even if the visibility was crap for the shallower divers. The icing on the cake was that all the popular dive sites were only between five and ten away minutes by boat. The afternoon dive was a short duration bounce to one hundred and ten metres. We both wore double tanks of air plus a deco tank of seventy percent oxygen. The couple of beers from the night before, combined with a restless nights sleep, must have affected me somewhat because I felt very depressed and negative on arriving at the maximum depth. I knew it was only symptoms of nitrogen narcosis and otherwise felt fine.

Although the water was clear, the ambient light was only equal to that seen an hour before sunrise. I noticed that I was squinting as if the light down there was very bright and this was definitely not the case. John and I had separated during the descent and I could not see him anywhere. The visual symptoms concerned me more than the negative mood and made me finish the dive early. Oxygen toxicity was likely the culprit for me feeling as if I was being dazzled by bright sunlight. I wanted to leave the deep water before these symptoms escalated to something more overpowering. This is the first dive when I have likely felt oxygen toxicity symptoms, but it was of more concern that it was not extremely deep and I was always totally relaxed. The ascent was like I had taken a sleeping pill, and as soon I did anything I instantly would forget having done it. The all-bad feeling vanished like a tangible cloud lifting out of my head during the shallow decompression stops, during which I breathed the richer oxygen tank also. I found John on the surface within a few minutes, he said he felt quite normal down there. I thought maybe there was some oily air or carbon monoxide in my twin tanks, as this would have a sedative effect as I got deeper. On the boat, John produced some more cereal bars like the ones we ate moments before the last dive. I scanned the ingredients list on the back and found that they contained Aspartame and other artificial sweeteners. These diet additives can have a very negative effect on deeper dives. I have noticed before that after eating several of these nutrition bars as snacks, I would get an instant bad mood lasting thirty minutes at least. Oxygen Toxicity symptoms have been linked to consumption of diet products in the past and may have been causing my visual problems and mood change at depth today. I removed all diet products from my favourite food list, and haven't noticed any further similar symptoms while technical diving. John was working the next few days teaching a trimix class and tomorrow was scheduled for some shallow practice dives, before the course started. Once a week, the dive centre organised a boat trip to nearby Verde Island. I joined the trip, despite the weather turning ugly and the promise of two hours in an un-seaworthy boat. I actually like rough sea conditions as long as I'm dressed for the occasion, be it in a wetsuit or a drysuit.

Verde is a pretty island, still inhabited by fisherman and tradesmen seeking a simpler life. The day trip is popular because you could still find shards of ancient Chinese Pottery both underwater and especially, washed up on the beach, plus there was a Bar-B-Q lunch laid on. John told me of an area where larger pieces of pottery could still be found. The site was at least ninety metres deep, and virtually unvisited except for him and his technical students. I took my video camera along to capture any images of the unusual that might come my way. On the boat was an English couple from Eastbourne, who had just bought a funeral headstone business of all things. Despite their sombre professions, they had an excellent sense of humour. They were looking to rename their company to something that stood out a little more. I suggested calling the firm Monumental Erections, as it was both descriptive and eyebrow-raising, but they doubted if their typically elderly clientele would see the funny side - Oh well. The trip across the bay was exciting, as the boat shuddered to within inches of breaking up for most of the journey. We arrived, shaken and stirred but ready to dive. We had taken some casualties due to seasickness, but still had enough to go diving. The dive guide was a trainee Divemaster from Korea and said he would join me going down to ninety. I said that wouldn't be necessary as I was being accompanied by Jesus and he would be taking care of me today. The guide, with his limited command of English, said to make sure we checked each others air supply often as ninety feet was very deep. I went in last and headed down the slope to ninety metres. The wall was pretty, but I only wanted to video the intact bow of an antique Chinese Junk before plundering all the priceless pottery. I turned on the camera when I reached the bottom. Looking through the viewfinder I could see strange black shadows running across the monitor display and wondered if my deep air diving days were over. I turned the camera over to video tape myself and to see if I looked funny in any way.

Staring into the lens, I was horrified to see an entire ants nest running around inside the camera housing. The ants looked clearly agitated, as I doubt if they were fully prepared for deep diving today. They must have entered in the night, after I prepared the camera before sleeping, I left the housing o-ring out to stop it getting squashed any more than necessary. I didn't think I would have to consider stowaways when I assembled it in my bleary-eyed early morning state. Taking video was useless now, but not really necessary either. The surrounding seabed was very bland, with not so much as Ming Dynasty coffee mug to take as a souvenir. I had a slow ascent to look at the reef scenery, multi coloured Anthea's filled the canvas and I was fascinated by the dozens of types of Nudibranchs and Spanish Dancers. Decompression stops swelled the dive time to seventy minutes, but I surfaced at exactly the same spot I entered. The boat was no more than one hundred metres in the distance, but was heading away to pick up some other divers I thought. Two hours later, I was still bobbing along, getting a nicely sunburned head. The boat had picked everybody up (well almost) and they sat in the distance for ninety minutes before the customers went diving again. There was not a roster to add my name to, but I did expect that someone might have done a head count at least. The sun was roasting my head and the current was picking up, taking me away from the island. I started swimming to shore, but it was a very slow process and I ended far down the beach by the time the water was shallow enough to stand up in and wade ashore. In the distance, I could see the dive boat approaching the shore to drop people off for lunch. After twenty minutes traipsing barefoot across the hot sand carrying my ridiculously heavy video camera still full of freeloaders, I rejoined the group. I was expecting some concerned questions as to whether I was alright and that they had been searching everywhere. The English couple I met earlier just asked me if I had a nice dive. I climbed back on the boat to get rid of my dive tank and to let my ants out for a walk. My face was frazzled from the sun and I didn't fancy another reef encounter so had a heavy lunch to console myself.

Three dives were planned today, but the third had to be cancelled after the beer-filled captain let the boat be blown onto the submerged reef. Everybody did go back in the water again though, even the screaming and seasick, as the boat had to be evacuated to lighten it up and nail a plastic bag to the hull to stop it taking on water. The journey back was awful, the skipper and wave combination even managing to shear off one of the stabilizing outriggers near the halfway mark. At one point I even donned a life jacket on top of my wetsuit. I also put the captains own life vest onto my video camera housing to protect the evidence and tell the story if we all came off worst against the perfect wave. Nobody on shore believed the story until they saw the video footage. The usual stories of 'it was a new boat captain' and, 'we won't be using him again', filled the bar. A better night's sleep purged today's memories from RAM. John Bennett taught his Trimix course along the guidelines of a competing training agency to the one I used. He was having problems with his local office and asked if I would cross him over to the one I recommended. As there was already a mix course on the go, this was easy, and I joined the class to do some evaluating and complete the paperwork. An e-mail from Koh Mao came, asking if I would come back to teach some tech courses for a new group of diving instructors. Flights were cheap enough to country-hop so I headed back to Manila for my Egyptair red-eye flight. Three hour flights don't give much jet lag, but travelling long distances, by road in the Philippines can knock the stuffing out of anybody. A crashed Coca-Cola lorry caused a river of brown tooth rot to delay my minibus several hot and sticky hours. I was glad to be back in the virtual civilisation of Thailand, at least they have more than one main road.

My work in Koh Mao consisted of four instructors wanting to complete several tech diving courses, ending in Extended Range diving as deep as fifty metres. We did some evaluation dives that showed I had my work cut out for me this time. The first of the dives was to just thirty metres, but the conditions underwater had deteriorated to have a virtual cloud base at twenty-four metres. The water was perfectly clear at the shallower depth but it was like swimming into a layer of Baileys liqueur at thirty metres. Everyone on the dive was at least a diving instructor and most were full of war stories about how they dived deep all the time. At twenty metres I started to hit the brakes, as did the three most experienced others. We hovered above the murky brown cloud and I signalled for the two others to not go any deeper. Buoyancy control was not in their vocabulary nor, it seemed within their grasp and we watched them career downwards into the thick sediment below. The seabed must have been almost fifty metres in this area. We watched the two divers exhalations get faster and faster as the bubbles rose from the primordial soup. After five minutes they had still not appeared, so I went looking. Following the Jacuzzi of bubbles, I found the two guys holding hands and breathing heavily. They made no effort to ascend, even when I gave them some signals to do so. Grabbing their tank valves, I inflated my buoyancy jacket to pull them into clearer water. Both remained inert until we reached the better visibility, and then the head shaking began. The dive was aborted early and a valuable dive de-briefing took place on the surface. This is what happens sometimes even during evaluation dives, the two instructors said that they were just frozen on the bottom with blank minds. One of the duo rolled a joint on the boat ride back to relax, so I had to dissuade him from continuing the course and a future in deep diving. I'd imagine that many divers smoke and do all sorts of things that contradict common sense. As long as they didn't do it in front of me, or weren't visibly performance-challenged by their evenings entertainment, it was game on. The four divers that were left proved very adept at deeper diving. It's not enough that divers mirror some drills and listen to lectures, I can only certify them if I feel that they could surface alone and in comfort, making all the right decisions. About a week into the training, I caught Dengue fever. The first few days of elevated temperature and painful bones were tolerable, but when I developed the whole-body itchy red rash, I felt pretty grim. A local nurse prescribed me 1000mg Aspirin to lower my temperature, but I felt worse and worse. Because of the mini Dengue outbreak on the island a specialist came over, I went to see her. When I told the doctor of my current medication she was horrified, and I stopped taking that type of painkiller in favour of Paracetomol. A day or so later, all that was left was the irritating skin rash and only the cold water from scuba diving would help it.

Some dives I would dive without a wetsuit, such was the relief, although getting hit by jellyfish stings more often and in sensitive places, was no picnic either. The diving course came to end and I returned all the rental equipment to its source. One of the requirements was that everything was disassembled and serviced thoroughly as it had been a long time since someone last looked at it. I incorporated the strip-down sessions into a service technicians' course. Thai wiring is not known for its safety standards and during one demonstration I was given a really good knock-down electric shock from the ultrasonic bath. I took an extended lunch break to recover from the jolt, and proceeded to ride home on my moped. Most of the beach roads on Koh Mao double as footpaths and I had to brake heavily to avoid some dreadlocked drunks that fell onto the gravel in front of me during the journey. A stoner on a much bigger off-road bike roared up behind me, oblivious to the obstacles now blocking the way. He crashed straight into the back of my bike and we all tumbled into some filthy puddle. My knee cap took the brunt of the collision, and when I stood up it had so many stones stuck in the wound it looked like a red apple crumble. The worthless stoner started apologising profusely, but had there been less witnesses, his injuries would have been much worse than mine - I was seething.

Koh Mao can be fun, but with so many pot smokers careering around on motorbikes, injuries are an everyday occurrence. The only protective clothing worn was the typical coconut shell crash helmet and suntan lotion. The $4 lids were mandatory for foreigners and Thais alike, but provided absolutely no protection. If the police saw you riding without one, at least they got some pocket money from the *literally* On the Spot Fine. Before I got Dengue fever, I would go for a run early in the morning to rid my body of alcohol and attempt to keep fit. One day, I saw some friendly locals pouring buckets of sand onto the road at a particularly nasty corner. As I ran past, they started grinning from ear to ear, like Cheshire cats. Locals did this when you caught them doing something they knew they shouldn't be. Moped rentals are big business in Thailand, foreigners are asked to leave their Passports as a deposit for the bike as accidents, and then the subsequent absconding of riders was epidemic. Having no travel documents tends to make riders a bit more likely to pay for any damage they cause. The next biggest business is running little health clinics that provide plasters and counterfeit drugs with a smile. Often, the motorbike renters also own one of these health centres, and when you fall off your moped the shop owners can benefit from offering the full service, the two dissimilar businesses complimenting each other perfectly. Sprinkling sand on the corners outside their shops just helps protect their investment and provides work for the extended families. This business model is called *Bend and Mend,* and can even be found in the underwater world where large dive centres buy their own recompression chambers to treat the injuries caused by their shabby instructors.

An e-mail from John Bennett advised that he had three people to do a wreck penetration course in Subic Bay in the North of the Philippines. He asked whether, if he gave me the business, I could give him a subsidised wreck instructor course. This was highly likely, and I could definitely do with letting my knee heal up away from Koh Mao's septic water supply. I travelled back to Bangkok and on to Manila with a nasty fever - it was like my dengue symptoms had returned with a vengeance. At Bangkok's Don Muang airport, some free entertainment was provided by a couple of British holidaymakers from hell. Two very loud and very drunk scumbags dressed in the usual uniforms of string vests and Tattoos, were having a fistfight simultaneously with each of their prostitutes. The ladeez were angry with them leaving for Manila to go whoring, and in particular, not leaving a large wad of cash behind. The rest of the queue was treated to a fireworks display of fists and tears and then a shouting of random swearwords after all the histrionics failed.

During my time in Pattaya, I visited Starbucks usually two to three times per day. I lost count of the number of times I saw the same girls asking many different men for money to get abortions for her families' pedigree buffalo or some such concoction over a Latte Macchiato. *Caveat Emptor* I suppose applies, as in all pursuits. I forwent the public bus option to Batangas ferry port in favour of a private taxi. The air conditioning helped to abate my temperature, but I can't remember ever feeling worse. I checked into the first hotel I stumbled across when I got off the ferry. I collapsed onto the bed a shivering and aching mess, with a dangerous temperature. Every scratch or old wound on my skin seemed to start bleeding simultaneously and I thought that I had caught the Haemorrhagic, or Jekyll version of Dengue Fever. I couldn't move a muscle and had no signal on my mobile to call in International Rescue and Thunderbirds. A power cut knocked the air conditioning off and I passed out from overheating. I didn't die, obviously...or did I? Who can tell? Late the next evening, I came to, miraculously feeling quite a lot better. My phone worked now and I called John to tell him where I was staying and that I was sick. He sent a nurse over, who said that it looked like I had dengue again or even blood poisoning. My scabby knee was black and horrible now. Whatever it was, it didn't last long and by the next morning I felt almost completely normal except from some light-headedness. I walked slowly to the dive centre and met the wreck course customers. I had another day to recuperate as we were leaving by ferry early the next morning to travel up to Subic Bay naval base some eighty miles north of Manila.

In its heyday, Subic was the largest Navy base outside of the United States and home to the US Navy's Seventh fleet with its many thousands of servicemen. A fall-out over rent payments between the Philippine government and the US navy saw the fleet sail away in 1992, and take with it the highly base-dependent prosperity for the entire area. The official reason for leaving was the eruption of the Mount Pinatubo volcano, which devastated a huge area. Subic Navy base is still one of the biggest toxic-waste dump environmental issues in the world today, but it also has a lot of sunken Japanese and US Navy vessels and makes a very interesting destination for wreck penetration divers. A relative prosperity has since returned to the base and neighbouring Olangapo city. After receiving extensive investment, the Subic area now sees even tourist traffic return, partly due to its duty-free port status and pretty landscapes.

The other wreck students were Chinese businessmen that would be meeting us up there, complete with their heavily armed bodyguards. Kidnapping of local and foreign VIP's is fairly common place and when these two guys arrived, they bought with them a virtual armoury to ensure that they didn't end up on an OGRISH webpage. I think these guys relished being targets because all day long they posed with their guns, and even shot them (badly) from their moving car on occasion. They must have actually *wanted* to be taken hostage by the disgusting ways they behaved most of the day. Still, underwater they behaved themselves and the below-the-waves attractions kept us all focused. A popular wreck was the USS New York, a huge battle ship scuttled just a few hundred metres from the shore. Within the calm protection of the bay at least a dozen other warships and freighters rested, all in relatively shallow depths. The only down-side was the constantly extremely poor visibility in the bay, caused mainly by the enormous volcano eruption some ten years earlier. Although there many wrecks to choose from, the outside visibility was bad enough that they all looked the same. Only until we were well inside the derelict wrecks did the water clarity improve. Bad conditions have one benefit, in that they often keep the group closer together by adding to the overall menace factor. Before we explored the rusty hulks, time was spent at the surface practising the following of guide-lines around obstacles. Once everybody was proficient in the car-park, we headed underwater to do laps around the dive centres barnacled support columns. This was the most painful exercise during the course as spiky sea-urchins often made their presence felt, despite our clearance dives moving to them to less prominent positions. Swimming inside large shipwrecks is my favourite type of diving. Artificial reef type wrecks are useful to learn the ropes on, but a proper wreck due to an unplanned sinking holds the most fascination. As you enter further and further inside, careful to pay a line out to mark the exit, the condition of the metal and clarity of the water becomes excellent. Even if the wreck lies on its side or up-side down, travelling through the ship is a weightless and highly relaxing experience. Swimming through engine rooms, now flooded with seawater and defunct, constantly reminds me of Mans sometimes painful duel with the ocean. Normally I just pull myself around inside the wreck with just my arms in an effort to save energy and preserve the scarce visibility.

The Subic Bay wrecks have had an estimated Trillion tonnes of volcano dumped on top of them and the even though the local tide just trickles along, it is enough to percolate silt throughout every compartment of the boats. The only good visibility is found in the vessels that came to rest in an upside-down position. We completed six training dives and two more fun exploratory dives during our five day Subic trip. Work came via e-mail from Koh Mao again, and I headed back on another one of my yo-yo journeys. More dive instructors had graduated and were eager to learn about decompression diving, these new skills would give them something interesting to do when they were not leading groups of intro divers around a reef at five metres maximum depth. I kept a room in Koh Mao even when I wasn't staying there. The new post office had included some brick-built accommodation above the main shop. Everything was new, and because of its second story elevation the ants and other bugs had not colonised it properly yet. Downstairs had a grocery store, complete with internet café, so was a convenient place to live. After a day to recover from the travelling, I was ready for antics...I mean, action. Getting us off to a good start on the very first morning of work was a possible case of the bends. I was assembling several sets of double tanks when I heard my name being mentioned. A crowd was hovering over a man on the floor nearby and I was called over to investigate. I recognised the guy as a newly graduated Divemaster candidate and he was saying he had decompression sickness. His symptoms included pins and needles in his arms and feeling very weak all over. I could see his eyes were also jerking erratically sometimes and was fairly convinced he had some kind of diving injury. I asked for the emergency oxygen kit and when it arrived, proceeded to set it up.

One of his friends asked when the last dive he did was, and did he come to the surface fast or anything like that. The patient replied that he had not been diving for almost a week. Hearing this, I stopped screwing the oxygen kit together. He added that the night before he had completed his Divemaster test, which normally meant drinking vast cocktails of alcohol through a snorkel while wearing a blacked out scuba mask. All manner of special additives are combined with the booze - from eggshell or rice, to toenail cuttings and beach sand. He continued that he had drunk a new derivative called Basils Mix. Basil was a stoner/diver with a reputation for drinking vodka after suspending a bag of weed in it for a week. Our buddy on the floor had polished off a large portion of Basils Mix last night, on top of God only knows what. Now he was paying for his sins with symptoms similar to those of decompression sickness. Even excesses need moderating; a couple of Divemaster graduates have died in a less-than-heroic fashion after attempting to drink their bodyweight in alcohol. It was back to work for me, and back to his hammock for the disorientated dive 'pro' on the floor.

Tech diving in Koh Mao has the added benefits of occasionally seeing whale sharks and the odd manta. Sites like Chumpon Pinnacle and Sail Rock often attract shoals of jacks and also turtles. The water is not particularly deep, although still too deep to stand up in most places, and if the visibility stays good, everyone has a good time. Challenges for me on this next course were similar to all those conducted previously on Weed Rock. Preventing people from over-indulging on whatever took their fancy had first priority as it was incompatible with deep diving, just as it didn't mix too well with crazy three-on-a-bike moped riding. I preferred to teach the more basic technical dive courses on the island, as they are more equipment and technique orientated rather than just jumping into deep water in a devil-may-care style. After some classroom theory about how to conduct decompression stops and what happens if you mess it all up, we progressed to a shallow sandy area to find out how much everybody breathed and to have a very long practice session manhandling the twin tanks and decompression cylinders without damaging the corals.

The initial dives used beginner's sites like White Rock or Mango Bay, which never plummeted much beyond twelve metres. Another nearby reef was called Japanese Garden and was famed for the number of Burmese staff that wound up sleeping under a soft coral blanket; usually after they had had a disagreement with their employers. Union officials tend to hit any noisy employees over the head in Asia, so it was best to not complain about much. Once everyone appeared happy with the equipment in the shallows, we would invariably head to Chumpon Pinnacle. Over the days, we progressed deeper until everybody felt like they were in control and not driven solely by the monkey on their backs. The finale for this group was a dive to the top of the nearby Unicorn wreck. It was all looking so good, until one of the team rolled off the boat wearing twin tanks right on top of the head of someone who was, at the time, telling them not to. The guy with the swollen gourd was bleeding profusely, like even minor head-wounds tend to do. The sea was a bit red surrounding the boat, so I shouted SHARK to try and ease some tensions as they were overheating a bit. Only I laughed at that one, but I'm sure some of the others grinned a little bit, as it was obvious the wound was superficial…ish. The patient even refused my offer of a neck tourniquet, but he decided not to come diving today nonetheless. Assured that we would not be coming back to a dead diver, the rest of us carried on in true Dunkirk spirit. The offending diver quite rightly felt a bit guilty about her causing the tanks-on-head incident, and decided to stay on the boat with her victim in sympathy. Despite his initial protests about his scuba nemesis staying on the boat with him, they became a romantic couple soon after. Down below, the visibility on the wreck was diabolical, the metalwork only appearing as a hard, dark shadow. With the recent blood in the water possibly acting like shark chum, we were constantly on edge in case Tiger sharks showed up, sadly though, this didn't happen. The other guys said that they didn't see anything at all after the dive but even my buddy Jesus would have struggled to see wreckage through the pea soup today.

The Unicorn wreck was a freighter that sank mysteriously on a flat, calm day some years before. The insurance claim paperwork detailed a cargo of expensive tuna fish. A team of divers found the wreck on behalf of the insurers and discovered only bags of pet food, and the total claim was thrown out. As the trip was such a success we headed back to celebrate. A few beer bars had got together to release some new turtle hatchlings into the sea that night, Koh Mao style. I got a ringside seat on a rope swing on the beach. The organisers had even shaped a little race track with the small brown Lipo bottles that littered the place. The beach that turtles leave from is the one they will always return to in future to lay their own eggs. I didn't think a busy beach bar was the ideal spot for these turtles to call home, but then I'm no expert in these matters. The crowds arrived to see the beautiful thing about to happen, and even the fire dancers had washed their hair for the auspicious occasion. Once everyone was suitably drunk or stoned, the organisers tipped the plastic containers of turtles onto the beach. These little wonders really had their work cut out for them tonight, as each time they exhaustedly reached the semi safety of the water someone picked them up and started them on their brown bottle gauntlet again. As people got more wasted, then the turtles odds improved - until the beach dogs turned up to claim their green shelled sushi feast. The bar did sell some extra booze though, and all except the turtles had a good time. Fire dancers went into overdrive and trance music filled the air. One guy had gone for a whole body tattoo look but it hadn't quite worked. In the candlelight his faded tattoos looked like he had slept on wet newspapers...or maybe that was the look he was after. People-watching is amusing, especially through drunken eyes, a heavily decorated body pierced type was explaining profoundly how, and why, he did this to himself, I thought he looked as if he had just fallen into a fishing tackle box really. The best was yet to come, as a new diving instructor started proudly showing off a huge PADI logo tattooed in full colour on his bicep. Some of the vintage dive pros (by which I mean certified more than two weeks) started laughing out loud at his little show and this caused a hysterical bitch-fight on the beach.

All the island antics were wearing thin and I needed another normality check, best achieved by flying home, plus I had started to miss my own boat. Before I booked my flight, I got an e-mail from a diver up in Pattaya who wanted to do a trimix instructor course. This is where I would meet a real-life rocket scientist, in the shape of Steve Burton. We chatted over the phone and e-mail for a couple of days before I upped-sticks again, bound for Pattaya. My previous stint up there over Christmas meant once bitten, twice shy, and I bypassed 'Sin central', going directly to nearby Jomtien. Steve was based in a dive shop near this pleasant beach town that was, coincidentally, the one turned black by radiation over Christmas. I got my anti-radiation jabs in a friendly beach clinic and felt ready to confront the Pattaya fracas again. The local diving scene is surprisingly busy due to its proximity to Bangkok. Hundreds of divers come here each year to become dive instructors and they generally stay for many months. Staying in Jomtien was a good move, as it allowed sorties into Pattaya's night life and then a good nights' sleep away from the throng. My earlier trips' hotel choice was too close to the belly of the beast obviously, especially considering my sensitive disposition, and Jomtien was far less hectic. I joined Steve as he finished some other tech diving courses. They have a couple of deep scours in the seabed, used in the past to dump ammunition. Conditions in the area were always dark, with fast moving tides and choppy seas. Because of the array of smaller islands dotted around the Samesan area, localised eddy currents were commonplace and unpredictable. On all deeper dives we expected darkness below fifty metres and swift water-currents going in different directions on the seabed. If we were unlucky, then encounters with nasty jellyfish and unexploded ordnance added to the excitement. The first dive we did was so murky and dark that I was convinced we were swimming around on a wreck. Steve had his course students, and I swam along separately to another fun diver who had just arrived from Koh Mao with new technical qualifications (not from me).

During the ascent after this unpleasant dive, someone showed how it was even easy to mess up deploying a lift bag simply using a bare spool of line. The diver had the spool on his finger and let it spin around, paying out line as the surface marker balloon sped to the surface. He looked cool and smug...until the spool jammed tight and pulled him to the surface by his near-to-breaking finger. Another guy had his buoyancy wing burst from the outer bag through the zipper a minute later. It was his own custom design, and looked like it would not catch on, as it hung above him, grossly over-inflated, ready to take him to the recompression chamber. His problems worsened dramatically when he attempted to turn on the valves to his decompression tanks. The first one free-flowed violently and nothing could be done to rectify it. We all waited for him while the decompression stops were lengthened on the way to a shallower depth. Everybody switched to their richer oxygen mixtures at the new depth. Exactly the same fate happened with the new tank. Steve swam over to investigate the problem, as the in-water time would become uncomfortably long if this rich mix could not be breathed. Removing the free-flowing regulator revealed the problem instantly. Our newly qualified tech diver had placed regular yoke style first-stages on top of Din type tank valves. Before any dive, each person is expected to check that all scuba tanks can be breathed from. This check had definitely been done, as the noise of the escaping air could only have been masked by a nearby jet engine. It would have been worthwhile to let this guy hang underwater for the additional hour to learn a lesson, but this would have meant someone staying with him. Steve removed one of his own DIN regulators from his twin tanks behind his head and screwed it in place to the offending valve. That problem sorted, we surfaced only fifteen minutes behind schedule. The customer was adamant that he checked the valves and that the Din inserts had somehow fallen out. I had noticed him check the valves when we set up the equipment an hour earlier, but then he was reminded to confirm each tanks contents with an oxygen analyser by Steve.

The shops nitrox analyser fitted DIN valves only, and so the luckless chap removed the screw-in inserts and forgot to put them back. Technical diving does have many little fiddly additional pieces of equipment that always require a clear head and full attention. After all this fun, we started Steve's Trimix Instructor, together with a new student called Andy. For the classroom session, I asked Steve to prepare a couple of presentations. One was to plan a trimix dive including as many fine details as possible. His background included holding various world patents for aircraft collision avoidance algorithms. Steve's understanding of diving decompression algorithms puts him in a very small group of people on the planet capable of planning decompressions just using a calculator with exponential functions. It was an interesting performance, but a little beyond what was necessary for class today. I took some notes myself in case my laptop programs ever malfunctioned. Andy the student was rendered unconscious by all of the exotic math. I didn't know what Steve was talking about but gave him the benefit of the doubt. His penalty for baffling us was to fill all the tanks with trimix for tomorrows diving. We were to be joined by an Inspiration rebreather diver named Lars. Everybody was deep dive ready and the first three dives went mostly without complication right down to seventy-five metres, the only noteworthy event was when we found the anchor wrapped around a rusty 500lb bomb. Our final mission was to explore the deepest hole on the sea chart, which Steve had nicknamed the Black Hole of Death. Not only was it dark and horrible even on a good day, but had actually claimed a few victims recently. The last one to be swallowed up was a German diver who went out with a local fishing boat. He was planning to dive twice into the hole, to nearly ninety metres - breathing regular air. His first dive went fine apparently, so after getting back on the boat, he had a quick celebratory beer, before going down again. Round two didn't go as planned, or maybe it did, but the chap was never found after the second plunge, so we had something to look out for now.

Andy, the student, was my buddy and Steve, playing course instructor, oversaw all facets of the dive plan. I would simulate a problem student. The boat ride out was very boisterous and had half a dozen beginner divers in various states of nausea. A huge swell kept breaking over the boat which had a deck only a few inches above the waterline and no gunnels at all. The boats' 'low rider' look did keep the decks clear from seasick but, one shire-horse of a wave swept the decks and took some key pieces of the scubee doos' dive equipment with it. Some of them looked relieved not to be diving, although sitting on this boat for the next three hours would definitely re-educate them. We knew we had arrived at the deep site as the echo sounder's depth display went off the scale, this did not indicate an infinite depth at this area, just a cheap depth sounder with a maximum reading of 60 metres - if it didn't read the depth, it meant we had reached our destination. Another big breaker buffeted the boat and sent Andy the student's box of equipment into the brine. Instinctively he jumped in after it, but seemed to get upset despite saving his box of goodies. Discovering his new mobile phone no longer worked after its early bath in his swimming trunks pocket must have been disappointing, as it cost more than the wetsuit and odds-and-sods he saved from getting wet. Lars would be my buddy, and was having a difficult time standing up in his enormous rebreather complete with back-up scuba tanks. Ironically, if he had just taken the bail-out bottles themselves underwater, he could have left the box of death on the boat, improving his odds and comfort in a single bound. The sea state was not too rough to go diving; the borderline conditions were just compounded by the flat-bottom hull design of the dive boat, but I'm sure this tub had made an excellent fishing boat on the local lakes twenty years earlier. Today it resembled a plague ship, complete with ten contorted faces. Finally we were ready, and feeling very stressed as the boats deck constantly heaved as much as the rest of the passengers. I for one wanted to get off, and leapt into the green foamy water.

After some frantic swimming wearing four clanking scuba tanks, we all reached the orange buoy that supported the descent line. Dropping down into the maelstrom at least smoothed out the waves, but I noticed that a gang of jellyfish were hanging on our rope too. I had a full body suit on and gloves, and I hoped for Steve's sake that they were not the stinging variety as he had gone for a sporty-shorty wetsuited look. The banging of the dive tanks was loud and constant, but not enough to drown out Steve's screams as he found out the jellies were of the highly unpleasant variety. He indicated to carry on, so hand-over-hand we continued pulling ourselves down into the blackness. Andy the student seemed to be having an easy time of it, and I could see Lars (on his box) was still definitely in the game. The descent was truly horrible, with a biting current all the way down through the turbid black water. Eventually, we did arrive in the lee of the deep hole, and you could actually see a sandy bottom in the glow of the torchlight. Hitting eighty-six metres was like an aeroplane arriving above a hurricane into clear blue skies. For a metre or so above the seabed the water was clear and calm, although still totally pitch black. Shoals of fish and a huge marbled Ray had sought sanctity down here also and it looked as if the next fifteen minutes would be quite pleasant. We kept our eyes open for the lost deep-air diver who was rumoured to be hanging about down here, plus the myriad of explosive devices launched or dumped into the black hole by the Thai and US navy. Steve's hand looked nastier than the boat trip out today, welts were building on the back of his hand in fine style, but he carried on like a trooper, just whimpering occasionally through his regulator. In these surreal and tranquil conditions, Andy and Steve ran through some tank valve drills and even completed a deep water diver tow. When you reach an oasis like this after a long arduous journey through the wilderness, it's tempting to prolong the stay, but any successful diver knows that to extend the dive plan without a better reason is foolish, and our planned time was now up. Signalling to each other to ascend, we braced for impact. The anchor line used for descent had been pulled up by the boat captain already, and we planned to send up surface marker balloons to help our ascents and indicate our positions topside.

Tidal streams are always faster when close to the surface. Whoever sent up their signalling buoy first would be dragged away from the group by it as it approached the top. Steve and Andy sent theirs up at the same time and seemed to be spirited away faster than someone wearing red ruby slippers. Lars was fiddling with something, still on the seabed and face down, I went over to investigate. He could not reach his dive reel and marker buoy, but that was no reason to stay on the bottom. I pointed to go up, and he begrudgingly stopped what he was doing to follow. Sending my SMB up would be sufficient for both of us until Lars could inflate his own. Ascending back into the moving tide and dark water gave us little to focus on except for the job at hand. I started to hear an electronic beep coming from below me. It sounded like Lars's rebreather was unhappy about something. These complicated boxes of plumbing spares and wiring are renowned for their needing constant attention. Rebreather units are fun and challenging, much the same way as hand-guns, and in the wrong hands have the same deadly reputations - and coincidentally, both were actually designed to help the user kill others. After a few minutes of constant beeping, Lars switched over to his bail-out scuba tanks and both our tensions lowered. Andy was in good hands with Steve, plus he had shown himself more than capable of ascending alone if the McDonalds really did hit the fan. I spent the next ninety minutes drifting through the murky sea, decompressing with Lars. One thing more hazardous than deep diving in Pattaya was a formal 'Night on the Town' with Steve Burton. After three days dodging oil tankers and deadly jellyfish during decompressions, we were obliged and ready to face a night behind the enemy lines of Walking Street in Downtown Pattaya. It was customary to visit the Tahitian Queen 2 bar to place our brain-cells into checked baggage behind the bar. After getting suitably upside-down on Crème de Menthe shooters, we headed out to the various Go-Go bars and skanky hostess bars on offer.

Steve and Andy were joined by Japanese instructress Noriko, the three fully battle-hardened locals were seemingly impervious to alcohol but were easily overcome by the charms of the local nightlife. I, on the other hand, have my own hair and own teeth and as such am rendered completely invisible on Thai bargirl radars. I urged the others to head upmarket to the somewhat classier Hopf Bar and Grill on the beach road. It's hard to imagine such a place offering live Italian Tenor singing while the audience tries their best to finish huge three litre classes of German Weiss beer. On the way to the bar, intrepid drinkers are constantly clawed by vendors offering EVERYTHING from a troupe of Midgets to Boa Constrictor snakes wearing pink feather Boa's themselves. The trick is to avoid eye contact with anything, animal OR mineral, while trying to drunkenly walk as quickly as possible. Despite my best efforts this evening, I was hit by the Tractor-beam of a stall selling shiny gadgets. They had electronic Taser gun's both obvious and disguised as beard shavers or even flashlights. The ingenuity of such devices from Chinese craftsmen always fascinates me, and I was attracted to a particular stun gun that sprayed out flames and mace. Some drunks next to me had a narrow escape when they pressed a button on what looked like telescoping baton. The device ejected a metal bolt that stuck into the table top almost an inch deep. As they laughed hysterically, they scarily paid for two of them before 'trousering' both and stumbling off. I picked up a three-in-one stun gun from the table and asked how much. Instantly a calculator came onto the table and I was asked how much I would pay, after a few moments of frantic haggling we couldn't agree. The vendor seemed a little annoyed by my reluctance to 'Part with my Baht' and showed me another, much bigger stun gun. This one said Big-Boy-Elephant-Gun on the handle and I was eager to press the zapper's button. I don't remember hitting the floor, but I definitely remember getting back to my feet, my whole body shaking and vibrating. The Vendor was shouting at me while holding broken pieces of the stun gun up for me to see. He was insisting I pay for the device now in full, as I had dropped it when it rendered me unconscious. I looked closer at the handle and could now see some bare copper wire showing on the handle, it had been fiddled with to inflict its donkey-kick like charge on the holder, which I'd agree is quite an ingenious little scam. Although I would have rather used the stun gun repeatedly on the stall holders' testicles, I offered to go straight to a cash machine to get his money, but of course went straight into the bar instead to join the others and tell them of my adventure. I was hooked by the Pattaya lifestyle, and made plans to go back to Jersey, sell my boat and jeep, and come straight back to waste the cash in style.

A number of customers had asked if Leviathan was for sale and it took little more than a week to swap my red RIB for hard cash. My Nissan patrol jeep went a week later to my scalloping buddy Tom. Selling the boats fishing license took a little longer, but everything superfluous to travelling was gone inside six weeks. I had no intentions of staying in Asia for ever and thought my future lay somewhere in Europe, as at least I have some basic human rights of employment and healthcare there, which Thailand obviously lacks. Before I returned to Bangkok I wanted to make a quick trip to the Algarve in Portugal to find out how easy it was to run a dive business in that neck-of-the-woods. My various rights were protected by Portugal's membership in the European Union and it was almost as sunny year-round as Asia. I was so serious about moving down there I bought a brand new van to ship over my dive equipment and self to set up a new life. Coincidentally a dive buddy Joao, known to many as the monkey boy, was heading down to Lisbon by car with some of his pals. It made sense if we went together. The journey was ill-fated from the start due to constant arguing about his lack of road safety awareness. The 1400 mile journey was covered in just 19 hours and was very stressful. This short time included getting hit from behind by a speeding truck as Joao reversed along a motorway after missing an exit, and eventually blew up the van engine up just outside Lisbon. Conveniently for me this happened right next to a train station. I couldn't wait to get a hire car when I arrived in Lisbon, and doing so I headed further down to the Algarve in peace and alone. Strong winds hit the seaside towns for the three days I stayed there.

Most of the dive centres were closed due to the rough seas and I couldn't find much out about anything. The normal holidaymaker in town looked tanned but over sixty, and the general entertainment trend was for bingo halls. I figured that opening another scuba centre specialising in technical diving would be a sure way to lose my entry stake. A little disheartened, I headed back to Jersey via train. To cap it all, the journey took three days of sitting in cigarette-filled carriages travelling through virtually all of Western Europe to avoid track repairs. I was sitting on a Thai Airways Jumbo jet within a week, my new van left sitting under a tarpaulin sheet needed for its extended stay under the stars in London. Koh Mao still had plenty of diving going on, and I immersed myself in teaching tech diving courses to a steady stream of stoners. Christmas was coming and the island got super busy again. Rumours had the owners of the two biggest dive centres planning an enormous joint enterprise. Each would build a luxury resort at opposing ends of the island, the beds would be filled from a new inter-island ferry boat service also jointly owned by the resorts. All new visitors would be delivered directly to the resorts, bypassing the islands 'other' options. This would have effectively put a noose around the necks of the other centre owners, so clandestine arrangements were apparently made to scupper the grandiose plans. Mr Ban, an owner of the Banana Diving resort, where I usually stayed, was shot 5 times by an unknown assassin. In the frame for the slaying were many local businessmen and half a dozen were implicated. Mon, from Buddha-Vista Diving, the other partner in the big ferry project, disappeared from the island shortly afterwards. Mon likely thought his own safety was in jeopardy too, as so many competitors were now being implicated in the shooting. The assailant was not found straight away, so Thai culture required that the victim not be interred until the guilty parties were found. Mr Ban was kept refrigerated at the dive resort for many months, during which time the mainland police conducted enquiries.

Every now and again, a troop of commandos raided various businesses and took away some quite high profile individuals to assist with their enquiries. Gunfire on the island was not commonplace but occasionally Thai businessmen shot at each other when drunk and *usually* only succeeded in ruining some western party goers evenings. Even in low season every night is party night on the islands, but during the festive season people really pull all the stops out. No festivities in Asia are complete without fireworks and because of the proximity to Christmas, Chinese made pyrotechnics and mind altering substances were available on every street corner, this meant accidents abounded. There I was, sitting on the beach at the BANANA resort on the evening of the Bearded One's birthday, getting drunk and exchanging bullshit dive stories. The bar was mobbed, more than usual, and it would have taken twenty minutes to get a new Gin and Tonic. I didn't want to leave my spot and miss the mostly disorganised firework display arranged for soon on the narrow strip of beach exposed by the ebbing tide. Some drunken revellers decided to start the flashes and bangs early but on the other side of the bar, on a small sandy road just 3 metres across. I could see some of the usual suspects holding fireworks bigger than twelve litre scuba tanks over their heads, clearly battered on drink and drugs and totally armed and dangerous. Right in the middle of the crowd on the sandy road, they lit the big bangers. For thirty seconds, smoke filled the air as the huge firework smouldered and built up momentum. A waiting Thai taxi driver could not be expected to wait for anything, and proceeded to drive through the smoke at the same time as the ground mine exploded. The tyre on his pick-up truck burst, and he lost what little control he had over the vehicle and crashed through the windows of the adjacent dive centre. A few seconds of muffled screaming followed, until an enormous boom shattered the windows of a nearby supermarket. The big firework had ejected an aerial bomb, designed to detonate near 300 metres of altitude - unfortunately the charge had been deflected into the shop, with some predictably undesirable results. Now the screaming began again properly, my ears were ringing but at least the crowds at the bar had thinned out. I grabbed another drink and retook my seat to watch the next display of skyward ooh's and ahhs.

Chapter 9: Coniston Copper Mine

My stint in the Orient went on for two years in total, travelling mostly between Koh Mao, Manila and Pattaya. On the whole it was an excellent experience, but I definitely needed a rest now and a change from the Wild West lifestyle of South East Asia, as it can take its toll on sensitivities and make you unfit to re-enter polite western society, if such a thing exists. I came back to London to spend a couple of months catching up with family and friends while I looked into finding the next destination. Not working, and living in the UK, always gives me a financial migraine, I even had to suffer the indignity of *paying* to go diving now. I tried to keep my finger in as much as possible, and drove to a couple of inland dive sites like Stoney Cove and Dorothea Quarry. Diving here was fun, but not too challenging and usually bitterly cold. I bought some dive magazines and read about some deep dives done in the Lake District. Reading about Richie Stevenson's adventures in Coniston Copper mine was fun. He wrote of eighty metre exploration dives in the narrow shafts while his friends swam about in the shallows above. It was lucky for him he wore a crash helmet when his buddies knocked rocks and timber down on top of him. The mine shaft was over thirteen hundred feet deep according to the official plans. Richie and his pal Nobby tried to get as deep as they could over several dives. The article mentioned them getting down to three hundred and fifty feet. The mine shaft had many obstacles at various depths. They were stopped eventually by some flooring still present that prevented deeper progress.

After doing some internet homework, I got the address and the low-down on the copper mine. Stuart, from Scotland, was an invaluable source of information. His knowledge of the mine even included valuable details such as where the roof was still collapsing, and which parts of the floor crumbled like a Clinton Alibi. I phoned Caroline, a diver friend from the Channel Islands who was studying to be a doctor in Edinburgh. She was usually up for some adventure, this one promised rock climbing, pot-holing and crazy scuba diving in the same afternoon. I would endure the three hundred and fifty miles of road-works from London to the Lake District. Caroline would travel by train a similar distance from Eastern Scotland. I didn't envy her ten hours as a hostage of British Rail, but it meant we could meet in the middle, saving me a thousand mile round trip.

This project had all the trimmings of an Indiana Jones adventure, but without the reward of a golden statue at the end. This phrase would look good on my headstone and sums up life as diving instructor aptly. The first dives planned were simply for reconnaissance purposes and to get a feel for the place. We met at Kendal train station and headed straight for the copper mine. My scribbled internet directions advised us to head into Coniston village, turn right at the Black-something pub before the bridge and head for the YMCA at the top of the hill. The route to the old mine was designed for mountain goats, no more than a rough-hewn track up the valley. The scenery was fantastic, but hard to fully appreciate with the steep drop into an icy river on one side. The track came to an end at a series of holiday cottages and the youth hostel. Behind these buildings stood the famed Old Man of Coniston.

This Old Man is a famous mountainside and deep beneath it was where the copper ore was mined. Copper and other minerals had been taken from these hillsides for nearly five hundred years, but all mining activities had largely stopped by the turn of the century. The Ruskin museum in the village is dedicated to the mine works and the men who toiled there. I drove the van beyond the holiday homes, and attempted to get as close to the mine entrance as possible without falling into the river. The weather was perfect, with blue skies full of paragliders enjoying the thermals. To get to the submerged mine shaft you have to cross a river, then crouch along a water-filled tunnel for three hundred metres. The tunnel contains an ancient mini rail system used for transporting the copper ore from the back of the mine. The pumps employed to drain the mine were decommissioned in 1897, so over a hundred years of rainwater filled the main shafts and cascades down the access tunnel, before joining the river. At the time we didn't know any of this, so just put our coats on to traverse the tunnel. We waded through the water and rocks, stubbing our feet on the old railway tracks. The tunnel roof drops to four feet high in places, so heads were getting sore as we journeyed into the darkness and unknown, dragging our dive equipment behind. As soon as you enter the tunnel, you feel the bite of the icy wind that constantly blows outwards. Even though the sky is cloudless outside, the inside of the tunnel experiences perpetual rain. Caroline and I walked for about ten minutes along this access shaft until it widened out considerably. The main tunnel is then crossed at ninety degrees by similar workings going in opposite directions. The ceiling at this crossroads was held up with rotten, damp wood secured with promises. The loose rocks above looked as big as cars, we were told to get beyond this point quickly and quietly. The thick timbers used to support the ceilings had been removed when the mine closed. The mine owners probably did not envisage many ramblers visiting, and definitely were not expecting divers. Wearing hard hats here would have been a good idea, but more likely would just prolong the agony for a short second if the ceiling came down.

Normally, Caroline and I would be chatting at one hundred miles per hour about everything and anything, but with the echo of the rock walls and the never-ending sound of rushing water, talking was futile. Our lights picked out our destination further back in the mine. The area was roped off with green and blue rope, a torrent of rain poured down from an opening in the ceiling like a curtain of water. Above us was an enormous chasm, known as Cobbler Hole. In front was the entrance of today's dive site, a portal just two metres square and almost four hundred metres straight down. The water looked black and freezing, but I wanted to know exactly how cold. I put my wrist and dive computer into the water to measure the temperature. It was far too icy to endure much of that, so I took the gauge off my wrist and dropped it back, attached to some rope. It would take five minutes to get an accurate reading, so in the meantime we drained our flasks of coffee in an effort to warm ourselves up. I had a dozen or so chemical light sticks with me, and activated all of them to add some emergency lighting should our battery lights fail. I fancied a dive to seventy metres today to get some video footage of the side tunnels I had heard about from my internet pal. We exited the mine to get our dive-suits on and get the rest of our equipment from the van. Caroline was going to be very 'rufty-tufty' today. She intended to wear just a thick wetsuit on this first plunge. I assumed that because it was still summer, the water may have been a lot warmer. I suspect that I may have said the mine water was as warm as the sea, and this was why she brought the wetsuit along. The thought of the constant 8 degree water temperature sent shivers down my spine, never mind what it would *actually* do to hers. On reaching the van, I pulled out my extra-extra thick undersuit to wear under my drysuit, I wasn't taking any chances - cold water is for ice-cubes…not divers.

We wore our neoprene dive hoods for the journey back, as the extra head padding meant we could walk much faster through the low tunnels. Caroline being six inches shorter than me was far better protected than I when walking though the midget-sized passage ways. Even Snow White would have had to wait outside if her seven short friends ever came in here looking for mining work. Off we went again to see what we could see. All along the entrance tunnel known as Horse Level, you can see drill holes left from when the rock was cleaved. Gunpowder charges would have been placed in the holes to split the rock. These holes were made with hand drills or chisels combined with hard work back then. The miners would dry the freshly-made holes with straw and then pack it with black powder. A primitive fuse was then added. After retiring to an unsafe distance the charge was detonated. In the confines of the narrow passages, the report from the explosion would make a Baghdad bombing sound like a disco beat. A day in the life of a miner two hundred years ago would make a modern prison inmate go on hunger strike, or refuse even to tidy up his play station discs. The mine went deeper each year by sixty feet only. All the rock was moved by hand initially, before horses were invented.

To keep things simple, during the first dive we used single twenty litre tanks filled with normal air. A small side tank of nitrox with 60% oxygen would speed up any decompression obligations we might incur. I plunged into the water expecting to be frozen instantly. But as I was already cold from the surroundings, the water didn't feel so harsh. As Caroline jumped in I could hear her scream as the water coursed through her wetsuit. Initially, cold water can take your breath away as it enters every orifice. After a few minutes acclimatising, your body warms it up, making it almost bearable - for ten minutes. My drysuit was feeling toasty for now. Having a dive site with the same area of a large TV screen can get a little claustrophobic. This one was surrounded by piles of dust and rocks all the way down, the visibility was nil at the surface. We dropped initially to thirty metres depth. Here, the water was momentarily clearer as we hadn't stirred it up yet. Rubble continued to rain down around us, slowly the smaller silt particles caught up and it was time to move downwards again. The article I'd read about this place showed divers wearing crash helmets when they descended into the mine. I thought that this was excessive at the time, but now I felt a bit naked without one.

Three of the four walls were rock, but one was constructed of enormous timber blocks. Behind this wooden wall was the ladder way the workers would have used to descend the mine to work. In places where the wall had disintegrated, you could see the original diagonal sections of rotted ladders. Because we entered the water in such a whirlwind fashion, the visibility prevented taking any usable video footage. Looking downwards, you could see the first of the temporary floors that would complicate our descent. All that was left of the floor here were timbers crossing the shaft at right angles. We both navigated our way through this obstruction by feel alone, as the rock slurry had again caught up with us, destroying what was left of the limited visibility. By fifty metres we could see a little better, but I could hear that Caroline was clearly frozen already by the chilled, dark waters. Her teeth chattering sounded more like a giant woodpecker. The wetsuit she wore was black in colour, as were her buoyancy jacket, fins, mask, hood and gloves. The all-black colour combination is very popular with technical and recreational divers alike, as it looks cool and it helps them pretend they were once members of some exotic Army regiment. A lot of diving equipment comes in 'any colour as long as its black' but it does nothing to improve the chances of finding a missing diver. Today's dive in total darkness in black water made matters much worse. I could only really see Caroline if I saw the whites of her eyes or the glow from her dive light. Every thirty seconds she made a circular sweep with the beam of her dive light to indicate that all was okay. I was a few metres below her, when without warning I started being dragged downwards faster and faster. Initially I thought we were both caught in some kind of underground stream system. Reaching out to find a handhold and stop was impossible - the walls were just too smooth. Going past seventy metres, I crashed into another restriction and then felt the weight of some huge object on top of me. I couldn't see anything except flashes of my dive light through the silt and rocks that rained down. I tried turning around to see what was lying firmly on top of my tanks. Slowly I managed to lift the thing that was pinning me down and realised it was a length of tunnel ladder. It must have been four metres in length and seemed to be covered in various lengths of rope. Probably, our groping in the darkness earlier had accidentally dislodged it from its perch as we passed it. Caroline or I may have snagged one of the dangling ropes attached to the ladder, causing the ladder to topple down the shaft on top of us. Sometimes, all it takes is the force of exhaled bubbles to upset a delicate balance and send something heavy crashing down on top of the diver. I was surprised that I never saw such a big ladder on the way down, but then again I didn't see much of anything on the way down. I couldn't even see Caroline anywhere now.

Getting free of the ladder wasn't so difficult, but the lines that dangled from it were like tentacles. Some of these sticky arms had wrapped around my tanks, I was sure. The only way to check to what extent I was caught was to try and ascend. I managed to get almost ten metres shallower before my progress was halted. Now at sixty metres, the water was a bit less silty and I felt clearer in my head. Being less deep also meant my air supply would last a bit longer. I was glad that I had put wrist lanyards on my knives so that if I dropped them they would not be gone forever. I looked down and saw green and grey rope, tight like piano wires, and clearly preventing me from further upwards movement. I did wonder which to cut first, the red or the blue, but an explosion was not likely in this situation. Cutting the first rope caused me to now float upside-down. The second line must have been wrapped around my tank manifold or regulators. But being weightless underwater meant I could just pull myself the right way round and cut this other line quite easily. Getting free of the nylon fingers, I headed up into the murky soup to look for Caroline. She was nowhere to be seen down deep, but eventually we met up near thirty metres. My 'hardcore' wet-suited buddy was clearly looking a bit chilly, and I had had enough by now as well, so we both signalled to end the dive. Thankfully, this quite short exploration dive only built up twenty minutes or so of decompression stops. This time however, was spent shivering in virtual darkness hampered by the shallow water visibility, which was now resembling a slurry of cement.

Our dive lights had been reduced to orange coloured discs, as bright as a daytime moon, so were almost useless for reading the information from our dive computer screens. We had to rely on the wrist computers audibly beeping to say that we still had stop time to complete. When the irritating alarms stopped, it was time to surface, or possibly, that their batteries were flat! On getting out, the mine was so dark that we would have to walk with all our equipment for fifteen minutes with small back-up torches before seeing natural light at the end of the tunnel. A small river burbled along outside, purring like a sleeping Lion. There were some mini-rapids and several deep pools that indicated that the river had a darker side when fuelled by winter rains. It was still sunny and some of the pools looked inviting. Jumping in to wash our equipment and ourselves, we both agreed that any future dives would need a different entry approach if we wanted to see anything at all, also, the water was so cold that we would postpone the second dive until Caroline got her Drysuit sent up from Jersey. I drove back to London and Caroline returned to Edinburgh after arranging to meet the next weekend for round two.

We checked into a guesthouse in Coniston village the following Friday, before heading for the pub. The Black Bull in the middle of town was famous for its scores of different ales and bitters. Though not normally a beer fan, I joined Caroline in a pint of Bluebird XG with its raspberry flavour. Over dinner we planned the next plunge. Staying suitably sober we agreed to get up early enough to visit the copper mine museum before the dive, to chat with the staff about the mine. In the morning, I filled up on a full English breakfast, with double helpings of cholesterol as Caroline is a vegetarian. I always find food tastes so much better when someone else cooks it. After fully saturating my arteries with grease we had a walk down through the village, this also helped me to decompress from the breakfast. We met Jeff, the museum custodian, and advised him of our plans to get some film of the copper mine. I mentioned the ingots I had salvaged from the cargo ship that sank in 1917 off of Jersey. I showed him some literature from a French company which had refined the ore that came from the Cumbria area of England. There was a good chance that the ore that made my ingot came from Coniston in the 1890's. When I told him of my plan to dive and video tape an area showing a vein of copper, his hair almost stood on end. Jeff then produced an old plan of the mine system, and showed me why he thought the venture was so dangerous.

The old plans were quite detailed and showed all the phases of work over the last two hundred years. As each ore vein was exhausted, it was walled up and a new level was worked upon. The wooden wall on the plan was complete all the way down to one hundred and thirty fathoms, about two hundred and thirty-seven metres. This indeed would be a challenge, and definitely not manageable today. Jeff added that some divers had tried to explore the mine already, but were stopped by a solid floor near 60 fathoms. This would be the story I had read about in the scuba magazine. The gas in my tanks for today was ideal for a seventy metre dive. The Trimix in the tanks contained 20% Oxygen and 30% Helium. The helium content would come in useful for minimising narcosis when working in hard conditions, especially with my heavy and hazardous video camera. Caroline would act as a support diver today, remembering last week, she decided to bring her drysuit. The warmth and protection of the drysuit meant she was able to stay in the water comfortably, for much longer - bringing me spare tanks to breathe during my two hour immersion. We carted all the equipment back through the tiny entrance tunnel, and this took over an hour. Putting all our equipment inside the mine the night before would have been nice. Pre-dive exertion should be kept to a minimum, but I had visions of local yobs or Tramps going in there to sniff glue or sleep rough. They would have definitely either stolen everything or thrown it down the hole. My pessimism earned us a bit of exercise and helped burn off the sausages from breakfast.

Before planning the dive to 240 metres, I needed to see if the various floors in the shaft really were impassable. I slipped into the water a lot more gently on this second dive. I did not want to jump in using the giant-stride 'avalanche' method of yesterday, trying to save some visibility for later. The water was a whole lot clearer today, to the extent that you could see from one side of the six foot passage to the other in places. I quickly got to the first restriction at thirty metres. I stopped for a second and noticed a side tunnel that looked interesting, but that would have to wait. Being able to see today meant passing the timber floor spars easily. Within a minute I approached the next restriction at seventy metres. The ladder I had tangoed with yesterday was there, lying awkwardly. If I didn't secure it properly now, it would undoubtedly fall on top of me again later. Tying it to some metal fixings took another minute, but there was no real hurry. Dropping to one hundred metres, my head still felt fine, despite my breathing mixture being only ideal for seventy metres. I paused here and studied the passageway beneath. I could see for at least another ten metres below and could not see any floors to impede a deeper dive.

Although I couldn't see anything, it didn't prove that nothing was there. I would feel stupid if I returned to do a deeper dive to find myself forced to stop halfway down. Helium is expensive in England and I was paying the full customer price.

Not knowing what was below could prove expensive. I dropped deeper. By one hundred and twenty metres, an obstruction did come into view. I approached it slowly, to find it was not impassable but just some loose timbers covered in silt. The previous divers must have seen this from a distance and thought it looked solid. I moved some of the wood, which was bloated with water and weighed nothing. I pushed most of the rubbish out of the way, but now the visibility was zero and I couldn't see my hand, never mind below. It would need at least another dive to check what lay beneath. The next dive would have a squirt more helium in the tanks so I could work a little harder. Today's effort was constructive, and the thought of what lay below was like honey to a Bee. Caroline would be getting into the water at thirty minutes elapsed time to bring me a spare decompression tank. I had turned the dive early, so had time to waste exploring the little side-tunnel I noticed on the way down. Ascending upwards slowly gave me a chance to do some sightseeing, but three grey walls and the brown wooden one were hardly a Nile cruise. Travelling up through the ore shaft felt quite cosy really, there were lots of reference points when the visibility was okay and I noticed it wasn't completely vertical, but curved like a giant banana. The trip back up was unremarkable, Caroline was on time to hand me a spare tank, but it didn't get used.

On surfacing, we chatted about what I'd seen below, and the fact that it needed another dive to clear the debris from the shaft. Caroline said she would be happy to come back next weekend and help. After a rest by the waters edge and after some sandwiches, we carried the equipment out and packed the van. The cold water had not been a problem today, but if my drysuit leaked or was cut in some way, the low temperature could be a serious problem. The next day, I went to a plumber's merchants and bought a huge water tank made of reinforced plastic. Cave divers sometimes took huge plastic rubbish bins underwater to decompress inside, this helps to avoid the chilling effects of long immersions in cold water. Because of the Coniston mines' low ceilings, I couldn't get a traditional 'double wheely-bin' through the mine entrance – never mind down the narrow shaft itself. My loft tank was almost two metres long but only one metre across, and it fitted sideways in the back of my van perfectly. My idea was to fix it to the shaft walls with ropes and fill it with air. The fixing ropes would be in three metre lengths, as I completed my nine metre decompression stops, I would get out of the plastic habitat and cut the ropes. The next ropes would be ten feet longer and, in a perfect world, would allow the tank to move up to the six metre mark. I would repeat the procedure for the three metre stop depth. It all sounded so easy that it hardly needed testing before using it for real. Unfortunately, it's not a perfect world. The plastic trough could hold 450 litres of water, so therefore would need the same volume of air to fill it. A litre of air has an upward thrust of 1 kilo. Even my diver-brain could see that to keep this underwater, I would have to find a manky, rotten piece of timber that was sufficiently strong enough to hold down almost half a ton of upward thrust. The wooden wall in the mine was constructed of timbers over twelve inches across. However, their appearance belied their strength, the wood was so waterlogged that you could punch your hand through in places. I drove back to Coniston to test my theory. I actually managed to find somewhere suitable to tie the lines much deeper down. Then I attempted to fill the water container with air and initially all went smoothly.

When the tank was only half full, the ropes were tighter than cheese wire. The sides of my improvised decompression chamber looked quite strong in the shop, but the force on the ropes now ripped them straight through the tanks sides. The plastic tank shot to the surface in a second, snookering my plans for a warm decompression with it. During the long drive home, I telephoned the company I bought my drysuit from and told them of my problem. The next day, I was the proud owner of an electrically-powered suit-heater system. During the week I jumped into a freezing quarry on the outskirts of London for five hours, to test my new Ready-Brek heated suit. The attractions included an old black taxi and some large plastic characters from a fairground ride. Three hundred minutes swimming around in the freezing and murky pit with seven metres maximum depth was not very stimulating, but every fifteen minutes the ground did shake as the trains to and from London went past. I stayed warm enough throughout and that was the main thing.

Caroline was still up for being support diver over the weekend. We met up as planned at the same station as before. To spice things up, we stayed at a different bed and breakfast though. The first guesthouse charitably charged me seven pounds to fill three flasks with hot water. That mistake I would not make again. I had been toying with using some new computer software to plan today's dive. I wanted to spend twenty minutes or so around 130 metres depth. There was the debris field to clear, and some side tunnels to explore. Traditional means of decompression would suggest I spend over five hours of waiting in the shallows before my body would be fully off-gassed and ready to surface. I tried a similar program before on the second BADEN wreck dive, it shortened my stops dramatically, but I got the bends on surfacing. I had used it conservatively during shallower dives several times afterwards though, and felt okay. The company even sent me an updated version to try. I could hear screaming coming from the compact disc as the program installed, no doubt from all the original guinea-pigs writhing in agony after their earlier dives. Today I would road test a competitor's software called VPM. Again, it promised all sorts of things that contradicted common sense but, like so many other divers, I was blinded by all the internet propaganda and it also seemed to provide a longer deco than my RGBM program. When you are considering jumping into freezing water for many hours, you can actually make yourself believe that something will work just because it fits nicely with your plans. That evening I showed Caroline the runtime for the dive using the new planner, and how it compared with a more established method. She confirmed that nobody would have marketed such a system if it was not okay to use, surely?

The dive tomorrow would have roughly 95 minutes of deco time, the software advised me. I wrote these losing lottery numbers on my slate, and also made a back-up copy. Sometimes you can remember all the various deco stops and times, but this plan had so many stops along the way only a magician would remember them. In the morning, we drove back to the mine and began taking the equipment inside. The trips back and forth along the tunnel became routine, and our heads ducked automatically at the right places almost without fail. Getting ready to dive took no time really, my equipment was prepared days before along with the filling of the tanks. Memory-enhancing trimix would be used today with 12% oxygen and 45% helium, the balance nitrogen. Down I went. As this was the third dive in here, I could descend quite quickly, as I knew where and when all the obstructions would appear. In three minutes, I arrived at 120 metres depth. The water visibility was now clear and my torch beam picked out every detail in the pile of wood and rocks below. Lifting the bigger lumps of wood and stacking them to one side allowed all the rocks and silt to fall away. In a few seconds I would be working in complete darkness, as the silt mixed with the water. The silt would settle down again with time if I waited. But not in my lifetime, which was fixed today by the amount of gas I carried on my back. In the darkness, I could feel that the hole in the obstruction was almost big enough to pass through. I couldn't see the elapsed time on my gauges but it was probably near ten minutes by now.

Lifting the deco tanks clipped to my side out of the way, I slipped underneath this temporary floor. The water underneath was thick with silt, so I moved deeper as quickly as possible. Getting to 130 metres, I could now see clearly downwards. There were no further obstructions as far as my torch beam penetrated. I got a chemical light stick from my pocket. The pressure of the water had crushed the small glass ampoule inside and had activated the chemical process already. An eerie green glow filled the shaft for a few metres. I had brought along high intensity glow sticks that only lasted thirty minutes. I dropped the light below me. Slowly, the bright green stick descended down the old engine shaft, illuminating its path. A minute later it had gone out, or was obscured by the gradual banana curve of the tunnel. Now I knew that the path was clear and I could attempt a deeper dive. I looked around for cross-tunnels to explore at this depth, but in the poor visibility the dark walls revealed no openings anywhere. Time really flies when your breaths are carried in tanks on your back. My twenty minutes were up, and therefore time to head home. I was quite still warm, and had yet to use my suit heater system. I didn't really want to test it early on in the dive in case the batteries died earlier than expected. It could turn out to be a lifesaver later as my suit could leak at any time, especially with all the old nails sticking from the walls at various depths. I performed all the decompression stops as required, and exited the water on time without too much drama. I stayed in the water for a few minutes to take off my equipment.

Caroline pulled my tanks from the water and we chatted about what I had seen below. As I was climbing out of the water, pain started to fill both my arms. I asked Caroline to pass me the cylinders containing 50% oxygen and 100% oxygen. I dropped down to 21 metres breathing the nitrox 50. Getting to depth eased the pain considerably. Obviously the decompression time was not long enough, and the subsequent excess gases in my body gave me decompression illness. For the bends to come this quickly, the stops were far too short. I re-descended to twenty metres and spent an hour slowly ascending to 6 metres, then another hour there breathing 100% oxygen. The software I used this time was free and from the internet, and I suspect I got what I had paid for. Getting out after two more hours decompressing properly did the trick. I was pain free now, but you can never really tell how long it will last. Feeling a little fatigued by the whole experience, we left the equipment in the back of the cave for the night. I thought that any self-respecting glue sniffer would have better plans for Saturday night than hanging out in a mine shaft. I just wanted to get out of the mine, throw off my drysuit, get some food, then sleep. After a few pints of Bluebird Raspberry Ale, I felt myself again. The bends did not reappear, so I felt like a deeper dive next Saturday could become a reality. The suit heater had worked, but even without it I felt fine for over four hours in the chilling water. With a short bottom time, maybe just a couple of minutes, I could complete a dive to 237 metres in under four hours - hopefully without getting the bends.

Such a deep dive would need multiple support divers. There would be more gas mixtures involved, all breathed at different depths. Changing of breathing mixtures on ascent are mandatory during deep trimix dives using standard scuba equipment. The gas used at the deepest depth cannot be breathed too shallowly, for fear of oxygen starvation or hypoxia. Similarly, at the deepest point a diver will breathe a mixture containing a large proportion of helium, and this gas will be very inefficient to decompress from if breathed continuously to the surface. To ascend safely, a diver should increase oxygen to the same extent as decreasing the helium content. Eventually, many divers would end up breathing a mixture containing no helium or nitrogen at all. Adjusting mixes in this way makes for a more efficient decompression. It gets complicated because a diver cannot carry dozens of different tanks safely, so compromises must be made. Generally, a maximum of five large scuba tanks can be worn without overburdening the diver. Any additional tanks used at shallower depths are bought by support divers when needed. Because this dive site is only six feet across it crossed my mind to simply hang the tanks from ropes at the appropriate depth. Rebreather equipment is another form of scuba equipment that solves the ever-changing gas mixture problem. Some units can electronically adjust the breathing gas and supply a gas ideally suited to the depth and decompression obligations. Solving this one problem is unfortunately not enough. A rebreather has its own specific limitations when used at extreme depth. Maybe in the future a rebreather unit will be designed with deep divers in mind, giving increased depth capability combined with suitable redundancy. Such a unit is still not currently available, so I needed to find some vertically-challenged support divers willing to carry heavy tanks through the low tunnels.

I phoned a few buddies and finally got through to Brian, the tech diver who operated a commercial diving company in Liverpool. We met during the Carpathia wreck trip and he was proved invaluable to the project, even though we didn't even dive. On the phone he said he would be happy to help and could organise some of his pals to join the party as both support divers and tunnel rats.

I had a week to organise everything for this deep dive. I wanted a descent line for this dive, clearly marked with the depth at one metre intervals. Electronic depth gauges used by scuba divers would not function at my planned depth and would most likely fail or lock out far shallower. I also needed to get more flasks for coffee, as there would be five divers in this project. Surface lighting had been a problem in the past two weeks, so some lanterns that would last five or six hours in freezing damp conditions were sought. The bill for the alkaline torch batteries came to over £150, with three dive lights for everyone plus some spares. I bought a pile of sweets and cakes for the group and litres of different liquids to drink. I contacted a company in Scotland called ITDA, about getting some cheap helium and oxygen for my dive tanks. The gas bill for this deep dive was so high that a drive of five hundred miles to Fort William was justified by their cheap gas prices. They were a commercial and technical diver training provider, with massive supplies of Helium. I left for Scotland on the Thursday, when I got up there after a ten hour drive they kindly filled all the tanks for free, plus lent me lots of spares. The trip was very worthwhile, Simon, who ran the technical operation, cheerfully filled my tanks late into the evening during very bleak conditions outside. The horizontal rain and howling winds were apparently typical of the summer weather experienced in this part of the world.

I drove back to the Lake District on the Friday morning and picked up Caroline from the train station. We decided to put most of the equipment inside the mine that night so the following day, would be more relaxed. We had only seen blue skies and sunshine over the Coniston hills so far. When we arrived at the shaft entrance that afternoon we were faced with biblical winds and torrential rain. Even the cloud level had descended to meet us, and this obscured the little stream that normally trickled past the doorway into the hillside. The little stream was now an angry swollen river complete with treacherous rapids. This was the first time that the weather inside the mine was better than outside. We put on our drysuit's and buckled down for a strenuous evening. All the tanks were put on luggage trolleys, but it was still more than four hours of heavy work before the bulk of the tanks and kit were safely dragged through the Horse level tunnel. Caroline worked like a trooper. It was a shame we couldn't go drinking tonight, as it was definitely justified by all the hard work. I don't like to get up early, so we arranged kick off for 10.00 the following morning. Brian came knocking on my door before 8 am, and it was like waking a vampire with a garlic breakfast. I sprang into action like an octogenarian full of sleeping pills. I needed a heap of fried animal parts sprinkled with beans and mushrooms, plus a litre of coffee, to bring the room into focus.

Brian's pals had phoned in sick after a night on the tiles. To top it off, some one had popped the window on his Land Rover during the night and run off with his diving equipment. I had so much spare kit that this was no problem, even my spare drysuit fitted him, although somewhat snugly. I always dive with a spare suit ready if the water is cold. Having lots of deco stops to complete cannot wait even if your suit floods, decompression is similar to Time and Tides in that respect, waiting for no man. At home, I practiced cutting a wetsuit off myself and putting on another fresh one. Drysuits are easier to take on and off, but success can only be assured if all bases are covered. The cold water here could be brutal if it touched my skin, hours of decompression could not be accomplished safely. Diving in cold water over the years has given me a good insight into the pitfalls, and they are very real. Drysuit wrist seals do fail, suit material can get punctured. I vividly remember when my chest valve simply fell from the suit whilst six hundred feet down in the English channel a few years before.

Loading the cave the night before was a good idea, all that remained today was to set the descent lines and go over some *what if's*. Brian would act as deep support diver, coming down to the seventy metre restriction. Caroline agreed to do the long stint in the shallows. Because we were down a couple of helpers, I rigged up the spare tanks on long ropes and lowered them down to the appropriate depths. I used an RGBM deco schedule to calculate the deeper stops of my ascent plan. I had no faith in the short stops it predicted for the shallower phase of the decompression, after getting my fingers burnt in the past. All the stops from 18 metres and upwards were lengthened to reflect a more reliable schedule. We all got ready for action when the plan was clear. Sitting on the edge of the shaft, I went through all of my equipment to check it was working and accessible. During the checks, one of my back-up lights fell into the black water and was lost. I grabbed another one from the spares box and then slipped into the water. With a wave to Caroline and Brian, I was gone. I didn't have to wear much extra lead weight to sink down, it was fresh water and I was wearing five heavy steel tanks. I took some weights anyway, in case I needed them in few hours time when the tanks became lighter as they emptied. Divers don't realise that the gas in the tanks can have significant weight. In my set-up today, the various gas mixtures weighed over ten kilos when the tanks were full. When the cylinders approach empty, it's easy to float to the surface unintentionally, especially in shallower water. The additional small lead blocks I might need later were placed in the small cross tunnel at 30 metres.

As I dropped deeper, I checked that all the extra deco cylinders that were hanging on lines were at the correct depth. Each tank was on its own line. Placing all my deco eggs in separate baskets ensured that they would still likely be there when I needed them. As everything in the mine was so rusty or rotted, each rope was tied somewhere differently. If I travelled quickly down the deep shaft, I would be rewarded with clear visibility all the way down. I had two primary lights and several back-ups, plus six chemical light sticks. During the descent, I paused to signal to the surface crew that all was okay by pulling the descent line twice at various depths. If I got stuck I would pull the line quickly a pre-arranged number of times, to indicate the depth. I asked Brian and Caroline not to attempt a rescue below the 70 metre restriction.

Passing the 120 metre restriction went smoothly, soon I was seeing virgin scenery. My most expensive primary dive light became the second torch casualty when it flooded abysmally at 130 metres. I switched the soggy HID dive light for a shiny blue new one from Finland. My newest light had a halogen bulb, which was not as fashionable as the HID variant for technical divers but was always reliable. Additionally, the older technology cost less than half of the HID hybrid and still cut a welcome swathe into the darkness like a light-sabre, whereas the HID light with its wet long-life battery pack was as useful as a cactus enema. Seven minutes into the descent I arrived at 150 metres. The next big restriction came into view now, it was a solid staging platform covered over with debris. I carefully started to remove the timbers and pile them up on one side so I could get past. As previously, all my efforts in moving the old wooden floorboards ended in zero visibility. I moved enough of the bigger lumps of wood out of the way that I could drop underneath. I only managed to descend ten more metres before another pile of timbers stopped my progress.

Like before, I worked carefully to remove them, the visibility was bad, with the results of my work just two minutes ago still pouring down all around. These flooring areas had been submerged in rainwater for close on two hundred years. The deeper ones had less rocks and silt on top of them, letting the water do its worst. The areas covered with debris seemed much stronger than those without. I changed tack here, to just concentrate on moving enough bigger timbers so that I could slip through. Piling all the timbers to one side, like I had been doing before, caused so much disturbance and bad visibility for below, that it seemed pointless. Dropping through my smaller access hole, I could see the results. Something immediately struck me as strange, the water was clearly illuminated below me. I had no idea what this could be, but was shallow enough at 160 metres for the helium in my breathing mix to allow full optimism. I switched my primary light off to allow my eyes to fully adjust to this highly unusual glow. I felt very uneasy now, there were small balls of green phosphorescence in the water all around me. The green bubbles seemed to be floating upwards. I figured that whatever nastiness this was, I was totally immerged in it, and it was probably bad. Reaching out I pressed a green ball between my fingers, my fingers where stained the same colour now. I was stumped and anxious. It was time to evaluate the dive and check equipment. Checking my head-mounted back-up lights, I noted the pair were, in fact flooded and useless. I checked my larger back-up torches and was very relieved when they both looked functional. My tank pressure was at three quarters full. The video camera was still turned on and the video lights fired up when I flicked the switches. I looked more closely at the camera housing. I had duct-taped chemical lights to the body to illuminate the controls that were in shadow from the camera lights. The plastic bodies of the glow sticks were distorted and split, I pulled one free and inspected it closely. The green chemical that filled them was leaking out. This explained the mysterious green balls in the water around me. That was one less thing to distract me, but the next thing was the yellow glow from below. I did not suspect alien life was hiding underneath the Lake District, but a government toxic waste dump from the paranoid 1950's seemed quite plausible.

The water clarity here was good. I fired up the video camera and headed down to make posthumous history. Approaching slowly, the camera lights picked out the source of the mystery glow. The mini dive light that was dropped before I entered the water had managed to slip past the different restrictions and was sitting safely on a ledge in front of me now -incredible. I picked it up and stowed it in my suit pocket. The ledge seemed to be some kind of window. I shone my light into the hole, to see it was an access-way to a work area. The water took on a sepia tinge but was otherwise clear. I noticed some shovels and other tools just leaning against a wall. The whole scene looked like work for the day had just finished. The digging tools looked strong, but if I grabbed them would likely crumble to nothing like all the other wooden objects I had encountered here so far. I had deco stops to perform at this depth during the return journey. I would take a moment to do some sightseeing then.

Back on track but a few minutes behind, I pressed on. Physically I felt quite normal, but noticed a dull ache in my spine area. Sometimes, helium breathing divers get all sorts of strange aches and pains when descending, so I wasn't overly concerned yet. In the deeper parts of the mine the rock must have yielded more ore, hence the wooden floors were now coming far more often than in the shallower areas. The next one was just 7 metres lower than the last at 168 metres. This staging consisted of the two solid diagonal timbers which each bisected the shaft. Thicker timbers lay loosely on top. I moved these by pushing them to one side. Dropping through the gap I'd made caused my back mounted twin tanks to get wedged on something. I tried to pull back up but my side mounted cylinders were now below the level and I was stuck. Visibility was almost zero, and fading fast. I shut my eyes to relax. Alarm bells started ringing in the back of my mind, as I was pretty much trapped. It was time to leave for the surface at twelve minutes descent time, but all of the restrictions had slowed the descent and I had not gotten close to the planned maximum depth. I could afford another seven minutes at this depth to catch up with the dives original time-plan. Any longer than this would make my decompression stops scheduled for later insufficient.

I tried to free myself upwards, but could manage nothing. The minutes were passing, but I had made no progress to free myself. Concern flickered across my mind, I looked at my back gas contents gauge. The visibility was so bad I had to hold the gauge up against the glass of my mask just to see it. The gauge needle indicated 100 bars of pressure. Struggling would increase my breathing rate, making me run out of gas later on. I slumped down against the wooden platform to relax. My back was aching even more now so I lifted my legs up in an effort to stretch my lower spine. This action caused my back tanks to spring free but only going downwards. I had to bite the bullet and drop below the restriction. The depth now was 170 metres and seventeen minutes into the dive. I checked the pressure in my tanks, only 70 bars remained. The second stages of my breathing regulators were bubbling now, adding insult to injury. The situation was dire. No situation is insurmountable, but I was in an avalanche of disaster right now. 'Focus...Prevail' I remembered telling other deep divers, lets see if it worked for me today I turned off all the tanks except the one I was breathing from. Looking up at the underneath of the floor, I started searching for a way through. I moved across the shaft, put my hand up and started to fin up. Some loose timbers lifted, but the effort from my legs was exhausting. Inflating my buoyancy jacket would add some much-needed lift. I could not afford to waste valuable breathing gas this way, but didn't have the time to consider an alternative. I inflated my jacket fully until the overpressure valve started burping. With a combined effort of positive buoyancy and finning hard, I was through. The plan called for a first deep decompression stop at 147 metres depth after an elapsed time of 21 minutes. I got there almost on time and started the thirty second stop. My mind started to slow down. My trimix breathing mixture at this depth made me feel like I was at the equivalent of a fifteen metre air dive and this helped enormously. My remaining tank pressure was very low but these back tanks were huge, with a combined capacity of forty litres.

The next stops trickled along, but by 130 metres my back gas tanks reached twenty bars pressure - this was too close to the surrounding water pressure and they refused to supply more gas for now. I turned on my left deco tank of Trimix 14/33, but was rewarded with a violent free-flow from the regulator. The rush of bubbles didn't abate my urge to breathe, so I had put the regulator in my mouth and breathe anyway. Taking a quick but wasteful breath I turned the tank off and put my thinking cap on. This tank was to be used at 90 metres and shallower, but without alternatives I had to use it even though I was currently 40 metres too deep. Onwards and upwards. With all the excitement and poor visibility I forgot about the next restriction near 120 metres. It wasn't much of a restriction taken on the correct side, but I ascended into the wrong side and was wedged in to the cross-timber. On this new trimix, my equivalent narcosis value was like 60 metre air dive. I had a stop here for a minute and used the time to signal to the surface I was trapped, with twelve pulls of the rope, I don't know why I sent this signal really. I got a response asking if I was OK. I wasn't, and definitely needed support diver Brian to descend earlier than planned, bringing the spare gas. There was no rope signal for this, so it didn't happen. Improvised rope signals are generally a bad idea anyway - if misunderstood, things can get far more bent out of shape. Experiencing problems at extreme depth are bad enough, but the outcome is the same as running out of air and trapped in just one metre of water. I personally find shallow water problems more frustrating than deep, as the feeling of stupidity gets higher inversely with reducing depth. Dumping the gas volume from my wing and suit, I started to sink back down with less struggling. I got free, sidestepped the obstacle and began the ascent once more. With the free-flowing breathing regulator still going mad each time I turned the tank on, it didn't last as long as it should. By 100 metres, the tank stopped breathing completely. I closed it and switched to the next deco tank of trimix 20/30. Every few breaths, I would swap to my remaining back gas to average out the high excesses of oxygen. All the deeper stops lasting longer than 30 seconds were reduced to 30 seconds maximum. I did this in an effort to reduce gas consumption, and thought that many were now unnecessary because I did not reach the planned maximum depth anyway.

By the time I reached 70 metres I was ahead of schedule by almost 10 minutes, Brian wouldn't be coming for a while. It left me breathing whatever was left during the stops. At the remains of the restriction at 70 metres, I settled on top of the woodwork. I dumped all the gas from my buoyancy wing and replaced it with exhaled trimix 20/30, this might be useful...soon. Staying relaxed in difficult situations is important, but so is knowing how to fix them. All my tanks were now almost empty, and Brian was still some minutes from even entering the water. I considered swimming shallower than my decompression ceiling allowed, getting the spare breathing tank hanging at forty metres, and re-descending. But there was still gas to breathe in my back tanks. I weighed up the dangers for both scenarios. Breathing the back-gas might complicate the decompression, but ascending past the virtual ceiling of my stops looked the dicier of the two. I opted with staying on the stop schedule and breathing the high helium breathing mixture behind me. I intercepted Brian somewhere deeper than 50 metres. He carried with him the tank I needed to complete the stops ranging from 70 metres to 40 metres. Taking this cylinder of weak trimix completely in the dark was the next concern. With two of us in the water and side by side, the silt was a thick as a swarm of bees...and just as dangerous. I recognised the correct breathing regulator by feel alone - to breathe a gas containing the high-oxygen mixes used in the shallows could be disastrous. Mistakes with oxygen are the most unforgiving, and in these conditions would go un-witnessed. We ascended together until Brian had to leave and carry out his own decompression plan. Caroline would be in the water soon, meeting me at forty metres and bringing something warm to drink. Although the cold was still not knocking at my door, some prevention now would be most welcome. With sufficient gas to breathe I was coasting smoothly through the stops now. The shaft here was featureless, and I was disappointed that I did not record any video of the work area and antique equipment on the way back up as I had planned to do while descending.

From 42 metres, I could see Caroline had arrived a little early. I beckoned for her to drop the flask of coffee down to me. The plastic flask was as light as a feather when underwater and took seemingly ages to float down towards me. The drinks trip down through the cold water had sucked most of the heat from the beverage, but it was still lukewarm. I gulped down almost a pint of coffee in no-time. I hoped my pee valve system was properly attached as the first test for this dive was coming soon. As the copper mine was filled with fresh water I thought it would be okay to eat chocolate bars of a softer nature than my usual rock-hard seawater favourites. Energy bars soaked with rainwater should not taste much different to their surface cousins but, disappointingly, the heavy silt and constant trickle of grit made the whole dining experience quite unpleasant on my teeth. Changing some tanks with Caroline, I carried on decompressing quite normally. Arriving at 21 metres though, I wondered if I was feeling subtle signs of decompression sickness. Sometimes you can't put your finger on any specific symptoms, but still something is not quite right. I switched tanks again to a twenty litre tank of nitrox with 50% oxygen. With all the antics and switching from mix to mix far below, it was time to add some conservatism to the dive plan. Although the software predicted just 6 minutes to pause at 21 metres, I increased this to 50 minutes. The mixtures I breathe are most efficient when breathed at the maximum depth permitted for them. If a diver ascends shallower than the maximum-permitted depth, the mixture becomes less effective at flushing the excesses of nitrogen and helium gases from your body. There are, of course, other insidious hazards associated with spending long periods at the maximum depths permitted for high oxygen concentrations, but I needed to prioritize here. The extra forty-five minutes spent at this depth were beneficial and all the unusual feelings went after the first twenty. I was surprised by how warm I still felt, Brian and Caroline seemed to be shivering even by the time they reached me. Even my hands still had life in them despite wearing wetsuit gloves in the 8'c water.

From here, I had still almost three hours of stops to complete. I turned my dive lights out for most of it...time seems to fly faster in the dark - only seeing flashes of light through the poor visibility can be very distracting also. Caroline continued to bring down hot drinks, and thankfully my pee-valve continued to work like it should. I noticed that as the decompression stops got closer to the surface, the temperature of the coffee got hotter and hotter. By six metres from the surface, it was almost too hot to drink. I had ordered some special super-long regulator hoses to allow the tanks of 100% oxygen to stay at the surface while I breathed from them from as deep as 9 metres down. The post man ensured they did not arrive until a week after the dive, so large cylinders of oxygen had to be lowered into the mine shaft from ropes. Spending long periods breathing 100% oxygen or other rich nitrox mixtures can take its toll on the lungs. This condition is called Pulmonary Oxygen toxicity - whilst it's not life threatening, it can affect the overall efficiency of your decompression stops. A colleague advised that a new technique had emerged, where you breathed your trimix back gas for five minutes after breathing the oxygen for twenty minutes, in order to minimise the condition. I read stories on the internet of divers doing this back switching technique and, as usual, they swore by its effectiveness. I learned that the internet is very effective at getting other divers to test all manner of bar-room theories from the safety of ones armchair. All you needed to do was recommend a new theory from personal experience. The more outrageous the theory was, the better, really. All explanations are best hidden in jargon or mysteriously justified with code words like 'George said' or even better, 'those KPP boys do it' (both subtle references to apparently experienced cave divers). By the following weekend, the tone of your mailbox would indicate the outcome of all the people stupid enough to follow your advice. My buddy said this worked for him, so at 6 metres I tried switching from 100% oxygen to 5%. His web theory hinged around the body having a reserve of oxygen that would easily last the five minutes of virtual starvation from breathing the hypoxic mix. I would feel the benefits almost immediately, he was right. Within thirty seconds of sucking the dregs out of my trimix back gas, my vision collapsed and immediate unconsciousness loomed. I hooked my arm around some spare tanks just in time to stop my one-way trip back down the abyss.

I kept my 100% regulator in my mouth throughout the rest of the decompression. To counteract the oxygen toxicity I simply moved the rest of the stops a metre shallower, this effectively lowers the dose also. I was saved from further drama for the remaining decompression stops. My surfacing was more of a relief for Brian and Caroline than myself. I quickly explained my adventure, both sights and pitfalls. Brian said he was ready to carry me from the mine if I felt unwell, but I felt quite normal, not withstanding the bends possibly coming post-dive. I inflated my drysuit to float horizontally on the surface and relax. Caroline jumped into the water to unclip my equipment and handed it up piece by piece to Brian. I stayed in the water breathing oxygen for some time. If decompression illness symptoms presented themselves, I was to grab some tanks and treat myself in the water like I had done here previously. Time is of the essence when treating the bends. In-water recompression is effective treatment, but needs careful thought and practice to avoid a possible worsening of the symptoms. Although I did not get to 240 metres today, I did see the work-face of the mine - sadly the images on the video were too silty to produce prints from. Despite all the dramas and entrapments, I would actually like to return to Coniston Copper Mine to explore and take video of this historic monument. We didn't remove any equipment from the mine that afternoon, exhaustion took its toll on all concerned. After a slow stroll out of the tunnel still breathing 100% oxygen, it was again time for a shower and an evening in the pub. Jeff, the curator from the Copper mine museum, was amazed when I gave him an account of the dive. He was even happier when I donated to the museum a copper ingot I had recovered from the Copper Wreck, sunk by the German submarine UC18 some ninety years earlier.

Chapter 10: The Deepest Dive – An Ocean of Problems

After the dive into Coniston Copper Mine, I was ready for phase two of my deep dive plans. This would take me to 260m, some two weeks before attempting the scuba depth record. The venue was not yet decided, but I had thought of either Puerto Galera, in the Philippines, or the Cayman Islands. Late November 2002, a phone call from Phuket, the resort island off of Thailand, possibly confirmed the dive site. The telephone call was from a dive centre looking to get into the technical diving market. I spoke with the shops General Manager - Hilde, she had been recommended by a training agency to contact me as a candidate for setting up their tech dive programme. We exchanged phone calls and e-mails for a couple of weeks, before I booked a flight to Bangkok and started work on the 1st of December. Before I agreed to work in Phuket, I did some homework on the area to make sure that there was water deep enough to fulfil my plans. Phuket sits in the Andaman Sea, which has several kilometres of water depth. The rest of Thailand's popular dive sites are in the Thai Gulf, which has an average depth of just one hundred feet.

Phuket is probably the epicentre of the Thai tourism industry, and as such has all the trimmings and extremes that South East Asia has to offer. The first night I arrived in Patong – Phukets' busiest nightlife hub, I had stupidly taken the advice of my taxi driver. He took me to an area known as Paradise Villas. I was tired and didn't notice the warning signs when I checked into my Hotel. At about midnight, the noise coming from the street was unbearable, many Thai men were screaming...although it may have been singing. My previous journeys to Bangkok and Pattaya had prepared me for Asian nightlife, but I had checked into a hotel above a cabaret show called Ka-Toys- R- Us. The war cry of lady boys screaming was ten times worse than fingernails being dragged down a blackboard.

I couldn't sleep due to the feral shouting in the street combined with my jet lag, so I dared to venture out into the affray outside. I moved quickly through the hordes of emaciated men clothed only in skin-tight neon coloured gym wear. Arms appeared from everywhere grabbing my arms and legs. "Where you go...sexy man Patong?" seemed to be a popular phrase. I remembered to never make eye contact for more than three seconds and walked quickly into the somewhat friendlier Hetero part of the town.

In Thailand, 'Hetero' is a subjective word, and strolling along the beach road after midnight trying to avoid men dressed in women's clothing is like navigating a minefield. I saw an Irish pub called Molly Malones, it looked upmarket which in this part of the world translates to: *No transvestites,* unless they were attractive even when the viewer is sober. A few Gin and Tonics later (Irish Tonic naturally) and a plate of sausages and mash, I was ready to attempt the treacherous journey home. I bought a Saddam face-mask from a vendor, and quickly put it on to improve my anonymity. The offers of sex-then-marriage rained down even with my mask on, but I declined all the generous offerings and stumbled along to the safety of my deluxe room, complete with foreign television programmes.

The next morning, I woke-up and headed straight to the dive centre, Hilde greeted me and we had breakfast in Starbucks while working out a plan of attack. I had bought all of the technical equipment the centre needed - over 90kg's of it, with me – unfortunately, the airline had lost two of the four bags. There were many things to prepare whilst waiting for the equipment to catch up with me, so the loss wasn't a train crash. The next three weeks would be fun-filled anyway, preparing all the scuba tanks and regulators, making them clean enough for the use of pure oxygen which can be extremely hazardous if it comes into contact with oily residues or other contamination.

Just before Christmas 2002, the equipment preparation was completed and training courses were being run for both customers and even staff. I looked at the tide tables for the area most days, and knew that an ideal Neap tide was forecast for 25 February 2003. This would be the day I wanted to make a dive to 260 metres. The technical training courses were proving popular and I dived most days with groups of customers, either on regular scuba equipment, or rebreather units. The repetitive nature of the tech-dive classes had me diving twice between sixty and ninety metres almost everyday, but seldom deeper. Although the depths were not quite as deep as I would have liked for practice purposes, the repetition meant that I was staying dive-fit and I felt totally match ready.

When you have a goal, time seems to fly. Three days before the dive, myself and three or four others started to fill the scuba tanks with all the various Trimix and Nitrox breathing mixtures for me and all the support team. There were many support divers and it was important that they breathed gas mixtures that I would be breathing. We would fill the tanks with oxygen, helium and air until midnight, and then wait for the constituent parts to homogenise overnight. After breakfast, we would use gas analysers to verify the mixtures - if they were incorrect, it could mean draining the cylinder and starting again, although, depending on the error, the corrections could be made at full pressure. I felt very confident and relaxed about the whole build for this deep dive. The previous adventure in the Copper Mine had more sharp turns and excitement than any previously and I had managed them all without drama and surfaced totally in one piece. These experiences are invaluable for the success of future projects. The upcoming dive would be my deepest plunge to-date, but my previous deep dives had seen up to twenty minutes spent at depths between 170 and 180 metres, these long bottom times dwarfed the two minutes planned for the 260 metre one. The dive team and I met many times to discuss the dive-plan in minute-by-minute detail. During these gatherings typically dozens of 'What-ifs' were thrown at me. We went over as many solutions as possible to best fix any problems should they arise. I preferred it if as-many-as-possible team members were part of the discussions, so that the filtering-down of misinformation was avoided.

The company had let me use the day boat for the deep dive, this was great because it meant we could load and prepare the boat the day before, and also this boat had its own compressors and a large scuba tank selection that might come in handy if shit and fans were to meet. The other instructors I worked with were happy to help and donated their time to the project, thankfully both during the build-up weeks and during the dive itself.

The dive site I chose was about 35 miles west of Phuket, the dive boat travelled at 8 knots, and I had calculated that the ideal time to make the descent was 11.30am. None of these figures were conducive to a good nights sleep though. The 5.30am meeting time meant I needed to get to sleep the night before by 8pm if I was going to receive my normal sleep quota. By 3.00 am I was still wide awake, with thoughts both good and bad sniping at each other. Hilde was fast asleep next to me, and at 4.45am the alarm clock would go off. I even tried to talk to myself about myself, I was sure that this would end in immediate unconsciousness, but even this tried and tested method failed to draw the sleep curtains. I managed a few hours sleep that night though, my eventual recipe for success was to try and memorize my dive plan with its dozens of decompression stops.

Waking up with such a big day ahead had me firing on most cylinders in less than an hour. I forced a healthy breakfast of bananas into my mouth, washed down with a mug of coffee. The coffee was the first of many before a bacon and sausage, egg roll. I think the caffeine pre-heats my boilers before the junk food fuels the fire. After a shower, it was time to face the day, but even still half asleep I still felt crucially optimistic. All the support team phoned my mobile in the morning to check-in. We met at the dive boat called Scubafun, which was moored at Chalong Pier some thirty minutes drive away. The trip out to the dive-site would take over 4 hours, so plenty of time for going over the days' plans, after a short snooze. Virtually everybody had a nap, even the boat captain must have grabbed forty winks when I noticed how off course we had got when I woke up.

With an hour's journey still to go, the dive team and surface coordinators met on the upper deck to fine-tune the dive plan. We discussed at length the procedures for dealing with me should I get affected by decompression sickness triggered by counter-diffusing gases. This particular flavour of the bends concerned me the most as it rendered the sufferer helpless with extreme vertigo and vomiting. Without a big support team the condition would within minutes lead to disorientation and drowning. It was ailment that had affected many commercial deep divers in the past and more recently some extreme scuba divers. Counter-Diffusion has been likened to abominable snowmen sightings by the usual crowd of *internet* experts, a bit like the way lack-of-education fuels religious extremism. The most recent case was John Bennetts' scuba depth record attempt the year before. His dive team held him to the anchor line for over eight hours as he suffered vertigo and nausea. The dive plan I had decided on for today contained legions of deep-stops that would help me avoid *fast tissue* bends like inner-ear decompression sickness, the type typically associated with counter-diffusing gases. My dive plan used the RGBM algorithm for planning the ascent. I knew that this software program gave far too short decompression times during the shallow phase of the dive considering the plethora of deeper stops, but on this plan I had deliberately lengthened the last portion of the decompression stops to avoid *slow tissue* bends, the type that typically give debilitating pain and cause long-term bone damage.

I had used the RGBM decompression program possibly more often than any diver and definitely much deeper, each time making it more and more conservative and therefore minimising pain at the end of the dive. I added almost ninety minutes of decompression stops in the shallow areas (21 metres and up), which made the dive more than fifty percent longer than the computer program suggested. I had liaised many times with the software providers, and my dive plan was a sculpted work that was going to be the defining moment for the algorithm...well, except that I had made it much more conservative than the *virtual-experts* insisted.

Language barriers are often insurmountable, and Thailand gives many examples of this. We had organised a rescue speedboat that would meet with us and bring a team of medics to the position of the dive. I gave the rescue boat's captain the GPS position of the dive site, and should have sensed a problem when he still asked where the position was. I told him west of Phuket, about 30 miles. I think the word *west* rhymes with *south* in the Thai language. Luckily mobile phone signal coverage was sufficient occasionally so that we could shout at each other and confirm where they should meet us if they still wanted payment. Anyone who has travelled by boat in Asia will remember how the marine VHF system is used as a means to broadcast dance music amongst fishermen. Any mariners needing to raise the alarm in Thailand would have to make do with listening to the Thai top ten pop songs played over and over, while their boat sank or burned.

I had a snooze for an hour, to ensure my brain voltage would be kept at optimum for later. On waking, I quaffed a few bananas and had some coffee. The rescue speedboat had appeared on the horizon, so things were falling into place. I asked the captain how much time was left before we arrived at the dive site, "30 minutes" he said.

The dive team were busy organising their personal equipment and looked ready for business. As we neared the area, the sea was flat except for some unusual white topped waves that seem to rise and fall for a few hundred yards. We crossed this rough area and headed further out to sea to avoid these bumps caused by the moving tide hitting the ocean's road-works here. The seabed dropped fairly steeply from 300 feet to 1500 feet in less than a mile. The tidal movement was running west to east currently (free pun), so I thought the mini tidal waves we were seeing were caused by the water reflecting off the bottom and being forced abruptly shallower by the nearby wall. The tide would change soon and the conditions should flatten out.

I had decided to wear a wetsuit on this dive, this was unusual because the sea temperature in deep water here was between 4 and 6 degrees Centigrade. My time at depths below six hundred feet would be short today, and the water temperature would be positively tropical from one hundred fifty feet and up, where most of my decompression time would be spent. I sold myself on the romantic notion that I would jumping into an ice-bath before spending the afternoon in a sauna. The moment for action was getting near so I finished getting ready. It took just 20 minutes to go from my swimming shorts to wearing my wetsuit, booties, hood, buoyancy wing, with four large scuba tanks attached. The heat under the midday sun was unbearable in my 7mm thick wetsuit, so one of the dive team would pour buckets of seawater over me so I would not overheat.

A rope would be used to control the descent into the depths, the rope would be marked every metre with gaffer tape that indicated the depth. I would, as always, wear half a dozen digital depth gauges, but on extreme dives, electronic devices are as reliable as British train timetables. The depth under the boat was over one thousand feet deep and my decent rope was just over 900 feet of Thai *quality* mooring line. I felt it was time to go, so the guys threw the anchor weight and line into the azure blue. As I shuffled down the boat towards the dive platform wearing over one hundred kilograms of equipment, many of the support team started taking photos and video, which would be highly entertaining and more sought-after if my underwater extravaganza became a one-way event. I stood at the back of the boat staring at the rope as it snaked its way down into the abyss. Support divers were talking loudly and jumping into the water, together with the photographers. Hilde, my girlfriend would join me for the first 50 metres down, as I had nothing in the tanks I wore that could be breathed shallower than 90 metres. She would give me a spare hose from her scuba tank, then I would descend very quickly breathing from one of my own tanks. Bruce K would be my first support diver once I returned from the depths. Bruce would wait at 300 feet from 5 minutes before, until 10 minutes after my planned arrival time, bringing with him spare breathing gases that I would need until the next diver appeared at a shallower depth. It is very difficult finding reliable support divers for the deeper depths, most candidates would rather use my descent line to set personal depth records and then have costly accidents, but I like to leave all that action for me!

I jump into the water with a full buoyancy wing, I bob back to the surface in a few seconds and start swimming the short distance to the descent line. I lie on the surface facing the sun, and relax. Two photographers have to swim for ages, as they jumped into the water far from the down line during the excitement. I turn over and look into the blue, the visibility is perfect, like a Mexican cave. My subconscious body clock is saying that its time to leave now. I look over at Hilde and wink, she looks pale and anxious. I say something glib to defrost the scene, but it achieves nothing. I grab the long breathing hose from her that I will use as a slingshot into the depths. Deflating my buoyancy wing, I pre-pop my ears as I hear photographers shouting to stop or something. I ignore everything that's not important. I pull Hilde below the surface with me, and off we go.

Gripping the down line between my legs, I reach around my equipment to make sure that everything is in place and working like it should. My eyes are closed now, but I sense camera flashes close to my face so the photographers must have fixed their earlier concerns. Feeling like my world is slowing down, I signal to Hilde with a thumbs down to get this ball rolling. Unknown territory is about 10 minutes away, so there isn't really anything to worry about now. Scuba diving below 200 metres must be similar to mountain climbing above 8,000 metres without supplemental oxygen. In this dead zone the body is running on empty, only experience and a sprinkling of luck will get you through.

Modern Climbing has evolved exponentially faster than scuba diving. Climbs to the summit of Everest are being regularly undertaken by groups of weekend thrill-seekers in the summer months, but Everest climbs in poorer weather need the same level of commitment as a scuba dive to just six hundred feet below the waves. Only the most technical of climbs in the most arduous conditions can equal dives below eight hundred feet, but then I don't climb very often so I imagine I will receive hate mail from hard-core climbers rubbishing the above comments!

I like to descend very quickly when possible and only slow down when I have to, and the first one hundred and fifty feet came in less than a minute. Hilde joined me during this first furlong, I returned her breathing regulator and began using a gas mixture of ten percent oxygen and fifty percent helium for the next 300 feet of the descent. I gave Hilde a wave and a smile before carrying on down. The videographer Andre, from Russia, had followed us down so far, but had to turn back now also. The rest of the journey would be made alone.

I had made a plastic device to help slide down the line quickly and protect my hands from rope burns. I don't like to wear gloves on deep dives, as the pressure always shrinks their insulating abilities down anyway, and they can badly affect any tasks that need an immediate hands-on solution. By 500 hundred feet, the plastic shield had worn through. Up until this point the dive was pretty easy. The water temperature had cooled down to about 14 degrees but I was still warm. Natural light was still evident and I could clearly see my gauges without using my electric or chemical lights.

At about six minutes elapsed time, I had reached 600 feet depth. The sunlight had disappeared and it was as dark above me as it was below. Some kind of tidal stream seemed to be driving freezing water towards me as well as turning the visibility bad. Simply slipping down a line getting deeper and deeper and colder and colder sounds like madness, but the feeling of increasing depth and the gradual reduction of light are intoxicating. Approaching 700 feet, the freezing water was taking effect and I was now shivering uncontrollably. My hands were shaking as badly as the rest of my body and I assumed this was symptomatic of High pressure nervous syndrome complications caused by breathing lots of helium and descending rapidly. The seawater was taking on a brown and murky appearance and I remember travelling through what seemed like a jellyfish breeding-ground. Hundreds of brown saucers of jelly with 6inch tentacles slipped over my face and body. Fortunately they didn't seem to sting me, but I doubt if I would have felt anything at this point as the cold was becoming paralyzing in itself. The cold and the shaking were taking a toll and I didn't know how much more I could cope with, it seemed like some kind of underground stream was now building strength. The freezing water felt like it was being pumped directly into my suit.

The force of this torrent of water was building, and slowing my descent speed. I looked at my digital depth gauges - amazingly they had not flooded yet, and although the analogue gauge that told me of my gas supply had flooded with water, the indicating needle was still in place and it showed 60 bars. The two 20 litre tanks on my back were connected with a manifold system and this manifold was currently closed, so effectively, when I opened it, my tank pressure would increase to half full again. The breathing regulators were becoming very light to breathe from and I noticed that they were bubbling and losing gas. I made sure that every tank that I wasn't breathing from was turned off to make sure there were no catastrophic loses. Still dropping, I saw a tape marker on the line, it read 217 metres, I checked it against my wrist computer and was surprised to see a similar figure of 219 metres. My mind felt unusually clear. I had planned to feel like I was on a 45m dive with regard to narcosis levels on this dive, at the moment I felt a little deeper than this, but still felt like I was pretty lucid despite serious discomfort from the cold. Giving up with my plastic line guide, I started using my *Phantom* dive-light handle to glide down the line. Alarm bells started ringing when I noticed that the descent line was now angled about ninety degrees to my body. I was slipping downwards faster than I could swim forwards. The dive-light handle was hooked around the down line and I was holding it with both hands. If I lost my grip on the handle, the line would pull away from me and it would be lost into the icy black water. Losing the line at this depth would be similar to parachuting at night with a tangled chute and no reserve. Managing to reach the line with my right hand, which now felt like an icy stump, I started to slow down my drop speed. Apart from the cold, I felt in good shape as I saw the figures approaching 840 feet register on one of my dive computers.

The end of the line was in view now and I stopped just before it, careful not to let the line slip through my frosty fingers. It had taken twelve of the most unpleasant minutes of my life to get to the end of this rope, but now I was here it felt amazing. I added air to my buoyancy wing, and at the same time, swung on the line like a monkey on a vine. I wondered why divers before me could have felt so bad, as their accounts detailed feeling near unconscious at similar depths. This depth had been achieved just four times before, three divers receiving knock-down bends for their efforts, only one escaping Scot-free for a dive twenty feet shallower. The depth record for scuba divers was just 45m below me now, and I felt like that record would easily be mine in less than two weeks time, when I would re-enact today's stunt.

This was going all too easily, I even had the audacity to recall my favourite phrase, "A lifetime of pain for a moment of glory".

Had I got the saying the wrong way around? I knew I had, but I was feeling very smug at the moment. I started up to the surface to begin just 3 hours of decompression stops. Travelling up the line, however, I quickly started to feel like I would not make it, the previous elation had faded into a sleeping sensation, fuelled by the un-abating cold. I had treated the hypothermia effect with contempt and now it was robbing me of the fight I needed to climb the nylon beanstalk back to the surface. The first decompression stop was at 590 feet, with subsequent stops every ten to twenty feet. Once I got into the decompression stop range, my travels to the warmth of the surface would be slowed even more dangerously. My brain worked slowly, I had neither the energy to think or shiver. I did not want to abort the deeper portion of the deco stops, but wondered if I would make it even to see Bruce, the first support diver at 300 feet.

With every fifty feet closer to the surface came a few extra degrees of warmer water, but giving myself little false-hope parcels was little consolation as I felt my conscious levels dwindling to Neanderthal levels. I remembered the cold water test I had endured almost ten years before - it felt similar to now, but then I was only 6 feet from a surface covered in thin ice, and if I succumbed to the cold I would be rescued. Now was different, my body felt as if it had fought enough, and all I wanted was to stop and sleep. I felt no cold, just confusion and disappointment. I carried on - with every conscious breath, I would carry on following the ascent plan. The wetsuit was a huge mistake in these water temperatures, to compound matters the helium I was breathing was chilling me further with every breath. There was little to be done except get closer to the surface so that the support divers could help. Gradually the darkness turned into a blue twilight, somewhere between six hundred and five hundred feet. Travelling from eight hundred feet to three hundred feet where help would be waiting would take another thirty-two minutes, with most of it spent in freezing black water. The water temperature was less of a problem than the freezing gases I breathed - commercial divers would use a heating system to warm the breathing mixtures at these depths, unfortunately I had no such system, and each breath of sub-zero gas robbed me of more and more energy.

At roughly 400 feet I had a glimmer of hope, the visibility had been restored to very clear and I could just about see the dive boat above. I planned to send a marker buoy to the surface to say that I was still alive and everything was fine. Even with my frozen confusion I sent up the lift bag without problem, but I remembered too late that the plan called for me to send this balloon up only if I had come away from the descent line. The bag had gone to the surface at around the same time that Bruce should have started his descent to meet me. I stared upwards looking for his silhouette coming towards me, but all I saw was an empty line. The marker buoy I sent up was tied to a very thin line that would be difficult to follow, this would delay Bruce's descent further. The rendezvous plan for us agreed that we would meet at 50 minutes elapsed time.

The time I had on my wrist watch was 48 minutes and I could not see anybody coming yet. My dive plan called for a breathing gas change at 300 feet, Bruce would be bringing a spare tank of this gas with 14 percent oxygen and 33 percent helium. I had already started breathing this mixture, but because of the cold breathing gases and stress, my breathing rate was ridiculously elevated to near 60 litres per minute. Normal breathing rate for me was approx 12-15 litres per minute. The tank I was using would only last a couple of minutes at this rate. I still had my deep water breathing mixture in the big tanks behind me, but breathing this could compromise the decompression plan and the 80% helium content would make me dangerously cold once more. I tried in vain to curb my breathing rate and make this tank last a little longer. As the decompression stops had become shallower, the water temperature had increased to double figures. I noticed that I had started to shiver again properly, a good sign. I started to feel much more alert at around 300 feet. I was shivering so badly that it was hard to hold onto the descent line. If Bruce was not coming, I would be forced to breathe my back tanks while ascending much shallower, thus making the cylinders last longer. This seemed logical, as the alternative was drowning, but to ascend shallower breathing the wrong gas mixtures would mean guaranteed decompression sickness in deep water - rocks and hard places sprang to mind. I looked up again and was happy to see Bruce on the line, dropping quickly down the thin rope. I dropped my dive reel so the two lines would be brought together. Bruce noticed I was still on the main line and changed over to the thicker and more hand-friendly mooring rope that I was on. The dive was getting back on track.

I like suspense movies as much as anybody, but being given minutes to live every half an hour can get very tiring. Bruce arrived, asking if I was okay. I responded that I was very cold, to which he replied "me…too…". Bruce had decided to wear a 3mm shorty wetsuit for a 300 foot dive, not ideal! I grabbed the regulator from the spare tank he carried and breathed deeply. Tensions in my body were at meltdown just a few minutes before, but now I was just shivering madly with whole body shakes. Although I wasn't in a laughing mood yet, there was a sense of comedy in both of us shaking like wet dogs side by side on the line. Despite feeling as chilly as Captain Oates, the situation was looking far less gloomy now. We stayed together for about 15 minutes while moving up the line, until the next man would take Bruce's place. I tried to write on my slate some comments about my recent tango with depth, but the shakes in my body made my handwriting resemble a lie detector printout.

By two hundred and forty feet I had started to feel warmer and much more optimistic, even getting some semblance of breathing control as the helium levels dwindled in my gas mixtures. The next support diver was Mike, who arrived at two hundred feet or so. I was just cold now, as the water temp had climbed to 21 degrees Centigrade. I was still breathing a little fast and went through the decompression tanks of Trimix 20/35 like a greedy pig. From two hundred feet I was back to feeling myself. Another Mike, together with Glen, would bring me a change of equipment and still more fresh tanks at one hundred and fifty feet. I felt completely fine now and comfortable in my present buoyancy jacket, so I kept it on while simply clipping the extra tanks to me, things were going great.

I had just another ninety minutes of decompression remaining due to this radical decompression RGBM profile. This dive depth was achieved by Sheck Exley some 15 years previously, with the unfortunate result of minor decompression illness even after a whopping 15 hours deco stop time. I would achieve the same depth with a total dive time of one hundred and eighty minutes, and I wasn't bent yet…unbelievable!

The next support diver was Sveinung from Norway, he would meet me at one hundred and thirty feet and bring the next gas mixture. Andre, the videographer, was with him. I took the scuba tank from him and smiled for the camera. Switching my breathing regulators, everything seemed okay for about ten seconds…Then it changed forever.

Suddenly we both started spinning around quickly like we were caught in a whirlpool. I gripped the line tightly, at the same time I felt strong vertigo and the immediate need to throw-up. I gestured to Sveinung that something was wrong. I wasn't sure if it was affecting both of us or just me. I started to be violently sick, and felt a very unusual feeling in the left side of my head. It felt like I had stepped onto a speeding fairground ride, after just getting off a boat full of seasick passengers. My mind was insisting that I was spinning faster and faster and over and over. I motioned to Sveinung that he should cut the anchor line because I thought it was caught on something and pulling us around. As this was not actually the case, he could not understand what I meant.

Sveinung cut the rope anyway, at my insistence. Now I was spinning round and round being violently sick and getting tangled in the descent line. After a minute of this, it dawned on me that the spinning and sickness feeling were only in my head, I must be experiencing decompression illness to my inner ear and balance centre. The feelings came on just ten or so seconds after switching gas mixtures, and now virtually everything was beyond my control.

The gas mixtures I had used were pretty much text-book, in the past I had read of similar incidents likely caused by rapid ascents. My ascent plan called for more deep water decompression stops than ever used before, this gave me a very slow and controlled ascent. I had briefed the dive support team for this very eventuality, but reassured them that this would a remote possibility given the method used to plan the ascent. The plethora of bubble stops was way too many. I had spent far too long in deep water and this only caused me to absorb more gas. The RGBM stops were meant to push the decompression ceiling away but instead had bought it dangerously towards me, and now my body was likely a long way above the safe ascent ceiling.

Even the control of my eyes was lost to me - if I opened my eyelids, my eyes would dart back and forth making me vomit even more. I swapped the arm that was holding the rope so that I could catch a glimpse of my depth gauges and have a rough idea of my depth and the dive plan. The dive plan must be followed, because death was waiting just a few metres above me if the plan was aborted. Support divers were briefed that while I still breathed unaided then I must perform the decompression stop plan. I held the line, spinning and vomiting with every breath. My eyes were closed unless I grabbed a second's view of my dive slate and depth gauge, I could make depth adjustments just using my fingertips as necessary.

The support team removed my equipment, as during my seizure-like vomiting spasms I was hitting my head on the tank valves. The big steel cylinders were also giving me trim complications now that I had lost my sense of balance. During my equipment removal, it became apparent that I would float to the surface without a belt of lead weights around my waist. As I twisted and convulsed, I could feel the efforts of many trying to attach a weight belt as I spun around vomiting. I helped the situation by taking the weight belt and stuffing it down the neck of my wetsuit. At least that problem was easily fixed.

Initially when you get injured, concerned people constantly signal asking if you are Okay, but after an hour of repetitious vomiting and being shaken like a dog's toy by whole body convulsions, it was easy to see that I was not alright and that no further questions were necessary or welcome.

At times I could feel like I was upside-down and others like I was lying on my back. I tried to position myself in a head-low position, as It was becoming difficult to stop myself choking on sick, and fluids were starting to enter my lungs and make me cough violently. Unfortunately, with my head in a low position, the stomach acids would simply run out of my nose and straight into my eyes. I had to flood my mask with water constantly to prevent them from burning, but at least I wasn't cold any more!

Although the vertigo and constant vomiting underwater were horrendously unpleasant, I did think I would survive it, but something new was beginning to overtake the discomfort with a level of pain that would fit well into a torturers handbook. From about thirty feet under, I felt the spread of pain that must surely be serious decompression sickness. I had planned to make the decompression plan much longer to avoid such problems, but the action that had gripped me for the last hour was difficult to endure for longer than necessary, and I followed the original shorter plan without adding the extra stop time. Planning to spend an extra ninety minutes from seventy feet and up seemed like a sensible idea, but my problems had begun from one hundred and thirty feet underwater. Spending extra time in the shallows was supposed to add conservatism - now any extra time spent underwater would increase my risk of drowning on my own vomit. I followed the bare bones decompression plan from seventy feet up, because as the horse had definitely bolted now, there was little reason to improve stable security!

The last three decompression stops were easily the worst experiences I have ever endured. My body was racked with vertigo, vomiting, extreme exhaustion and now, debilitating pain. I wondered how much more I would experience before unconsciousness drew the curtains on this fiasco. The support team were doing an excellent job, giving the right gas mixtures according to the dive plan. I nodded my appreciation when it was possible. I stayed awake all the way to the surface - fortunately or unfortunately. When I had had enough and my dive watch said that three hours had elapsed, I floated to the top.

Lying there staring at the sun was no relief, I may have survived the drowning ordeal but it was far from over. I had gone deaf in one ear completely and the other ear felt as if someone was stuffing a finger through it and into my head. I could hear people saying that I was now dead. I couldn't think of anything to add to that, maybe I was dead.

A support diver swam over and asked out loud if I should be put onto the speed boat for a fast ride home, or on the slow boat, as time was not an issue any more. I remember opening my eyes and managed to utter the words "speedboat please", then closing them.

Divers were all over me now, lifting me from the water, across the outboard engines, and into the waiting speedboat. An oxygen mask was put over my face as the engines of the boat sprang into life. The journey to shore was fairly unpleasant as you can imagine. My wetsuit was removed and the medics revealed that my body was covered in a purple marmoreal rash. I continued to retch and convulse as the boat charged back to Phuket at full speed. This journey took less than an hour, but if you have exited the water likely more than 6 hours early, then your body will be experiencing highly damaging and painful decompression sickness which can be life threatening if not dealt with immediately. I needed to get back under pressure in a recompression chamber as quickly as possible. The Thai boat captain generously beached the boat to save some time. The ambulance would not be coming as apparently they had less messy emergencies to attend to, so the dive medics simply called a taxi to meet us. Dragging me up the beach to the road was symbolic of the muppet show, with Hilde and one of the chamber staff trying to help me stumble incoherently across the sand. Note to self: bring stretcher next time.

The taxi driver was understandably reticent to have a puking foreigner in wet and sandy clothes in the back of his car, but after some frantic re-negotiations the price was adjusted to ease his reluctance. I had to draw quite deeply on my resolve that afternoon, especially as there also seemed to be a problem with the chamber, i.e. getting me in it quickly.

The attending doctor did not want to go into the chamber with me, and was insistent on putting IV lines into my hand in the observation room. I had such low blood pressure because of all the fluid loss and shock, that his repetitive tries to find a vein resulted in numerous broken syringe needles. I found this very frustrating and painful. The doctor was clearly mistaking my apparent calm for a less serious condition - that could wait for his botched efforts at needle insertion.

After some protests from me, I was placed, still puking constantly on the floor of the chamber about an hour after first arriving. I put the oxygen breathing mask on my face and tried to time my inhalations for when I was not being sick. The initial treatment was seven hours long - the chamber tender said I was breathing heliox, but it didn't feel like it until about an hour from the end. It was a very surreal situation. The chamber staff were projecting the South-Park cartoon movie through an observation window onto a *widescreen* white sheet that was clipped-up across the entry lock door. I was lying so the blanket screen was both behind me and upside-down, although this orientation didn't really ruin the acting. My status as a captive-audience meant listening to a lecture about how decompression diving was dangerous, and at the same time overhearing the inside tenders' concerns that the chamber should not be pressurised below one hundred feet, as one of the view ports was only pressure-rated to eighty feet. The current depth in the chamber was one hundred feet. There was a risk that the window would blow and we would all be extruded through the small hole.

My eyes darted from side to side throughout the ordeal and my mind span around like a maniacal carnival wheel. I repeatedly filled my BIBS oxygen mask with my stomach contents. I managed to vomit almost continuously over the next three, seven hour, chamber runs, and every day and night in between. When I was finally able to hold them down, I was given anti-emetic drugs to curb the puking during the following seven sessions. I ended up being treated ten times in this chamber. After each of the first three therapy-rides, I was transferred to a nearby hospital to sleep under observation. The only room available there was on the third floor and there was no elevator access, the manhandling up all the stairs by the tiny nurses was very uncomfortable. After treatment number three, I'd improved sufficiently to be allowed home to be sick in my own bed.

One morning, before the fifth chamber visit, I was treated to a trip to a McDonalds. With all the anti-vomit drugs doing their job successfully, I felt able to drink a strawberry milkshake. Without help I tried to walk into the burger bar with a walking frame and order for myself. As it was early in the day the staff actually refused to serve me, saying that I was too drunk. I did even manage a smile as I attempted to back out of the store with my eyes darting about like a savant's. I tried unsuccessfully to keep my balance unaided, my patient car driver had to go and order my junk food for me - as I sat sweating outside and being sick in a paper bag. Realistically, I should have ordered my food at night - after dark in Patong even Stephen Hawkins dressed as a nun would appear normal in comparison to the normal clientele.

My shake did the trick and I felt a lot cooler *and* less sick after it. I hadn't taken off my stylish hospital clothes all week, except to shower, so all I had to do was shuffle into the big metal tube for the next treatment. Today, I would see a fellow diver join me for the treatment, someone who was far worse off than I was. My new chamber buddy was a Burmese lobster fisherman. He had used the Hookah Pipe system to spend way too long, far too deep. Although he spoke no English *or* Thai, a translator explained that when the diver was down at one hundred feet checking lobster traps, the boat had drifted into water some fifty feet deeper, but he continued to work - quite oblivious, as he was working without a depth gauge. The boat captain saw his error, and moved the boat back towards shallower water. He drove the boat a little too fast. The divers breathing hose that snaked from the surface was pulled from his mouth. He was left no alternative but to swim quickly up and suffer horrendous decompression injuries. Normally such a lowly paid diver would be left to his own fate, but as the chamber was currently in use and being paid for, the unfortunate diver was allowed to ride alongside me.

This diver had luckily lost consciousness after reaching the surface, but he was in a terrible condition. He was laid in a foetal position on the floor of the chamber and the treatment began. After an hour or so, the man started to moan loudly while still clearly unresponsive. The chamber tender looked into the divers' ears and said that the guy had apparently no eardrums left at all. He grinned that this guy would have no difficulty equalizing during the chambers pressure increases. Apparently, the younger shellfish divers are actually encouraged to puncture their own eardrums, as this means more days available for diving work because of no complications from colds or congestion. The Thai boat captain came to the chamber facility grinning suitably through the chamber windows, he was obviously pleased with himself for doing such a selfless thing. His charitable act was to take the rest of the day off work to check on his five-dollar–a-day employee that he had negligently almost killed. My chamber treatment fees were on average $800 per hour - this was the typical rate in Thailand charged to divers' insurance companies. Injured divers with no insurance coverage would be given a discounted rate if they still wanted treatment. The ever-grinning boat captain was getting the lower rate for his worker, around $150 per hour, on finding this out he stopped grinning. I could hear the argument developing outside through the chamber's internal speaker system. Apparently the boat captain was not happy with having to pay anything for this man he suddenly barely knew. The boat captain left and the helpless diver was removed from the chamber after the short treatment. I never saw him again.

This episode was a little depressing really, the chamber operator put on another movie to lighten things up. I was not in the mood for Shrek the Revenge, so attempted to read a magazine. Unfortunately, my jerking eye movements prevented any literary stimulation unless I learned to speed-read like Rainman.

Receiving seven Table-6 recompression treatments back to back left me feeling a little sore in the lung area, so I had a days break. I was allowed home and instantly took on the role of a pregnant mother, asking for all manner of ridiculous meals and having Hilde running around at my beck and call throughout the day. Over the past week I was only able to consume horrible, artificial strawberry-flavour electrolyte drinks in the chamber. I had almost stopped throwing-up now, so I thought I qualified for some solid sustenance. Hilde came back with an All-The-Toppings-Pizza, marinated anchovies and coconut ice cream. I ate everything and was nearly sick *again*, but for more traditional reasons.

The chamber staff were suggesting that I had been treated enough when I arrived the following day. They said that I had shown no improvement and more treatments would be unnecessary. I spoke with the attendant during the day's session, he confided that the real reason for the ending of my treatments was that my insurance company were complaining about the bill. I got a copy of the bill and noticed that the chamber company had inflated the number of treatments and added some bogus exotic gas mixtures. I sent a letter to the insurance company soon after, saying that I thought the treatment bill had been inflated - also, I was concerned when the door of the chamber needed a fat man to lean against it while pressurizing every time. The inner-lock door had been welded badly and was heavily distorted. The chamber owners had massaged an extra $14,000 for the inconvenience of having to work with their 25 year old creaking chamber, while I simply had to ride inside this death trap.

The chamber company agreed to give me a couple of extra *shorter* treatments as some kind of consolation prize. They would have to be a maximum of an hour long, and I would have to climb in and out of the pressure locks myself. Despite the shabby treatment, over the ten days I did manage to stop being sick and even succeeded in standing upright for a few seconds. I was still mostly deaf, constantly nauseous and disorientated, plus my eyes darted from side to side in a very disconcerting manner. The doctor at the recompression chamber kept banging my head with a tuning fork, asking if I could hear anything. Although I was completely deaf on one side, I definitely knew that I had a developed a pretty healthy tinnitus, the high pitched squealing noise was one hundred percent on my left side and fifty percent of my right. The doctor kept re-stating that I had "no enough power in head". Obviously his time spent at a top Thai medical school enabled the following suggestion to "give back power". His inspired offering was that the skin of an octopus be placed over my head! I declined the offer and showed some obvious contempt for his nonsense diagnoses. The doctor was annoyed so much that he said I should leave right away. The chamber staff helped me to the front door - I stumbled through it and managed to bounce my way across the car park like a human Pinball. I had no mobile phone with me, so I had to walk for about half a mile to the dive centre and arrange a ride home. I managed to get to the busy main road just ten yards away before exhaustion and the worst of my symptoms returned. I lay on a parked car, trying not to collapse in the blistering heat. I needed to cross the road, but it was like I was constantly spinning round and around, totally disorientated. Blaring car horns and screeching tyres told me to collapse to the floor and I crawled back onto the pavement, sweating profusely. Some elderly westerners asked me if I was OK, probably thinking I was just another drunk. The old couple helped me across the road, thus avoiding another spell in a Thai hospital for me. Once on the other side, I stumbled along in my own time grasping bushes and walls. The final two hundred yards took nearly half an hour. I arrived at the dive shop feeling similar to when I surfaced ten days earlier.

Over the next three months, I made slow improvements. Phone calls to doctors in the UK recommended that I danced a lot, or ran on sand to improve my balance. One doctor even suggested I get a set of skateboard pads and a crash helmet, to minimise my injuries when I constantly fell. I had been diagnosed with inner-ear decompression sickness and this had damaged my vestibular canals. I was prescribed elephant doses of Valium as these had helped in other cases. I thought I would try the exercises first, before I jumped into the twilight world of drug dependence. Spending the day balancing on one leg, or jumping up and down with my eyes closed sounds like great fun, but it can get a little stale, and quickly. I filled my waking hours exercising, and when my eye movements allowed, I went over my dive plan again and again. After some weeks I started corresponding with the individuals who had helped sculpt the final set of decompression stops and gas mixtures. I was ultimately responsible for my dive plan of course, nobody made me do it. I was now injured and disappointed, but at this point blamed no-one. There were many unknowns with such deep dives, I would be the first to admit this. However...

During the course of e-mailing the designer of the RGBM dive software, I told him of the recent dive, and the outcome. I said that as soon as I could, I would change what I thought was responsible for my injuries and attempt a deeper dive. The reply (see appendix) from this scientist at a famous US laboratory was incredible in the extreme. He had obviously had a bun fight with his cohorts and sought to explain that my problems were caused by their computer programming ineptitude. Additionally, the lack of understanding of decompression theory of the design team led to the program giving inadequate decompression stop times. My injuries were apparently caused by relying on these ultra-short dive times, rather than the usual rapid ascent or bottom time overstay. The scientist had gone on to advise that I should not use the product any more, but stopped short of globally recalling the algorithm as this might harm the business interests of his other franchise holders. I was speechless, after some deliberation I showed this to some lawyers, who filed complaints immediately. This case has dragged on over two years now, with all the corporate mud-flinging, bankruptcies and denials you could imagine. Tree huggers often jump to the aid of make-up wearing rabbits and smoking monkeys, but tens of thousands of divers need the very same protection. Technical and Recreational divers have been experimented on for the last five years in the name of pseudo-science, and most even paid for the privilege. The tactics employed by Bubble model software writers seeking the spotlight would have animal rights groups worldwide signing petitions and burning bras en masse, had it actually been tested on sheep or apes in this way.

All this aside, I did now have plenty of time on my hands to look in depth at what had happened to me during the ascent, comparing it to accounts from other divers that had suffered similar outcomes. I phoned my buddy Steve Burton who, in addition to being a technical dive instructor, was a genius with maths. He set about incorporating the current knowledge behind decompression theories with data I had collected from many people's problem dives over the years. Speaking most days, it took two months to build some software that would compare dive plans with outcomes from the past. We called this analysis software Decochek, and its predictions would be the basis behind any further deep dive adventures planned for the future.

By the end of June, I was walking in much straighter lines and even contemplated diving again. I thought that being underwater might actually be less challenging than the surface because of a decreased need for a sense of balance. One Sunday, I booked myself to go diving at Phi Phi Island with Hilde. The weather was a little rough but the medication for balance problems is the same as seasickness tablets, so I was already well prepared. I did not know what would happen, but I was pretty sure that nothing bad would occur. When we arrived at a reef in twenty feet depth, I lowered myself tentatively into the blue. As I thought, no stumbling or swaying occurred whilst under the water, I felt quite normal. I did a second dive to seventy feet, and from this awarded myself a clean bill of underwater health, despite Hilde following me about like a super-glued Remora.

Being underwater was one thing, but moving around on the boat with the finesse of a Saturday night drunk was a nightmare. It would be impossible to return to being a dive instructor feeling like this, I would have to sit down like 'Ironside' all the time and let others run around for me. That sounded like an excellent idea and I would definitely include my arm chair-based management strategy on any future resumes. My bad balance seemed to stabilise right up until July, when I had resigned myself to it never recovering beyond working outside of a comfy chair.

After retiring early to bed one rainy evening in the middle of July, I woke up during the night to go for a pee - normally this could not have been possible without turning a light on, as darkness worsened my balance drastically. I got up and found that my standing ability had improved incredibly and now I could walk almost normally, despite the twilight. I lay back down and thought I would wait until morning before telling the world, as it was probably a transient improvement or a dream. Even stranger was that I woke up the following morning at seven, rather than my habitual *jobless* eleven. I wanted to test my new balance skills, so I tried to get out of bed with my eyes closed and incredibly was able to stand up without falling over for almost thirty seconds. The real test was to be able to balance heel to toe with my eyes shut. I practiced this little sobriety test at least six times per day, normally I started swaying out of control almost immediately. I got Hilde to time me, and although it felt like twenty seconds before I started wobbling like a suspension bridge in a hurricane, by the time I fell towards the floor only ten seconds had actually elapsed. Still, this was a huge improvement. I was pretty pleased. I felt like my deck of cards had been reshuffled and the pair of twos I had been dealt in February had just been changed to a straight flush. Over the last few months I had put on weight, due to being very lazy, but now I could plan to be very constructive again. I went running that afternoon, although I only managed a few laps of the jogging track - this would change, as I would need a lot more fitness if I was going to attempt a thousand foot dive in December when the weather improved. With my improved balance, I returned to teaching diving again, even completing trimix training down to three hundred feet a couple of times a week. Moving around the boat some days was still more luck than judgement, and I did start to collect some new scars and plenty of bruises.

One group of customers wanted to complete a mixed gas course in the Similan Islands in November. There were 2 trimix students and an Instructor candidate. The weather was unusually calm, almost as if this was high season, but this would not arrive properly until late December in Phuket. The Low season had been renamed the Green season, quite ironically. During this Green season it rained almost continuously and the wind never dropped lower than typhoon force. It was always a competition to see which was greener, the surrounding countryside or the passengers on the dive boat. Still, the customers were very lucky this week, as the seas were flat like an ironing board around the Similan islands and the rain seemed to hover solely over the mainland some fifty miles to the east. We dived twice a day in perfect visibility, the calm ocean giving me no topside surprises either as I moved around the live-aboard dive vessel, with nothing more than a John Wayne swagger. We dived one afternoon at a submerged rock and reef system called Elephant Head, I had the two trimix diver students Matt and Sveinung plus Evan the Instructor candidate, as usual. As this was a relatively shallow dive to two hundred feet, the boats tour leader, Sylvie, came along as a sort of 'discover technical diving' experience. Sylvie completed sometimes ninety dives per month while leading dives around the Similan's, she knew the area better than anyone, and admitted to the occasional deep air dive when not sheep dogging customers round the reef. I always bluffed that technical divers saw masses of sharks and rays on all our deep dives. In reality, we only got to see common or garden varieties of deep water sand, sprinkled with not much else.

Letting Sylvie lead us through the rocky outcrops, we steadily got deeper and deeper. As our planned maximum depth approached, we were met by a shoal of Eagle rays and six or seven leopard sharks. Sylvie instantly assumed the role of dutiful tour guide and turned on the fire alarm in the form of her underwater rattle. All our peace was shattered with the constant noise, and I swam over to extricate the annoying din-maker from her. I pretended not to notice the wildlife parade, to fit in with my usual story of us seeing this stuff all the time. I indicated that we should carry on swimming and when Sylvie looked away, I quickly stared back to the incredible show along with the other three. The dive went as planned, our twenty-five minutes slipping away faster than normal because of the unusual fish carnival. It was time to ascend, so up went our surface marker balloons to mark the beginning of the decompression stops. By the time we arrived at the fifty foot stop, jaws dropped as gigantic Manta rays swam through the group. Divers just stared upwards as the majestic creatures swam through our bubbles. The fun turned slightly more serious as two of the rays got entangled in the ropes of our marker buoys whilst doing somersaults. Manta rays seemed to like the tickling effect of our exhaled bubbles on their skins, and now they were using our reel lines like dental floss. It was an incredible tech dive, unfortunately there wasn't a single camera in sight - quite typical when scenes of Harp-playing Mantas or Alien abductors are on offer.

All of the decompression stops came to an end, so we surfaced and stuck our heads into the fresh air. Sylvie was gob-smacked by the scene we had just witnessed, and despite our re-stating that this happened all the time, the rest of us were equally amazed. The next day would see a 2 metre Sail fish probe a couple of the group with its long nose while we swam across the sand at three hundred feet. The feeling at the time was more of apprehension than excitement. Being skewered like a kebab at this depth would upset anyone's day. The week of training dives in the Similan Islands would be remembered long after the ink in our log books had faded.

Chapter 11:   313 metres - My Own 18.12 Overture

The tides were ideal for a deep dive on the 5th of December, this was a month away and I felt ready. The support team would arrive from many destinations a couple of days beforehand. I had been keeping match fit by teaching tech diving courses at work, and even on my days off I would still go diving. A drysuit would be worn on this dive to avoid the problems with temperature variation I had experienced ten months earlier. It was very uncomfortable wearing a membrane drysuit in the tropical seas even with a thin undersuit. I would often be soaked from sweat and condensation after diving, even if the suit never leaked. Mentally, I felt totally prepared for a thousand foot dive, even my body seemed to agree, just a few weeks remained before D-DAY.

With just two weeks to go, I stopped teaching diving and just concentrated on diving with my full complement of deep dive equipment, including my drysuit - I had to feel totally comfortable on the day, even if it meant some unpleasant training days. Rough seas and twin twenty litre tanks can get complicated, one day saw the heavyweight twin tanks fall on my foot on the boat, nothing broken, just a blue and purple painful foot. Getting off the boat late that afternoon, I put the double tanks on my back as usual and walked from the boat transfer van to the dive shop car. Because of my injured foot, I leaned heavily on the other foot as I walked and stood. With my entire weight on one foot, I stood on a storm-drain cover behind the car, ready to offload my 110lb millstone. The bars of the drain cover broke and my foot slipped between the rusty jaws. I felt for sure my good foot was now broken properly, I couldn't even stand up with the weight of the tanks and my foot broken and wedged into the drain.

With two feet out of action, the only thing left to do was have a mini holiday. But firstly a visit to the hospital was called for. I went to the same doctors who had recommended the octopus-skin flavoured Viagra to fix my balance problems a few months earlier. The attending nurses and bar girls x-rayed my feet and miraculously said nothing was broken. I was happier for ten minutes, while they also x-rayed Hilde my girlfriend's foot for a possible unidentified drinking injury (UDI) sustained on Koh Mao a couple of weeks earlier. Hilde's x-ray plate showed a clearly broken bone and they prepared to put a plaster-cast on her leg. I noticed the toe jewellery on her toe in the x-ray picture. This was a little unusual as Hilde didn't have any toe-rings on her feet, Amazing Thailand.

Who knows whether we really had any broken bones at all - certainly none of the doctors or nurses, it seemed, but it was definitely time to take a few days off. We decided to do some touristy things like ride elephants and visit the many spa's that Phuket is famous for. The elephant trekking area was just ten minutes from our house, so we rode there on Hilde's Hardly Davidson motorbike, a sort of locally-made roadster that looked and sounded like the real thing, in the sort of same-same, but different way, typical of many things Thai. We got there for the evening cruise and picked our wrinkly grey steed. At the loading dock, I recognised some of the westerners as diving instructors I saw in the mornings at Chalong Pier, where the day boats left from. These instructors were buying elephant dung, maybe as a fertiliser for their gardens, but I rightly assumed an ulterior motive was in play. As we mounted our elephant, I asked a couple of the guys if the dung was for their vegetable plots, they just nodded and grinned. Our Mahout, or elephant driver, told us that they had started selling the dung quite recently, after a television documentary revealed just how much amphetamine powder the elephants were fed throughout the working day. As it was illegal to keep elephants in built-up areas, the keepers kept them a few miles from town, and then walked them into the city at dusk. This could take a few hours if the pachyderm was in no particular hurry, or feeling melancholy. Clever Thais would overcome this dilemma by pumping huge quantities of speed pills into the elephants' feed to get it to walk closer to marching speed. Our Thai driver actually thought that this was preferable for the elephant as it meant a shorter working day. He continued, saying that this was purely for the animals well being! The Phuket dive industry was just coming out of the Green season doldrums, and wallets amongst the scuba elite were getting emaciated. Desperate times called for desperate pleasures, so ingenious dive professionals were collecting Pachyderm-dung laced with speed and smoking it, saving cash and smoothing the rough seas of life. Elephants, however, would occasionally go mad, with the inevitable headline-grabbing outcomes that make Thailand such an exciting country for its expatriate and local communities alike.

The day for the deep dive drew nearer, making my mood turn darker than coal. I had seen this happen before previous *stunt dives* - the closer to the event, the worse my mood became. I normally tried to avoid people for a while unless absolutely necessary, it would take just a few days for these storm clouds to blow away. I went for a few deep air dives to clear my head, this usually helped. The weather was bad during the boat trip out and the tensions were rising between my ears to bursting point. Throwing on my twin tanks, I jumped into the water quickly, I hadn't noticed my drysuit zip was still open. The suit filled up quicker than a quick thing, I blamed everybody as I continued to descend, the water didn't matter – it was warm. Some equipment had fallen on top of my buoyancy wing during the car trip that morning, but I hadn't given it a second thought. I spent fifteen minutes at two hundred and fifty feet slowly unwinding. It wasn't until I'd seen enough sand and begun the ascent that the situation fully presented itself. My drysuit zip was open throughout, and although the water temperature was tropical and I was still warm, the suit would of course not hold any air. The lack of suit buoyancy would not have been a problem if my wing was working as expected. Every time I added air to the air cell behind me, I could hear the air pour straight out of an unseen hole. In my haste to get into the water, I had not checked the wing pre-dive as I should have done. On this dive, the plan relied on solely on my drysuit for buoyancy control as the tanks were the low pressure steel variety and therefore light enough to not need the back-up provided by my wing. This plan was officially out of the window now, as I was obviously too heavy to ascend despite finning like crazy. I instinctively sent up my surface marker buoy so I could it use to pull my way to the surface.

The line thickness on my reel was 2 mm and therefore similar to cheese-wire on my gloveless wet hands. With decompression time building at the same time as my air tanks were getting closer to empty, I had to swim towards shallower water to give me some thinking time. The area I was diving was about two hundred yards from the beach, and while the seabed was not exactly flat, it didn't resemble a wall either. Hand over hand and with my legs going like eggbeaters I headed for the shoal water. Five more minutes swimming at warp speed in deep water did no favours for my air supply, but the depth had gone down by one hundred feet. I could not breathe water no matter how shallow, but things were at least heading in the right direction. Getting closer to shore meant getting closer to the surface. I managed to get to fifty feet, then forty, at the same time completing some of my decompression stops. My only concerns were my nearly empty tanks and twenty more minutes of deco stops to do. The tank contents gauge was resting peacefully on empty and the breathing regulator felt very tight to breathe from. I breathed very slowly, to draw the last dregs from my tanks. The time to the surface on this very conservative dive computer said eight minutes to go at ten feet. This was not likely unless I held my breath for seven of those minutes, so I started to climb some nearby rocks that looked like they broke the surface.

My regulators delivered their last breath while I was still a few feet below the waterline, I had taken my fins off and climbed the rocks while exhaling the last few litres of air from my lungs. I remembered stories of deceased divers found strangely without fins or other equipment in shallow water. I pictured myself appearing as another scantily-clad newspaper headline during my scramble up the reef. Diving is very safe, right up until the point it becomes very unsafe. Sitting on the reef for about thirty minutes, while the boat went back and forth picking up the Scooby Doo divers, allowed plenty of time for reflection. I was pleased with the recent outcome, but highly irritated with myself with the show of complacency that got me into jeopardy in the first place. Today's little bimble was supposed to help clear the thunderstorm in my head that the dive in ten days was brewing up...it did not. These events just added to the growing list of 'what if's' now crowding my head. All these distracting thoughts of doom could have disastrous effects, especially when the McDonalds started to hit the fan in a multitude of ways as it undoubtedly would during the thousand foot dive.

The boat showed up, and I had a laughing audience as I attempted to climb the boarding ladder with a drysuit full of water. The water-swollen lower body proved a real struggle until I lay out flat on the swim platform like a stranded whale. I wriggled from the drysuit, turned it inside out and plunged it into a tank of fresh water. I was more interested in investigating my buoyancy wing for the cause of its failure. On closer examination, it seemed something had punctured right through the double bladder air bags, leaving it as water-tight as a Clinton alibi. Things would get much worse, as today I would have to pay $1000 for various boat hire fees, book and pay for the video-graphers, organise various photographers, plus confirm (with cash) all the helium and oxygen needed during the deep dive.

The weather was border-line the entire week before the dive - not really rough, but just crossing the line of unpleasant. I scoured the weather forecast hoping for a biblical storm. The Thai boat captains would not cancel, no matter how rough the sea, and now the boats were booked and paid for, only I could cancel, subsequently losing my payment. I felt very pessimistic about the dive - not that I would not get to where I wanted, but that maybe my preparation had ensured a one way trip. I felt a tension in my head I had not felt since my previous profession. I was aching everywhere but didn't seem to have the flu. Everything and everyone made me snappy and I just couldn't clear my mind. I knew I would feel better and that this was all just some kind of stress reaction, but getting so close to the dive day and still feeling like the grim reaper was highly frustrating. Three days before D-Day we started to fill the tanks, the noise and heat of this operation was a welcome break, at least I could think of nothing else. Many people helped, but it really was a job I preferred to do myself. The weight of tanks needed for this project would sink a small dive boat, so I had rented an eighty foot live-aboard dive vessel as the main dive platform. I looked at the boat a couple of times and it seemed OK and certainly was big enough. The cruising speed was only 8 knots unfortunately, and for the 40 miles to the dive site would mean certain seasickness for many of the support team if the sea stayed lumpy.

We filled tanks in the day, and I went over my decompression stop profile again and again late into the evenings. I had a similar approach to the previous 260 metre dive - although less deep stops than before, there was still many in very deep water. I had concerns that the cold water at depth would affect my breathing rates adversely, and that I could run out of breathing gas in several areas beyond the help of the deepest support divers. The deep stops were necessary, I believed, but just how deep and how many had never been established for a self contained scuba diver. I spoke with Steve in Pattaya numerous times, he repeated the warnings that the plan was too short considering the high number of deep stops. I would have to blow some of these stops off or lengthen the shallow time to over twelve hours to have a better chance of success. Just two days before the dive, I went for adding an additional tank to my already bulky configuration. Of course I needed to wet test this big steel tank that I fixed behind my even bigger twin tanks, so I jumped in the dive shops swimming pool. The extra weight made the whole rig unbalanced - if I ever let go of the descent line, I would go the same way as upturned Turtles. I could not wear the large additional tank for balance reasons and went back to the original idea of a smaller aluminium tank.

Diving extremely deep in Thailand's Andaman Sea exposes would-be aquanauts to strong tidal movements throughout the descent. To complicate matters, contra-flows of current will buffer the diver at many different depth levels, bringing with it freshly-frozen murky water. All equipment must be firmly attached to the diver, or it will be shaken loose. I yearned for the clear and calm diving conditions found in deep caves or the Egyptian Red Sea, and that was before I found out that the temperature remains virtually constant, even down to ridiculous depths... Shangri-La!

With one day to go, the tanks were all filled, with three thousand dollars in helium and oxygen and air. All the mixtures were analysed for oxygen content only. Helium analysers are available, but if the oxygen is correct then the other components must be right too, my back gas for the maximum depth analysed at 4% oxygen and 80% helium which was very close to the planned 5/76, and perfectly acceptable considering the time of night it was finished. The menu of gases created for this dive was a cocktail of Trimix's - 4/80, 10/60, 14/56, 20/50, 27/43, 50/25, 80/20. The first number refers to the percentage of oxygen and the second number refers to the helium content. One hundred percent oxygen would be used during the ten foot stop and above. The gas mixtures were chosen this way to have a similar percentage of nitrogen through out the ascent. The only exception was the first change from 4/80 to 10/60. This did jump fifteen percent nitrogen, but this I considered acceptable as it was to be breathed at a depth slightly deeper than the critical decompression ceiling. All the other gas switches came at depths that closely followed my body's current decompression ceiling. One of the hard lessons learnt from the previous deep dive was that Nitrogen values should not be raised if ascent ceilings are nearby. Traditionally, divers would reduce Helium in decompression gases to speed up off-gassing time. Dives of the nature I would attempt the next day have additional complications that cannot be hurried, keeping the Nitrogen content constant all the way to the surface, combined with sufficient decompression, would assure a better outcome than ten months earlier. Because of the cold conditions at depth, we filled the required tanks for me and everybody else, plus two spares of each ascent gas to be used. I would be breathing hard and did not want to introduce any funky gas mixes into my lungs if I inadvertently breathed down my tanks a bit quickly.

When we were filling tanks and checking equipment, it was all business and I forgot completely the task ahead. The negative moods disappeared during the almost relaxing time spent charging the cylinders, and even the measuring and marking of the down line was like a head massage, despite the many hours it took. Loading all the equipment into two trucks, we headed down to load the boat the night before. Normally, the public piers are off-limits to cars not part of the mafia co-operatives that run things in Phuket. I bought along some extra cash to oil the cogs of industry here, the equivalent of twenty-five dollars meant we could drive on public property, thus avoiding the transfer of tonnes of equipment from our cars to the permitted vehicles.

The weather was windy and raining, the forecast the next day was for more of the same. As we loaded the boat, the rain started pouring and the wind turned nasty like a winter squall. Thai people won't work in the rain, and they don't carry tanks if westerners are available to do it. All of the tanks containing gas for me I would carry to the boat myself, to avoid the damage typically caused when workers are underpaid. The weather was so terrible that I knew that this was all a waste of time, but should the wind drop overnight, we would leave at six in the morning. Doom radio started playing loudly between my ears again.

I drove home for a shower as tank filling is hot work, and although the constant rain was refreshing, I felt pretty grimy. Hilde and I met a few of the guys who had flown over to help with the dive and we all went for dinner. I didn't want to eat much, as seven hours spent in a drysuit the next day could have some highly undesirable effects if I went for the last supper approach.

Trying to get to sleep that night was impossible, I wasn't thinking about anything in particular, just everything at the same time. The weather outside the window was howling winds and strong rain. I must have dozed off at 3.00am, only to re-waken at 4.30am. The alarm clock sounded like an alien invasion, but this was birdsong, as in my head it was World

War III. The wind had dropped, but not enough - unless it was natural for palm trees to be lying down. Hilde woke up and asked if it was all over yet. Sadly it wasn't. I had a shower, and a couple of cups of coffee plus a litre of water to give my urinary system a rude awakening, but still my brain slumbered on in a dark place, firing on only eleven cylinders.

The car was already packed with all the peripheral goodies and miraculously had not been stolen, so all that was needed was a thirty minute drive in the pre-dawn light to the pier. Everyone was meeting at 5.30am for a 6.30 kick off. My mobile phone rang continuously from people needing reminders and confirmation that all was well. As we arrived at the pier the weather had abated, but still the journey out, of over thirty five miles, would be unpleasant for all concerned. I took a couple of Dramamine seasickness pills to help me sleep for three hours or so on the boat.

The entire crew had already arrived and were waiting at the end of the kilometre-long pier with piles of equipment bags, the contents considered too valuable to leave on the boat overnight. Some divers had so many boxes with them it looked like they were leaving home. The boat was scheduled to meet us for loading at 5.45am - it was, of course, nowhere to be seen. The boat was not on its usual mooring or even in the bay. Thoughts of the operators sailing off to Burma with our fifty or so tanks and crates of equipment instantly filled my jaded gourd.

Out came the mobile phones in an attempt to wake up the boat captain or his crew. The Thai automated voices in the speakers told of sleeping owners with phones switched off. The mood around the group was united now, everybody thought that the boat owner had sailed off into the sunset to set up a tech diving school with all of our equipment. If we didn't leave by 6.30am, we would miss the slack tide for this particular sea area. One of the support divers offered that he had been on the boat before, and it could go very fast - enough to make up an hour easily. I knew we wouldn't be going.

At 7.00am, the hired rescue speedboat arrived, virtually on time except for thirty minutes late. Someone managed to phone the office of the company who chartered out the big boat, waking an owner who was shouting in Thai something about drunks and boat captains and 'no worry falang'. At 7.30am, the sun was poking through the thick grey cloud as our dive boat came smoking into view. The support divers became animated and started readying to load the boat. The captain came hurriedly alongside the pier, a dirty window opened and somebody's hand gestured that we should hurry, as team members started tying the mooring ropes for the lazy boat crew who were sluggishly appearing, bleary eyed after a night of drink and drug excesses - paid for, no doubt, out of my very own pocket.

Bruce, the deep water support diver, asked how we should load the boat as the captain had brought the boat to the pier the wrong way around.

I calmly said "Fu@k it…Get all the equipment off".

A dozen faces looked around at me.

"It's too rough, and it's too late…We're not going now" I said to everybody within earshot. The instant nods confirmed that this thought had crossed other people's minds too. An enormous weight lifted from me, taking the storm clouds from the sky and stopping Grim Reaper FM from playing the requiem between my ears. No further explanations were necessary - this day would come again, before or after Christmas, I couldn't think now. We unpacked the boat, loaded the cars, and dropped all the tanks and kit boxes back at the dive centre. Six or so of the team went home to bed while the rest met at Clarets lounge, a Scottish owned, Thai managed café that did a respectable full English breakfast.

The next few days were spent relaxing, I played with dive plan some more to better suit the cylinders I could safely wear. The tides would be similarly suitable in two weeks time, the eighteenth of December. I did not relish the thought of

Christmas dinner in a recompression chamber, but for some reason seemed far more optimistic about the success of the whole project now. I think the negative thoughts primarily came from the bad weather which had been present the entire fortnight before, additionally some equipment worries had flickered in the back of my mind also. I now had two whole weeks to calmly re-plaster all the small cracks - the tanks were already filled, the line tagged and measured. After a week of lounging and doing as little work as possible except fun diving, my head returned to the place necessary to think of everything and succeed at a one thousand foot plus dive.

A couple of the deep support divers could not wait for two additional weeks in Phuket, so some places were swapped around. Instead of Bruce meeting me at three hundred feet, Sveinung would do the job. We had dived together a lot recently and I had total confidence in him performing on the day. The deepest support diver has the hardest job of all. Sveinung would have to do a three hundred foot dive for twenty minutes, arriving at the correct depth without fail. He would ideally get there early and wait for the full twenty, in case I had been delayed doing my shoelaces or something down deep.

I managed to get a dozen or so practice dives with full equipment, and several deeper air dives It was all starting to look rosy again. The rescue speedboat was arranged for the new date, but the live-aboard we had attempted to use before was not available for the same money - the money paid for the aborted day should have been enough to purchase the entire boat, never mind rent it for a day. Luckily, the company I worked for said that I could use a company boat on this particular day, this was perfect as this boat had compressors, fifty or so spare scuba tanks, and a great crew who were very familiar with tech divers. The dive centre would partially close on the dive day, so that would allow most of the resident instructors to join the project and help with the support diving. Those two weeks flew by and I can't really remember much of them. I did check the already filled dive tanks again and again - the helium in the tanks was prone to leaking past any valve or component that showed any signs of wear. Most of the tanks with trimix inside had a regulator constantly attached as extra security against gas seepage. I was especially paranoid with these tanks, because many times I had seen company drivers and staff sneaking a sniff of the trimix or helium so they could speak with a high pitched lady-boys voice for a few seconds.

The weather still remained unsettled, but the long-range forecast was for a high pressure system during the Christmas period. I was convinced the weather would settle, but just the day before the dive again saw wind and rain, with jittery seas. We loaded the boat at about four in the afternoon, some dive staff returning from a days' diving assisted and the job went quickly and smoothly. The Thai crew men on this boat, Scuba Fun, were Bau, Boy, and Captain Quat - they were always cheerful and helpful, and tonight they would stay on the boat to ensure the equipment didn't walk off into the darkness.

I went to bed at nine in the evening, during the previous two weeks I even managed to alter my sleep patterns to suit getting up earlier. This was probably one of my hardest-ever challenges, with my entire previous thirty-four years dedicated to getting up at midday.

Still, I could not sleep, but just rested. I managed a couple of hours, but I was totally relaxed, plus a little tiredness wouldn't matter tomorrow. I woke up ready at 04.30a.m and felt great. The darkness outside prevented seeing the weather, but I could see even the palm trees outside were sleeping soundly. Turning on a light switch woke up Hilde, plus countless Cicadas that broke into full song outside. My tinnitus was still present and stood to remind me of the consequences if today didn't go as expected. I didn't need tinnitus to remind me, as I had Hilde constantly re-stating what had happened before, and how stupid I was for considering a rematch. Today would be different, I recalled feeling excellent at nine hundred feet a year before – however, the ascent had had some creases, which today's dive plan would definitely iron out. My reason for going again was that I wanted to be the first to surface unaided from a thousand foot dive, and now I knew how to do it. Another reason was that I had told John Bennett, the previous deepest diver, that I would beat his record just because he had ripped me off over some clothes I lent him. The doorbell went; it was some of support team who had come over for an early fry-up. For my breakfast I would just be having some coffee and a mars bar, as in previous deep dives, I would be off solid foods for logistical reasons. We all left together, the mood in the car both jovial and buoyant. Some of the guys asked if I would lend them cash before the dive and if they could have certain possessions of mine if my plans went pear-shaped. Hilde said that she had first refusal on my belongings and she would E-bay the rest.

We arrived at Chalong Pier again at 05.30 a.m, the sun was just showing on the horizon, the sea was as flat as a pint left on the bar overnight. The journey out would take four hours or so, but with the ocean resembling glass, everybody could manage a nap...probably even the captain. We had a much bigger topside crew on this attempt; the surface coordinators would use huge white boards, with all the timings of the dive and who was to doing what and when. I set up my equipment while Hans, the videographer, and Morten, the photographer took countless images. I had a small sandwich then climbed the ladder for a snooze on the sundeck, lying in an inflatable dinghy. Waking up with sixty minutes to go, I stayed lying where I was eyes shut while Mark the surface coordinator ran over some points with everybody. We had gone over things again and again, both before the previous attempt and during the last two weeks. All I had to do was jump into the water, dive as deep as I could, and then fall into the arms of support divers at three hundred feet. How hard could that be?...I would find out soon.

Captain Quat, advised twenty minutes to go, according to his GPS screen. The dive site was chosen simply because the depth of water was close to 480 metres deep. The Andaman Sea starts to deepen quite quickly at thirty miles distance from shore. The eight hundred foot dive earlier in the year used a site just slightly deeper than required, but there were pesky pinnacles on the sea charts that crested at six hundred feet depth, and I'm sure that the descent line dragged into these during the ascent. The new site was miles past this area, right out in deep water, and far away from the charted wall area. Anything near this wall would be hit by up and down welling currents, and combinations of both. My descent would be timed to slack tide, which I assessed from digital charts and fisherman information. Slack today was roughly two hours before high tide at Phuket. The water would stop moving for less than one hour only. I wanted to be dropping down the line just as it stopped and be heading back up to the three hundred feet mark inside fifty minutes elapsed time, then the tide would run again. Tides today were forecast to run north then south, and at the end I should only be no more than a mile away from the start position. During my time spent planning deep dives on wrecks in the Channel Islands, I had more than enough experience at predicting tidal movement and dive times. During certain tides off Jersey, the tide would stop for just a couple of minutes before getting back up to eleven knots across the shipping lanes. Today, near Phuket, the sea was perfect, the sun was shining, my drysuit was on and the descent line was in place. Phil and Glen helped me put the 58 litres of bottom mix cylinders on my back. I clipped my safety reels to my buoyancy harness, put on my fins and neoprene hood with lights attached. The two extra fifteen litre tanks worn both sides would be clipped on after I jumped into the water, because I didn't want to give myself an hernia by wearing it all during the dozen-step shuffle to the water.

Hilde had a look of grave concern on her face, I tried to reassure her saying "If I can't do it…I won't". I think that helped, but looking at the dive video after the dive, you could see tears in her eyes at one hundred and sixty feet as I gave back her air regulator and slipped into the darkness. The video showed me dropping down to about three hundred feet, with showers of small bubbles cascading up, before I disappeared completely from view. I breathed my trimix 10/60 gas until about four hundred feet. From here, it would be the 4/80 all the way down and back to five hundred feet. I didn't like to breathe the travel mixes very deep, I would rather use the bottom mix up. I would definitely need all the decompression gas and more to make the ascent, but I didn't need the bottom mix. I would stop and turn back when I reached a tank pressure of 90 bars, regardless of the depth reached.

I felt no nerves at all as the five hundred feet mark came and went. Six hundred feet meant light levels falling to an eerie purple twilight. The water was still clear, but I noticed the colder water on my bare hands. I stopped to change hands on the line and check the gas supply situation. I noticed my hands were shaking as I studied my contents gauge. This was likely just the cold rather than the early effects of Helium tremors. On this dive I would wear my dive lights on my head, as this normally didn't shake as badly as my hands even when the cold had done its worst. I felt thoroughly chilled now as I crossed into a stream of dirty freezing water. The cold was biting my face and my hands were weakening. The gas in my tanks was filling my lungs with a freezing concoction of oxygen and helium. The shivering had moved into centre stage as I crossed the eight hundred foot mark. The depth readings on the line seemed to agree with my digital gauges, which was reassuring. One of my wrist computers had frozen way back at five hundred feet, and strangely the elapsed time had stopped also. Another gauge had given up the ghost and replaced all the usual information with the letters flashing 'Error' while beeping a very annoying warning alarm. I still had one good depth gauge, this displayed the figures nine hundred and six in feet, the rope marks confirmed two hundred and seventy metres. I had to stop now, I felt disorientated, both through cold and anxiety. How cold could I get without falling unconscious? I would find out soon. I checked my contents gauge again...disaster. The gauge read just 50 bars of pressure..

I had breathed way past my turn around point. I wondered if the figure was true. If it was, then I had just another couple of minutes before the show came to a freezing halt. I reached behind to check if the cylinder valve had been turned off as it slowly brushed against the descent line. It was fully on. I checked the centre isolator valve that connected the two big tanks behind me. It also was open. I had thirty bars now, not even enough time to write a stupid note on my slate and send it up. The cold was debilitating, I held on the line as wave after wave of jellyfish passed over me, thinking, "up or down", either way meant the same fate. I remembered the Coniston dive when the Isolator valve didn't open until after four turns, maybe that was it - the valve was only semi open. I reached behind again and started to turn the handle. I looked at the dive timer and eleven minutes showed, in one minute I would be out of time before having to ascend back up. Ironically, in one minute I wouldn't be *able* to ascend. I would try to head up, and travel as close to the surface as I could before breathing the knockout gas I had clipped to my sides. I would go the same way as another deep diver - Sheck Exley who likely passed out and died when forced to breathe a deco gas suited for a much shallower depth, while he was at eight hundred feet plus. Like him hopefully, I would not know much about it. The valve behind me kept turning, with each additional spin, my fate was confirmed. The valve stopped rotating all of a sudden. I had been turning it the wrong way - I span it counter-clockwise as quickly as my numb fingers could manage. I heard the sound of a jet engine roar behind my ears and the contents gauge needle started to climb. This had breathed new life into the project, in more ways than one.

The cold was way past too much, and I had spent far too long descending down. To top things off nicely, one of my wrist computers had obviously imploded, orange fumes poured from the battery case and the incessant alarm sounded distinctly strangulated. I had more gas than I needed now but time was almost up, common sense shouted abort. This was madness, I was constantly telling myself to abort the dive.

Another voice in my head (not that I hear voices often) was saying that to come this far without giving everything was a waste of time. My ego-driven hand hit my wing deflator button, and I noticed my ears feeling pressurised again. My hands were not listening to the battle in my head, they just pulled arm over arm down the line with what little strength they had. At thirteen minutes I had reached three hundred and ten metres,

I had eighty or so bars left of tank pressure. Although I had had a reprieve just two minutes back, I had thrown it away again. I had to head back up, while I still had a chance. Looking downwards I could not see far past all of the hydroids and sediment. I saw on the line the 315m marker, but also something huge in the water beside it.

At the time, I thought it was the head of a whale that had come for an inquisitive look at the funny diver. Then my view changed and it resembled a giant grey jellyfish. Whatever it was, I didn't want to meet it in this highly vulnerable state. The unidentified floating object was touching the line now - that was it, I grabbed the 313m piece of tape, stuffed it into my dive hood, and hit the up buttons. I had intended to dive to 320 metres today, but this wasn't to be, 313 would have to do, but I would still have to get myself and the tag back to the top. During the pause at the bottom, I had wrapped the down line round my wrist as my hands were too weak to hold on. The line had slipped between my Nitek computer and my Sub Mariner watch. As I tried to leave the scene, I couldn't free my hand and was momentarily trapped. I wasn't about to cut the line or my hand off, so I pulled as hard as I could. Something had to give, I watched in horror as the Rolex dropped off my wrist and fish-tailed into the abyss. Double Damn.

The air gauge read seventy bar, twenty bar too little to make the return trip. The bottom time was also over by at least a minute. I inflated my wing, hit my drysuit inflator with a curled-up, frozen hand, and pulled for the surface. I shut my eyes, I would use the inside of my eyelids as television screens to go over my now various problems. Periodically, I opened my eyes to check the depth markers on the rope. The first decompression stop was at eight hundred and twenty-five feet. Like the previous deep dive, the cold on the ascent was a huge problem. I was shaking violently, and had such a long way to go that I didn't have too much faith in getting there. I had been injecting trimix into my drysuit during the descent in an attempt to avoid skin bends. Some tech divers liked to use argon to inflate their drysuit's, mainly to appear fashionable. I associated argon with skin itching and rashes during previous deep dives. My undersuit was only 1mm thick and wouldn't contain much of any gas, but nevertheless I felt much colder than ever before, and the helium certainly wasn't adding any sense of wellbeing. I pulled my way up the narrow nylon line, my double buoyancy wing balancing the weight of my one hundred kilo burden of equipment.

On arriving at the first stop, my heart stopped as something bad started happening. The water all around me was vibrating and shaking, I thought that it might knock me unconscious it was so intense. As quickly as it began, the shaking stopped. I thought I was suffering some kind of bends event in my head, but then I felt the same as before, so couldn't be. Then I remembered the whale apparition at the bottom of the rope, maybe it wanted to have some fun or chat. I read about whales knocking out sharks and dolphins with bursts of sonar energy. Having my plans curtailed in this way was beyond my imagination. This first deco stop was more of a pause than any length of time spent, and it was time to move on. The deeper stops came and went, I was a couple of minutes behind schedule by the time I reached the six hundred and sixty foot stop. The shivering had gone a well-trodden route, and now I was too cold to even shake, my body exhausted now, with almost all energy lost to the ocean. The warmer water was coming, I knew, and it was a case of holding on. At this depth the water temperature was almost balmy at 12 degrees centigrade, at the bottom it was between 4 and 6 degrees centigrade.

During the ascent, I longed to breathe a gas mixture without helium for a few minutes to give my lungs a break, but this would likely cause horrendous decompression injuries almost instantly due to breathing dissimilar gases. The journey between the bottom and the first gas switch at five hundred feet will take twenty minutes, but each of these minutes is spent perilously, far beyond shivering, locked in a hypothermic twilight. My mind is completely shut down at this stage, autopilot carries me through this unpredictable section of the dive. Somewhere in my head a repeated whisper of 'Focus-Prevail' falls on deaf ears, I'm too frozen to even think positive. My back tanks are nearly empty now, and the gas comes slowly like a treacle milkshake. The increase in breathing resistance wakes me from my trance-like state and my first reaction is to check the depth, it is five hundred and sixty feet, deeper than the planned gas-switch depth, but needs must. I turn on the tank of trimix 10/60 and take a deep breath. The previous bottom-gas mixture had so much helium, that although I was half dead from the cold, the narcosis levels were equivalent to breathing air at just one hundred feet of depth, this dwindling narcosis kept my mind from stalling completely, up until now. The new gas mixture will be less chilling to breathe...but I would feel in my head at least fifty feet deeper than before. A see-saw of compromises was balanced before making these gas choices. A jump in nitrogen percentage could be very costly at an inappropriate depth, I could attest to this. This new mixture was not ideal, but breathed this far down would make the whole experience predictable with regard to the bends. I was very mindful of the implications as I took a careful breath, it would be like taking a mouthful of poison as antidote to negate the effects of another unknown poison swallowed before. If it went wrong I would be knocked senseless like ten months before, but this time I would be beyond assistance, spinning around, out of control, falling into the icy blackness. The theory worked, after two minutes of breathing the new mixture, I knew the rest of the dive would be relatively drama-free. The rest of the breathing mixtures on the gas menu were all chosen to complement each other. This drama could have been avoided by carrying yet another scuba tank, or having a support diver at five hundred feet. I was not happy with either of these solutions.

My breathing rate was far too fast - a combination of breathing gases containing lots of cooling helium, heavy stress, and the cold water. If you breathe chilled gases, your body compensates by breathing faster, the more you breathe, the colder you get - a vicious cycle. My only respite would come when the helium levels dropped as I reached warmer, shallower water. A solution for next time would maybe be to use a closed circuit rebreather for the ascent only. One benefit of rebreathers is that they supply a nicely pre-warmed breathing mixture. Unfortunately many have already died attempting to tame this emerging technology and at far shallower depths than mine today. Another complication would be that trying to put one on while already in deep water would be akin to skinning a live Tiger.

The tank I was breathing from would not last the course, as I'd breathed some of it already during the descent. Just how long it would last was a mystery, as the contents gauge was full of water and the display needle was floating in a mix of oily bubbles. There are no refuel stations underwater, so knowing when you will run out is little consolation anyway. My M1 dive computer, that had stopped working at five hundred feet earlier, woke back up as I returned to the natural light zone. The depth reading it gave was useless, the trip to double its working depth had left it with a permanent limp. I still had an old and faithful Aladin depth gauge and my TAG divers watch still functioned like it should. It's amazing how the ten year old devices continued to work perfectly as all of the state-of-the-art electronics either imploded or dozed off. The drysuit started earning its keep by four hundred feet, it kept the cold water from my skin as my bodies central heating system started to reboot. As the temperature climbed to 16 degrees centigrade I breathed a little relieved sigh. The shivering had returned, along with some optimism. My breathing mixture ran out then, and I was left with a fifteen litre tank of trimix to get to three hundred feet with. This tank contained a gas which should only have been used above three hundred feet, I sucked it anyway. The only thing hot about this mixture was the oxygen pressure - it was still less than two bars, easy-as-pie normally, but not while I was breathing like an asthmatic pervert.

Although things were going smoother now than recently, I could see a potential for a major drama happening in the next few minutes. This was my last breathing tank, it would not last until I met Sveinung, the deep support diver, in ten minutes time. Anxiety levels went through the roof - this was one problem I could not fix. From this depth, I could see the surface. I felt like a suicide jumper looking at the road below. If

I swam up to safety now it would be like leaping from a skyscraper. I had close on six more hours of decompression ahead of me. Without the support divers I would not live longer than five minutes at this depth, and I could not see Sveinung even on the line. I sent up my emergency lift bag to confirm that I was alive and on the line, maybe the topside crew were convinced I was already dead. I exhaled into the red bag and let it go. I kept my dive reel in my hand and the line spool spun violently as the lift bag accelerated upwards, then it stopped. The lift bag line had circled my descent line and began wrapping itself around and around the thicker rope - it wouldn't be confirming anything to anyone. My back-up reel didn't have enough line to reach the surface from this depth. If I sent it up, it would mark a position where I would not be. The support divers would descend down this line to find an empty reel, I would be long gone by then. I did some stock taking to see what breathing gases were still available. I turned on all my dive tanks and saw that the only thing left was a few bars of bottom mix. The tanks were huge and would last at least ten more minutes, but they were the totally wrong mix to breathe. I considered the alternatives and tipped an imaginary egg-timer in my head, ten minutes to go. I thought it a bit of a shame, as I had resolved so many problems recently and had reached a new record depth in crap conditions, but now I would simply run out of gas beyond the reach of support divers.

Carrying on with the stops was the only correct thing to do. The plan would be followed, but without a safety net. I mused that clowns and trapeze artists must do this every day. The time on my TAG watch announced that Sveinung should be getting in the water now, I wondered if he would see me as I fell from the line. I considered quickly ascending towards him as soon as he came into view. Telling myself to wait and be cool was hard. I moved up to the three hundred and thirty foot decompression stop - still no sign of Sveinung although I could see the dive boat in the distance and glimmers of sunlight mocking me. I saw a splash at the back of the boat, someone had jumped into the water. He would need to get his skates on to save this day. I waited through a couple more minutes of deco. God knows what was left in the tank, still it breathed normally until - it didn't.

I knew what it felt like when the tank runs empty, I had felt it many times recently. I can't take a full breath now, towards the end of each breath it just stops…dead. Slowly the end gets closer and closer to the beginning, until it's like attempting to breathe with your mouth and nose closed. I clipped my breaths to make the gas last, but the carbon dioxide in my lungs would build much faster doing this. It would get to the point where my lungs would scream for a fresh and full breath, at that point I would take another breath of the gas still left in my big tanks behind me. My eyes are closed, trying to force my lungs to stop complaining, I sneak a look up the line, Sveinung is coming, he is on time, but it's me who is out of time.

Sveinung is just a few metres away now, but is stopping for some reason, he is trying to equalise his ears. He starts moving again, but stops once more. Stopping tantalizingly out of my reach, Sveinung starts to unclip the tank he has brought along for me - there is no time for that. I am stuck underneath an invisible ceiling imposed by the decompression stops. I can't wait, I pull myself towards him frantically. I take the regulator he gives me but the cylinder valve is still off, *no time*, I take the regulator from his mouth. Sveinung looks startled but quickly recovers his spare. I take a breath, the relief is tangible, the tension levels rescind like a flash flood. He asks if I'm Okay, I signal back that I guess I am – for now, and follow up with hand-signals explaining that I had some problems in the deep. Sveinung grins, I grin.

The decompression stops were every ten feet from here to the surface, I was still breathing far too fast, but this would be managed, I was sure. The support divers themselves breathed what I breathed - on top of the tanks that they brought down, there would be enough.

Phil changed places with Sveinung at two hundred and forty feet. He carried extra tanks and took away the ones that I was rapidly breathing down. I still shivered uncontrollably. No doubt this would have an effect sooner or later, time would tell. The adrenaline of success was overcoming the discomfort from the cold, but when this was used up I would just be very tired and weak. Warmer water was all around now, together with warm drinks and gas mixtures with less bloody helium. Phil helped untangle the lift bag that I had birds-nested around the up line. Gai would be next bringing fresh tanks, he was the company's operations manager and a Thai diving instructor who liked a deep air dive now and again. On arriving, Gai, which means chicken in Thai, kept shaking my hand again and again. This was fine, but I was more anxious to unclip the fresh tank he'd brought down and get breathing from it. I started to relax by one hundred and fifty feet, my breathing rate had fallen sharply, from mimicking an Asthma attack, to my normal telephone voice. The scuba tanks for the shallower decompression stops were aluminium eighty cubic feet tanks, and I was gulping the contents of these down in less than ten minutes by the time I reached one hundred feet. Glen and Mike, the owner of the dive boat and the company I worked for, bought double tanks of trimix 27/43. Clipping these extra bottles to my harness, made it difficult to even see me underneath all the equipment, but it all remained quite balanced. Ten months back, Glen and Mike bought similar sized tanks to this depth. This dive saw a major improvement on my state of health compared to last time, when I was on the receiving end of some major decompression injuries. Still, it was early days on this dive with more than five hours deco still to go. I would be more vigilant than a watchman aboard Titanic II this time.

Hilde came to visit me at the 30 metre stop, bringing a spare decompression tank. She is smiling and happier now, as am I. I am sorry to cause so much anxiety and dread for her…again. Earlier, I did think about how she must have felt, watching me disappear into the gloom, maybe for the last time. It is difficult waiting for someone to come back from such a risky endeavour, especially when you have seen the result of when things go badly wrong – first hand and up-close. But Hilde knew why I had to go down again, to do it right and prove to myself that it could be done without injury. We discussed this deep dive many times and why I was prepared to pay the ultimate price to validate my theories. But it's impossible to prepare others to accept the consequences as freely. Hilde doesn't take risks underwater and thinks I'm crazy to risk everything in this way, but then I think she rides her motorbike crazily. It's just about experience and confidence in what you have done before and therefore think you can get away with next time.

I only started to feel comfortable and stop shivering after reaching eighty feet depth, where I breathed the remains of my 40/30 deco tanks. David "Hansom" Hanson arrived on time to bring yet another decompression tank containing helium. The following gas mixtures would see the nitrogen get minimised and then completely removed. With two hundred and ten minutes remaining for my exhausted body, I wanted to breathe gases containing some helium all the way until the ten foot stop. Despite possibly complicating the decompression, Helium would be easier to breathe, and might conserve my strength, although in reality, it made me so cold that it wasted even more energy. I would purge the Helium from my body during the last hour by breathing one hundred percent oxygen.

Because of the specially filtered and dried gas mixes I breathed, designed to remove all impurities, my body was dehydrating fast. Additionally, a condition called immersion dieresis was causing almost constant urination. I tried to remain as horizontal as possible to minimise the effects of pressure differences across my body from the water. Staying flat didn't seem to help much, maybe because of the enormous four hundred and seventy pounds of pressure I had just endured, albeit for a short time. The non-stop peeing was combated by drinking two to three litres of fluids every hour, but I think it just made me pee.

Fun-sized Mars bars were added to my list of hourly consumables, together with bananas. Dutch Abraham and French David brought me a surprising amount of these incompressible yellow wonders, maybe thinking I was very hungry. I gestured as to where I should put the four monkey snacks they handed me. Imagining their response, I painlessly pushed them into my drysuit pockets, with one under my mask strap, as sticking them in my arse was not possible today due to the constraints of my drysuit. As I dined on soggy fruit and chocolate bars, I could see that it was also feeding time at the zoo above me. Lunch had been served on the dive boat; this was obvious by the scarceness of support divers and an almost constant rain of chicken bones that drifted down around me. I dreaded the inevitable toilet flushes that would no doubt ensue, guaranteed by some of the support divers who nurtured dubious senses of humour. I would have done it to them, guaranteed. Four hours into the dive and everything was going quite smoothly. Support divers ferried down tank after tank, and some stayed throughout, watching me while away the hours. Long decompressions in the ocean leave no time for boredom. Compensating for the changes in buoyancy as scuba tanks empty over time, though hardly rapid-fire excitement is absolutely necessary. If I let my legs fall below horizontal for long periods, then the subsequent toll on the circulation causes a dead feeling, then pain. This has to be remedied, the discomfort endured, then plans drawn to avoid a repeat performance. I went through this again and again, as the excitement of the day took its toll and gave me a goldfish's memory.

During the shallower decompression stop depths, at both thirty and twenty feet from the surface, I breathed Heliox – a mixture of eighty percent oxygen and twenty percent helium. The reason was to remove as much as possible, the nitrogen content in my body tissues, nitrogen apparently a slower gas to eliminate. Helium leaves the body safely and rapidly if ascent speeds are kept very slow and as such is perfect for decompression. Helium is becoming more and more fashionable with technical divers as its lets the inept and inexperienced dive deeper than ever before. However, bends incidences continue to rise each year, due in part to bad buoyancy control, but also because of the equally fashionable modern deco-algorithms propagated through the internet. These 'Bubble models' promise much shorter, often inadequate ascent times. If deep divers combined traditional decompression methods with better buoyancy control - rather than simply buying cocktails of internet marketing, then advanced diving would have a steadier foundation. I have to admit to once staring into the dazzling headlights of bubble model decompression, they promised a great deal, but delivered terrible injuries both during and after extreme deep dives.

Where was I? That's it, I was breathing Heliox 80/20. Having to breathe it at thirty feet for sixty minutes meant adding insult to injury regarding my oxygen toxicity loadings. I knew that nobody has ever died because of cumulatively-high CNS loadings of oxygen toxicity, but the effects of pulmonary toxicity on my lungs were becoming very real indeed, my lungs began to feel 'tight' and I developed a raspy cough. After thirty minutes, I planned to breathe trimix 14/56 for ten minutes in an attempt to reverse some lung damage that I was sure was building, in much the same way as divers who take air breaks during recompression therapy. I took the new gas and started to breathe. After five or six minutes, I felt pain in both shoulders. I thought the bends would come, as I had cut this dive plan about an hour shorter than ideal. The pain had become quite intense by the time I returned to my decompression gas. After fifteen minutes or so, the pain went away and left me relieved for now, but also mystified. Another thirty minutes later meant it was time to travel up to twenty feet and make another break from the high oxygen decompression mix. Again, just five minutes or so into breathing the 14/56, the pain returned. I stopped breathing this mix straight away, vowing to finish the stops here continuously breathing the Heliox. The pain went and didn't return, just like before. I concluded that breathing the Heliox and then breathing the Trimix was the reason. The likely cause was the sudden increase of inspired Nitrogen levels - in this case from zero to thirty percent. This 'counter-diffusing' gas was causing similar complications to those that caused to my vestibular injuries sustained on the eight hundred foot dive. The key, I believe now, is not to have an increase in nitrogen at or near a decompression ceiling.

I was learning all sorts of things on this dive, this is the first text that details many of the points, maybe something more technical will follow. The down side with new discoveries underwater is that they are generally joined at the hip with pain and discomfort. The next hour decompressing at twenty feet was pretty painless, although I started to notice not so much discomfort, but not being able to breathe deeply and needing to make some unusually big yawns. Pulmonary Toxicity had arrived.

Being an hour away from the surface was great - I knew I would survive the rest, no matter what. The sun was low in the sky, the sea was still. My colleagues and friends who had helped me through the day were free-diving down to see me and wave. Hans, the videographer and Morten, with a camera, swam around taking shots constantly before night replaced day.

I breathed one hundred percent oxygen now at the ten foot stop. The gas was being supplied via a long hose from tanks kept on the boat. The first tank must have been quite empty, or small, as it ran out shortly after I started on it. The plan was for the surface to monitor the pressure gauge and give me something else to breathe from during the changing of the oxygen tank. A breakdown in communication between such an international support team was inevitable. One minute I was relaxed, breathing contently, eyes closed in reflection. The next minute I was fighting to pull my tongue from the regulator, it felt like it was going to be severed within seconds. My stamp-licker was dragged straight though to the back of the regulator, my eyes bulged with pain. I could see that the hose that snaked to the surface was collapsed flat. The familiar taste of iron in my mouth confirmed the blood that I was sure I would be swimming in shortly. With a huge and excruciating effort, I pulled my tongue from the regulator. I looked up to the surface and saw French David giving me the Okay sign. I let my tongue do a quick attachment check on itself and spat the rest of the claret out. I cursed the boat based chimp troop above.

My next thought was to find something to breathe from. I grabbed the discarded regulator and started pointing at it aggressively to David. He pointed back that I should breathe it and now it was fine. Apart from swimming up, my alternatives were limited, so I gingerly returned the oxygen regulator to my mouth and breathed. Now it worked again, and my tongue still worked, which was even better. I would be throwing some tongue lashings around as soon as I hit topside. I tried to relax again to conserve energy. The cold had returned, but in a way I had not felt before. I seemed to be shaking from the inside out, and now my lung problems were getting my full attention. This dive was plagued with problems, some major, some minor, some predictable while others incredibly unusual. Now I was concerned with my breathing, as I was coughing virtually non-stop with just fifteen minutes to go. The constant chill of breathing Helium for over five hours on open circuit had taken its toll on my lungs. I'm sure a sprinkling of pulmonary oxygen toxicity played no small part either.

The underwater phase of the dive was over, but just one metre below the surface I held onto the boat ladder coughing uncontrollably. I felt dazed and confused, and now my lungs were complaining loudly. Holding onto the ladder, I took my fins off and handed them up to an unseen handler. With both feet on the bottom rung, gripping the ladder tightly, I spent a few minutes getting my breathing under control. I surfaced and dropped my regulator, the breath of air tasting instantly different to the musty acidic oxygen that I had breathed for so long. The dive team were on the swim platform and cheering, it felt good. I was happy so far, but knew it was far from over. I pulled my mask and dive hood off, then rinsed my face with the sea. I grinned a bit and shook some hands from the water, but my mind was starting to go totally blank, strangely in unison with ascending the steps. In my confusion, I tried to climb the swim ladder still wearing my forty-seven litre dive tanks that seemed moulded to my bank after near seven hours. Mark, the surface coordinator, was in the water and helped me out of the equipment. I managed the steps up onto the boat, but had to sit down almost immediately, I felt exhausted. Camera strobes flashed away, my face was swollen and when I blinked it took three seconds or so to reopen my eyes. Hilde and others asked if I had the bends, I said that I did about an hour ago, in both shoulders. The pain was gone for now, but I was pretty sure some action was still to come. Getting onto the speedboat back to shore and breathing some more oxygen was my only goal. First though, we all had to go onto the top deck of ScubaFun and take some pictures with all the support team, and maybe sip a glass of champagne. When I sat down I felt sort of okay, but standing or climbing stairs was a monumental task. With some help, I mastered the steps to the upper deck and sat down to open the bottle of bubbly. Now I noticed my hands were shredded and painful. The rope had both cut and burnt into my fingers and palms. Holding onto the line for so long had curled my fingers like a catcher's mitt.

Many pictures were taken, my brain was a blur. I started to take my drysuit off but forgot to unzip the back first. I climbed onto the rescue speedboat with Hilde and Phil, who had grabbed the box with some spare oxygen for the journey back. The moon was in the sky now, I felt like I had missed a week of sleep, but I had become the first diver to exit the water without the bends and unaided from a thousand foot scuba dive, that was fine for today. I reached for the box containing the oxygen kit, opened the lid and was a little surprised to see the green tank had been removed to make room for lots of green TINS…of beer. I had a Heineken instead, it helped a lot, together with some therapy Pringles. Turning my mobile phone on, the text messages poured in from all over the place. Steve Burton's message was to rethink the dive plan before trying it. I responded with, 'Still alive, touch and go for a bit…313m', another friend got 'reports of my death are greatly exaggerated'. The boat raced back to shore, this time the occupants were all fit and well-ish. I wouldn't be celebrating tonight, just relaxing. The parties would have to wait a couple of days, until I knew the bends were definitely not coming and I had regained some energy.

I got home and immediately lay down on the settee, the television was on but the sound was off. I just stared at the pictures, a re-run of Sesame Street, which fitted my intelligence levels perfectly at this time. I needed to pee, which was a big relief - the indignity of catheter insertion from a sleepy nurse would not sit well with my current mood. I got up and tried to climb the staircase to the bathroom. I was standing next to the downstairs toilet, but my mind was blank and I just climbed the stairs instinctively. Each step was like a tall hurdle, I breathed faster and faster, almost out of control, just moving from one step to the next. After three or so steps, I had to give up, due to being so knackered by the exertion. I used the downstairs loo before collapsing back in front of the telly. Dozing off was not the plan, I definitely wanted to remain conscious for the rest of the evening. I fell into a dreamless sleep for almost five hours, waking only at the bequest of the pain that now shouted in my left arm. The discomfort was at the eight out of ten level when my eyes opened. I had an oxygen bottle in the house and Hilde assembled it. Taking a breath, I wondered where it was all heading, but knew that so long after the dive the symptoms should not escalate much beyond intense pain.

Taking painkillers was not an option after a scuba dive, the only medication was to breathe oxygen. After ten minutes the coughing was back, my lungs were producing fluid to combat pulmonary toxicity. I thought about visiting the recompression chamber, but with my lungs in this state I couldn't imagine not having exotic complications while continually breathing more oxygen at almost three times the surface pressure. When the coughing stopped I breathed more oxygen, four hours of this saw the pain starting to diminish. My arm was just feeling sore by the morning, but I gave it two further hours of oxygen therapy while sitting at my computer, the biggest challenge now was to avoid keeping all the drool from the regulator dripping across the keyboard as I typed. The feelings in my lungs meant not being able to breathe deeply or exercise harder than teeth-brushing. The majority of the symptoms lasted over five weeks after the dive. I corresponded with a guy from the German military and commercial rebreather development company, Draeger. When I described my lungs symptoms, he said they were typical after breathing super-cooled breathing gases like I had done for long periods. I had simply frozen my lungs. They had seen such symptoms many times before and developed a gas-heater system for oil-field workers. Unfortunately, this equipment could not be modified for use on such deep scuba dives. A local doctor advised rest and no-smoking, which sounded ideal to me as I could *NOT* smoke very easily, as I've never smoked anything. Newspapers and Radio stations from all over the world phoned around the clock over the next few days to conduct interviews and make news pieces. One of the press agency reporters said that the newspaper circulations covering the story around the world would top six hundred million readers in dozens of different languages. The story was carried by so many newspapers as it was up-lifting and had some nice supporting photographs. With so many depressing events in the world at the time, news of the dive had been a welcome break from the bleak war coverage. The tabloid stories had some unusual twists to attract the readers of course - one paper mentioned I was attacked by killer jellyfish, another by giant sea beasts.

My deep dive was done in preparation for a televised epic to a similar depth. To remove some of the unknowns, I had to prove to myself that it could be done, and to measure the risk to life and limb while I was relatively relaxed. Media involvement can add some ridiculous pressure as producers aim to get their 'way' above all else. Television footage of my death would have to handsomely paid for...up front. I spoke with a US life insurance company after the dive about the televised second phase, but they couldn't get liability coverage themselves in light of such a risky endeavour. Also, there were other contenders that seemed quite willing to do this kind of circus trick for free.

The fifteen minutes of fame was fun, but I doubt if I would do such a deep dive again, unless for a large amount of money. Evil Knievel didn't do too many stunts for free either.

Chapter 12: Victoria's Secret

I flew to London in March 2004 to visit family and friends and say hello to John the owner of Otter drysuit's during the UK dive show. Semi-conveniently it was being held in the dockland area of London, not too far from where I would be staying. Dive-shows are very similar anywhere in the world, with large and small dealers cutting the scuba industries throat by selling equipment at less than it cost them, for various reasons. However, the shows are great places for divers to view and buy new equipment at rock-bottom prices. The Saturday was busy and I showed my dive video's and signed lots of posters that one of my equipment sponsors had produced. On the Sunday afternoon, I was signing more posters at the Ocean Management Systems booth, when a guy called Christian, a dive shop owner from Lebanon introduced himself. Over a coffee, Christian outlined an intriguing project that he thought might interest me. He showed me some historical photos of a battleship, HMS Victoria, which had sunk after a collision with a sister ship in 1893. The story was more interesting as the Victoria was the British Navy's flagship at the time, and its sinking cost the lives of the greatest number of UK sailors in peacetime, both then and since. Victoria was lost off the coast of Tripoli, Lebanon in one hundred and sixty metres of water, and as such was beyond reach of virtually all divers, except myself. Christian asked if I would come to Lebanon and prepare him and a team to help find and dive the wreck of HMS Victoria.

We discussed the likely payment terms for me and from this I knew he was serious about his project. I receive lots of possible new wreck projects that need finding and diving, and each is always more interesting and significant than the last. Sadly, anything connected with scuba diving always becomes generally a pleasant way to waste your time, with no financial incentives apart from a free baseball hat, or team-fleece. If you want to make a million pounds from scuba, you had better start out with at least double that. I doubt if diving will become professional or mainstream any time soon, as it is not an ideal spectator sport because of often bad visibility - and the fact of course, that it's usually done underwater. Imagine if football matches were played at night by candlelight in the rain, they would not be so popular on television.

Christian had a very interesting plan and a realistic budget, so very soon his project could hopefully be realised, and I could get paid to do some cool diving...perfect. He sent me an air ticket from Thailand to Beirut via Dubai for July, as promised. In the meantime, Christian would further preparations with the boat and get some possible firm wreck co-ordinates. I went back to Phuket at the end of March and got back into work mode. When you complete the deepest dive you get lots of work offers, but continuous technical diving doesn't make you much richer - just more likely to ride in a recompression chamber. Customers would happily do two 100 metre dives per day if they could whilst on holiday, but it's important not to let their vacation schedule dictate the dive logistics, or it will all end painfully.

Nowadays most inquiries come via the internet, and I'm usually quite blunt when it comes to letting people know what's available or not. It would be great to farm the work onto other tech instructors, but the customers would not be flying from the other side of the world just to shake my hand and then get tuition from any old tech instructor, sadly. The usual internet enquiry for technical training has been shaped by the caveman tone that echoes around all the various technical internet chat rooms. An example would be the following: "I'm interested in doing ALL Trimix, Cave, Wreck and Rebreather courses to instructor level in one week and you must give me the best price, I am currently a NAUI open water diver with eleven dives". I would get a dozen quality enquiries like this every week, and found it difficult to always stay positive when responding to champagne taste, beer money mails. My local competition was a *one man band with two sets of (independent) twin tanks* and a glitzy website. He would usually give these web prospects everything they wanted and more, then send them off to breed the "friendly fire" mentality that diver training agencies love. The funniest thing was when the 'one week, ALL technical levels' instructors came looking for work. In contrast, recreational diving internet enquiries are still quite polite, but getting less so as people surf around for cheap prices. Only when there is a real customer in the shop will I go out of my way to inform and advise. Even phone calls involve a slightly less personal two-way exchange. Any time a conversation takes place where desires are translated into realistic needs and a mutually beneficial solution found is superior to swapping black text. The in-store customer gets to see the dive facility in the flesh and makes possibly even informed decisions, whereas the internet equivalent just saves cash - usually at the expense of safety and standards. Rant over.

I finished a trimix course for three Finnish scuba instructors who ran a dive centre on Ratcha Yai Island near Phuket. They mentioned going to look for a sunken temple and village that disappeared after a valley was dammed to create a reservoir. The valley was in Kao Sok National Park on the mainland, about three hours drive away. I thought it must be easy to find a village at the bottom of a lake but they advised that the flooded area stretched over 160 square kilometres, with 60 metre depths attainable in many places - also the valley was covered by forest before the flooding, which meant all dives took place under a complete canopy of trees now. The Fins, Janne, Janne and Adam, were planning to go back with a group of helpers and I was only too keen to join in. A group of seven of us drove up to the Park, which still has proper jungle with all the popular wild animals running around. Locals spoke of giant sea snakes and fresh water sharks that struck without mercy. The man-eating serpents had better watch out today as I'm quite capable of becoming a shark-eating man. We took with us a portable air compressor to refill the tanks, and provisions to stay three nights. Arriving at the Dam installation at before nine in the morning we met our boat drivers, who were still totally drunk from the night before. The area was deserted, other than some fishermen who lived in floating bamboo huts. We were the only tourists here at the moment and it was likely to stay that way; Koh Sok Marine Park sees the same number of visitors in one year as the more mainstream Phang Nga bay area gets in one day.

Phang Nga is popular for its James Bond Island famed by the film 'Man with the Golden Gun', obviously Scaramanga's summer house is much more of a draw than elephants and tigers. We loaded piles of twin tank set ups and deco bottles onto two long tail boats. Scenery in the area is breathtaking - sheer limestone walls extend up to three hundred metres on both sides and despite blue skies all around, some of the higher peaks have a mini cloud system circling up top. The water was like glass and when the huge un-silenced car engine that propelled the long tail boat along stopped, everything was eerily silent. The still-tipsy skipper seemed to be heading towards a certain spot about an hour away agreed with one of the Jannes. He constantly took nips of something from a plastic bag and straw combo. Rare birds flew from crag to crag, while monkeys could be seen leaping through the forest as our noisy transport shattered their morning naps. We headed into the middle of a three way gorge about a kilometre across, the boat captain kept shouting "Baan, Baan, Tinni" which meant his house was here. He pointed downwards as we kept moving along.

His old house must have been roughly the same size as Buckingham Palace because we had travelled easily 150 metres from the pointing part to the stopping part. On the boat was a small sonar device that gave the depth as fifty-five metres, but the rest of the screen was just full of distortion. The manufacturers probably didn't envisage it being used to see into a forest and it clearly didn't do that. One of the Jannes threw a weighted search line into the water so we could see where we had been. The captain was adamant that here was where he had lived twenty drunken years earlier, but who were we to argue. A couple of the team were apparently doing a 'discover tech diving' experience today, as they had never dived wearing twin tanks, nor done any decompression diving or been close to fifty-five metres swimming through tree branches. I wished them the best of luck and went over the side. The water felt very warm but was murky like a swamp, a smell of rotten eggs started to creep through my nostrils. This smell meant hydrogen sulphide was in the water, caused by rotting vegetation somewhere. I asked for some bottled water from the boat to re-clean my mask, as swimming with a fart smell in my face isn't too pleasant. I headed down, just two metres below the surface the visibility turned to thick fog, clouds of white obscured everything and the egg smell became so strong as to be nauseous. Sometimes during cave dives, bad smelling and milky coloured water hangs around near the shallows, but never extends all the way down. I carried on down into the enormous lake. Visibility was zero but the white milky colour was flavoured with green now. I could not see my bright dive light even when six inches from my face. Feeling something scratching my leg I groped around below me to feel tree branches everywhere. I was stuck in a tree in zero visibility at an unknown depth. I wiggled about and slipped down further into the branches. At twenty-five metres, the water was perfectly clear but with a heavy green tint. Shining my light upwards I could see all the bad visibility just hanging above, suspended like clouds. The horrible smell was now gone and I headed down to be the first into our boat captains living-room. The descent up until now was pretty nasty and would prove quite disorientating to the guys trying their first deep dive in such conditions. Swimming though the trees, now near sixty metres, felt very strange. The trees were in various states of decomposition and were covered by what looked like icicles made of silt. I could see for at least twenty metres with my primary light and headed over to what looked like a clearing with definite chainsaw marks on some of the tree stumps. I had heard about illegal underwater logging going on to harvest mahogany trees, this sounded like another horribly dangerous way to earn a living.

The descent line thrown into the water earlier had seemed a good idea, but as soon as it met the tree line it became tangled in the branches, so I had to let it go. I was just swimming around freely now, looking for signs of buildings and the infamous Buddhist temple. Bamboo plants grew everywhere, the waterlogged poles crossing each other at all angles. I could see the base of the old river that had been dammed. The riverbed extended away far beyond the length of the visibility so must have had quite a flow in its heyday - the valley took just two years to get this deep as the river ran its normal course with nowhere to go but upwards. Rumours about the dam said that the people who lived in the jungle valley village were communists and a concern to the government. The forest-dwellers were asked to give up communism and/or leave the valley. The villagers retreated to nearby caves and defended any attempts to move them on. The Dam project ensured that only the best swimmers would be able to spread communism throughout Thailand. If increased drinking water reserves were the official aim of the dam in the valley, the project had been unsuccessful - the water was rancid and fit for nothing but upsetting some villagers. I constantly kept one eye open for the fresh water sharks and giant snakes but didn't even see a minnow. There must be fish somewhere in the lake as a few fishermen worked the green water, and I had seen some prehistoric looking fish in nets as we boarded earlier. The 3mm wetsuit I had on was more than enough at the surface where the water temperature approached 30 degrees centigrade, but swimming along in the deeper clear water I started to shiver. I checked my dive computer and it confirmed a much cooler 21 degrees down here. The dive time so far was twenty-five minutes between forty and sixty metres, and already my wrist computer advised I would have to spend an additional forty minutes decompressing in the rotten-egg smelling, milky waters above me. I checked that my spare mask was easily accessible in case I needed it in a hurry later.

I did not relish the thought of spending even a minute without a mask submerged in that virtual sewer. As I had been swimming away from the anchor line for most of the dive, the boat would not know where I would be unless the skipper had been bubble watching, and I certainly doubted the captain was doing anything other than sleeping. I sent up my surface marker buoy to indicate my position. The orange balloon made a hole through the clouds above, all the way to the surface, and now rays of sunlight shone like a laser beam down through the trees. My exhaled bubbles had also left a trail of their own through the virtual clouds but as I had been swimming along as I breathed out, the effects were not as profound as the marker buoys'. Heading up, I wound in my reel line while following it to the surface. The nylon cord had caught branches in several places and I slowly untangled it in zero visibility while immersed again in the disgusting sulphur clouds. The water temperature was much warmer where it stunk the most and I started to retch from the smell. Hydrogen Sulphide can permeate through the skin and it becomes a nauseating full body experience. Today's dive site was very interesting, but I couldn't imagine a regular crowd of Scooby divers putting up with the smell and bad visibility. My mask stayed on my face throughout the deco stops and the smell stayed the right side of manageable, but reaching the surface was very welcome. As I thought, the drunken skipper was far away but I could see him lying in his hammock on the boat. I blew my whistle to wake him from his snooze. The others were still down and I sat on the boat alone for half an hour more until they surfaced. The boat captain strangely spent the entire time naked in the water, hanging onto the propeller shaft while singing loudly in Thai. Everybody's dive went to plan and once all were back on the long-tail boat we chugged along the river to see our floating hotel.

From a distance the accommodation resembled a tangled log jam. Once alongside, it looked like a like a log jam with rotten children's play houses sprinkled on top. I expected to see prisoners of war kept in underwater cages and the whole scene screamed Apocalypse Now or the Deer Hunter films. Some gap toothed locals stopped polishing their guns long enough to welcome us aboard. Tentatively we all climbed onto the floating bed and breakfast, with thoughts of nocturnal Russian Roulette action against bearded G.I's as tonight's entertainment. I had a look around and saw that there were no roofs on the sleeping areas and the mattresses were all soaked. Luckily I had decided to leave my laptop at home today. It may have been quite cheap for a night here but was definitely no bargain, as it had all the home comforts of a wet park bench - without the newspaper duvet. Our hosts started cooking lunch while we prepared to refill our scuba tanks. The portable air compressor roared into life for about five minutes before springing a leak. A torrential down pour stopped play at about the same time as we had the high pressure pump stripped down in pieces. I worked with two of the Jannes underneath plastic bags until we realised our efforts would come to nothing, a key piece of pipework was visibly corroded and broken. Lack of raw materials on the floating barge meant our improvisational options were limited to unrestrained swearing. The three day trip plan was snookered and even the lunch looked like it would have a maggot considering bulimia, even better was that someone would have to soon tell the locals using sign language that we would be not be staying now as our compressor was knackered and we couldn't go diving again. Surprisingly, lunch tasted fantastic and I vowed never again to judge a book by its cover...although my fingers were crossed behind my back, of course. Janne senior spoke enough Thai to explain our complicated situation and everything was now smooth again. If we had just decided to finish our lunch and pack the boat before leaving everything would have been fine, but sadly our dive instructor common sense took command of the situation.

A plan was hatched to do another sixty metre dive using the remnants of our dive tanks. Everyone agreed that this was the best idea, as we had come along way just to dive once and even the guys that had completed their first decompression dive an hour earlier were bang up for a report performance. We all went back in the water just before dark with nearly empty tanks. Conditions at the bottom at night were likely to be very similar to those experienced during daylight hours. With so little left in our tanks the dive plans were shorter than thirty minutes of in-water time. I went in alone, as the other two sharing the boat took their time getting ready. Dropping through the clouds of hydrogen sulphide this time was very spooky. What little light that was available on the earlier dive was now gone, and with it any clues as to orientation. I kept my legs firmly together so as not to get any tree limbs going anywhere untoward, and drifted down though the spiky branches. I always clipped my tanks contents gauge just under my chin and hardly took my eyes of it this time. The luminous green face of the gauge indicated that I had enough air to finish the dive as normal, but this time it had only just begun, I justified it to myself by the facts that we had come along way for just one death...err dive, and I was luckily diving alone and therefore wouldn't need to share any of my air supply with anyone else. I reached the bottom on top of a large mangrove bush at fifty-five metres depth. I thought of sending up my surface marker buoy to help the boat captain keep track, but realising it was dark above, and that the skipper was likely curled up asleep in his hammock before I went into the water, meant it would be even more foolish to waste the precious air needed to inflate the balloon.

Swimming around in this sort of stealth mode was very relaxing, the thought of scuba diving at night can be very intimidating for beginner divers, but after just five minutes of torchlight finning, apprehensions turn into enjoyment. I really like night dives, but I did have three underwater lights with me to help avoid darkness induced surprises. Some of the other guys carried only one light and when the batteries died they would realise that this flooded forest was definitely not Kansas - ascending through the gnarly branches and then navigating the stinking egg smell, all the time in total darkness, would be definitely similar to running a gauntlet of excited lady-boys. Oh well, better thee than me. Searching for the elusive Buddha Temple was as fruitless this time as before. The drunken skipper did point downwards from the boat saying that it was right beneath us again, but now he added that it was bottomless here also, or at least 180 metres, whatever was deeper probably. It was actually quite near 180 feet, but the similar numbers were purely a coincidence I'd imagine, as the only depth measuring equipment on the long-tail boat was a rotten oar. I thought I saw a clearing in some trees at one point, maybe it was an medieval car-park for a sunken drive-through cinema, or narcosis, boredom or the cold was playing tricks on me. I managed just twelve minutes swimming through the trees, like a sub-aqua Tarzan before I reached the tank pressure needed to allow a re-entry into Earths atmosphere with any degree of certainty. If I stayed any longer I would likely run out of air and be forced to ascend without completing my deco stops.

The thought of getting the bends in the moonless jungle tonight ensured I headed upwards on time. Ascending up through a bit of a clearing gave me a direct path away from any scratching tree branches, but like before, I was soon engulfed in the thick and warm sulphurous soup layer. My dive computer beeped that I should stay here for a few minutes and almost immediately the egg smell got to me. I started to retch and so held my regulator firmly in place to avoid it being lost if I couldn't control the vomiting feeling. One of the Jannes said over lunch that he had tried to clear condensation from his mask earlier by filling it with the cloudy water. Within seconds his eyes were burning and he was overcome with nausea. I hoped my mask strap wasn't about to break, as I had at least fifteen minutes to wait during my decompression stops. Thankfully it didn't, and I broke the surface on time and in one piece, with even a small reserve in my air tanks. The night sky was like a planetarium, every star in the area sparkling brightly. The water was flat like glass and warm like blood, nothing was making a sound. I just floated looking upwards for five minutes enjoying the view, contemplating what I had just seen. Shouting out to the boat captain, who was hopefully somewhere in the darkness - drew no response. With only the starlight to illuminate the area, I couldn't see either of the two long-tail boats. I turned my powerful dive light on and scanned as far as I could see...nothing. With no direction to swim in, I decided to float and wait. I turned on a small flashing strobe light to become a little more conspicuous, a passing aeroplane might see the faint flicker and call the Automobile Association in England - this was every bit as likely as the emergency services in Thailand effecting a rescue. I floated for at least forty-five minutes in the darkness without hearing or seeing any boats.

A few of the other guys were arriving back at the surface now and were starting to shout out to our hopefully still sleeping boat drivers. Some groaning in the distance identified our captains and reassured us that they hadn't left for an early night. We had obviously not paid the total amount to the drivers up front, but what they did get would probably have been a week's normal wages and more than enough to allow them to head to a bar. Still the boats engines didn't splutter into life, the only thing to do was to kick our flippers in the direction of the gruff coughing voices. I got to my boat in just ten minutes of finning, my dive-light picked out the skipper still working on the boats adapted car engine in total darkness. Climbing into the boat without help, I scanned the decks for possible indicators of aggravation to come - we were in no-mans land after all, and drunk and drugged-up boat captains in these parts had gained reputations for being unpredictable and sometimes mercenary. The boat seemed to be full of rainwater and it must have been raining hard when the group was below the surface. I shone my light onto the cursing captain to illuminate his engine project and could see that the entire head of the engine was off. Not speaking much Thai was no problem here, as anyone could see that we were not going anywhere for several hours or maybe even days. I shouted over to the other guys the situation on this boat. Someone shouted back a similar story from the other long-tail. Apparently, the captains had fallen asleep in their hammocks as soon as our flippers were out of sight. A rainstorm had lashed the boats for thirty minutes at least and the captains just sat and watched as the engine carburettors filled with water. There was no mobile phone coverage in this area, nor anything to eat, and definitely no internet connection, we were all doomed. We sat and shivered until eleven at night before the engines were successfully reassembled. The rain never stopped, but we witnessed some of the most amazing lightning storms I had ever seen.

Getting back to Patong in Phuket after three in the morning was hard work, and to make matters worse, I had a diving course starting the same day. I deliberately scheduled an academic day to kick off things and today was meant to be spent just checking the customer's pre-study reviews. Steve, the would-be tech student, had actually done his homework as agreed and this gave me a fairly easy day to recover from yesterday's adventure. I had training courses booked for the next twenty-one days straight, all these trimix dives were good for business but hardly salutiferous. After a day spent relaxing in an air-conditioned classroom and an early night I was raring to go again. Air diving courses are great because the boats the company owned all had air compressors on. This meant I could go home earlier and simply fill the dive-tanks on the boat on the way to the dive-site. Our first dives of this training course were quite shallow evaluation dives. We would do three of them on day one. A three dive day meant going to Ratcha Noi Island which was 3 hours cruise away, plenty of sleeping time. Most dutiful dive instructors would treat a 3 hour boat ride as if it was a day off and go out on the town the previous night – to have a large one. I stayed at home to do some planning and write some more of this book. At seven the following morning the staff met at the shop to get a ride to the boat pier, by the looks on everybody's face, most had come straight from a bar, and often we would pick up customers *directly* from their bar stools.

My customer on this course was a diving instructor himself, over from the United States to complete some technical dive training. He said he would not be drinking during the course, so I extended him the same courtesy, at least until he fell off the wagon first. The boat journey out was not rough, but still fairly spirited. The staff were all asleep as usual in various nooks and crannies, recovering from their nights excesses, and the customers were just warming up before getting into the full swing of seasickness. The cabin on our boat today was enormous and had close on thirty people packed inside it today, sheltering from the wind and spray, the windows were shut, the temperature inside bordering uncomfortable. Almost the entire group were yawning and salivating, waiting anxiously for the small yellow Dimenihydrine tablets to work their magic and stop the vomiting. When it became properly rough all the staff hoped the pills were not the generic or fake varieties that plagued Asia. Copy tablets were a bit cheaper than the originals, but meant that one of us would have the grim job of cleaning up seasick most of the day. I sat outside on the open deck with my customer Steve, to take advantage of the fresh air. I noticed one of the dive-guides' going in and out of the toilets, maybe he was being sick. This dive-guide was new and therefore was just being an instructors' assistant today. Our proximity to the toilet door allowed us to hear that lots of sniffing and groaning was going on inside the cubicle. When Jimmy the dive-guide came out he had white powder all over his face. He was brushing his nose profusely and said to Steve my customer, who was waiting to use the loo, that he had spilt prickly heat powder all over himself and the toilet floor. Barging past him to use the toilet, Steve came out shortly afterwards shaking his head. Jimmy the dive-guide had left lines of finely chopped 'prickly heat powder' on top of the toilet cistern. I went into the bathroom and threw a bucket of seawater over everything, so Jimmy didn't have to, because that's the kind of considerate fellow I am. I'm no expert but the lines did resemble lines of cocaine and they were easily the size of poodles' legs (and the same colour). Jimmy had been very quiet up until five minutes ago, but now he was bouncing around the boat waking everybody up.

Steve, the customer, was mortified that dive-guides took cocaine before going underwater...me too. I got Jimmy to stop irritating the seasick customers and come and sit down for a chat. I said that he couldn't dive with any customers now and that he could pretend to the instructor (that he was supposed to be helping today) that he felt too sick to do any diving. Jimmy started to get a little tearful, and started camply explaining his cocaine addiction saga. He said he could fix it and instantly proceeded to take two large brown tablets from a well-stocked tablet box in his backpack. The big pills looked as big as walnuts, but within a second they were both swallowed. Steve asked what they were and Jimmy calmly responded that it was just Rohypnol, his doctor had prescribed them for times when he needed to relax, or when he craved his nasal marching powder. He took both of them as he wasn't exactly sure of the dose. Jimmy continued to snore for the rest of the day but woke up fresh-faced as the boat re-entered the harbour that evening. Jimmy never came to work the next day, but he texted me saying he was going to a quieter, neighbouring island for a little peace and would maybe even start a much more chilled-out dive centre with some pals. This would be probably the last diving course I taught in Phuket, as I had had enough of all the constant antics. Thailand is fantastic fun, but you have to be careful not to get caught up in it yourself. Alcohol and drugs have dogged many a 'dive-professionals' career - even forcing some individuals to need psychiatric help. I had witnessed many customers and some instructors being taken away by the authorities to be put in sanatoriums or funny-farms while waiting for family members to fly over and extricate them. Constantly moving around Asia, or back and forth to home, means avoiding continual exposure to destructive temptations or friends, with their propensity to take down all around them.

After ten days of exhausting but drama-free diving with Steve, I was ready for a break. I went to Phi-Phi Island to relax and explore the many caverns and caves it offers. The islands sit on top of a myriad of limestone tunnels and swimming through them, it's a wonder the whole place doesn't collapse. I stayed at Phi-Phi Island village and went diving with some instructor buddies – Adam and Simon. They took time off work to complete some Cave Instructor training at the same time as we looked for more interesting small holes to swim into. The Emerald Cave on Koh-Ha, or the Maya Cavern on Phi-Phi Le were my favourite spots. You could swim three hundred feet into a warm, subterranean wonderland, accompanied by only the most experienced fellow divers and feel a million miles away from the outside areas of these popular cavern sites. The Phi-Phi island dive sites are so scenic and popular they usually teemed with hundreds of scuba Noddy's – all standing on the reef or impersonating coral wrecking-balls. Many were discovering ever-less intricate ways to drown themselves while pitting 'poorly applied diving instruction' against limited common sense and biblical hangovers. Being inexperienced underwater is hazardous enough, but even after surfacing, divers are faced with the unrelenting gauntlet of myopic or drugged-up long-tail boat drivers sporting buzz-saw like propellers. I was thankful I was not at the sharp-end of diver 'training' like this. After my very civilised cave-safari trip I was fully sane again and ready for the next roll of the dice. I had no idea where to go next, the Lebanon trip was still some weeks away, the lease on the house in Patong expired at the end of the month, as did my work permit and visa. I fancied moving to the mainland for the proximity to Bangkok airport and better choice of shops.

Steve Burton always seemed to promote Pattaya, saying it was not as bad as my memory painted it. However, I had 350 kilograms of personal possessions and Pattaya was over a thousand kilometres away by road - an expensive combination in Thailand. I checked the rates for a one-way hire car rental – it would have been cheaper to buy the car. The airline wanted sixty baht per kilo in excess baggage, but at least I would *probably* get all my stuff to my destination in one go. I opted for the flying option and rolled up at the airport with enough luggage to put Mariah Carey to shame. The excess baggage total came to more than the price of six passenger tickets. I swallowed hard and got out my credit card to pay. The clerk then advised that I could have a domestic luggage rate of just nine baht per kilo if I wanted - it seemed Jesus was also watching over luggage handlers today. My baggage would travel on the same flight, on the same day as myself, but would now only cost in total just 3200 baht, a little over forty English pounds...Fantastic - even if only half of it arrived in Pattaya, I was still saving money. Standing by the luggage carousel at U-Tapao airport I did feel a little pessimistic, I had a feeling that at least some of my diving equipment was just about to be used by someone else still back in Phuket. How wrong could I be? I chastised myself (lightly) as all of my dozen bags appeared one-by-one and trickled along the conveyor belt like a gaggle of ducks. A free courtesy bus took all the passengers to their respective hotels in an unusual non-circuitous route. The shock was so much - I had to lie down...I spoke of it for days afterwards. After a few nights in a swish hotel, I settled back down to earth and checked into the less salubrious Jomtien Long Stay hotel. Although costing just a hundred dollars per month, it had air-conditioning, hot and cold water, even a telephone and television that worked. Room service and a swimming pool were the icing on the cake.

The only downside was that the pool was a meeting point for transsexuals cavorting with their drunken western boyfriends.

Man on Man petting was acceptable, but any Male/Female untoward behaviour was strictly taboo and usually complained about. With all the floating used-condoms and small bottles of poppers in the water, the pool was off-limits to all but Gary Glitter wannabees. Other than that, the hotel was fine. I had some training-text writing work to complete in addition to scribbling some more pages of this book - just by concentrating on these, I could keep out of trouble.

On the 18th of July I flew from Bangkok to Dubai using Emirates airlines. I had a connecting flight to Beirut with Arab-Air leaving from Sharjah airport, a smaller regional airport on the other side of town. The taxi ride was a bit like Tom Cruise - short but expensive. I had a 'relaxing' 7 hour stopover in this airport but sadly it was neither open at this time of the morning, nor contained facilities to entertain me longer than the time necessary to drink one bitter coffee. There were multiple mosques of course, but I surmised that my sitting at the back playing Solitaire on my laptop all day would not be appreciated. My friendly cab driver was still outside, waiting expectantly. He gladly offered to take me to his friends' hotel near the airport I originally came from. I was a little miffed at him, considering he had taken me to the closed airport without telling me so beforehand, but there were sadly no alternatives to his scruffy Datsun estate car in the cab rank. Even at seven in the morning the heat was unbearable as we sat, prisoners to the traffic, his fare-meter ticking like a crazed metronome. I felt like I was about to suffer heat exhaustion as the cab had no working air-conditioning and the morning temperature nudged forty five degrees centigrade.

The taxi driver kept ranting on about oil-wars and the Bush crusades, infidels etc, although it was difficult to disagree with any of his sermon actually - especially given my current location in purgatory. Dubai hotels can be magnificent, however, my accommodation situated far from the emerald and glitzy coastline was also far from magnificent. Inside the dark and shisha pipe smoke filled reception, the clientele resembled those of a Heathrow airport immigration holding cell. I paid my 200 dirhams (£70) for the use of a room for the afternoon and headed straight for it. I was grubby, but delirious from sleep starvation - pillow first…shower second. For the next two hours there was a steady knock at my door as every nationality of prostitute paraded their wares without speaking a single word I understood. I put a musty cushion over my head and tried to snooze through the nightmare. After a couple of long blinks my alarm went off and it was time to head drearily back to the airport. I asked the taxi driver from before to come and pick me up an hour *after* I actually needed to leave. The new drivers fare was a third of the firsts' and this guy only spoke of English football teams to himself, as I know nothing about them. I checked my bags and went to find some awful coffee to wake me up. The thimble sized cup contained a 'black-as-bitumen' syrup, the very essence of caffeine. As it touched my tongue its effects worked with the startling efficiency of a cactus-enema. I was energised with a dark mood full of contempt for anyone or anything…Perfect for travelling with locals in this part of the world.   The plane journey was uneventfully appalling and, as in any religion controlled environment, alcohol flowed thick and fast as soon as the aircraft crossed an imaginary border high in the sky.

Lebanon is as much a Christian country as an Arab one, liberal attitudes and western decadence contrast with impoverished conservatives on every corner. Landing at Beirut airport I saw many passengers discarding their all-black robes in favour of skimpier and revealing western alternatives, before driving away in chauffeur driven Hummers. I was met at the airport by Christian's girlfriend, the lovely Lara. We drove straight to the north-west coast of Lebanon to the town of Enfeh, home to the resort of Las Salinas where Christians dive centre is located. Situated overlooking the Mediterranean Sea, Lebanon benefits from the influences of many differing cultures and cuisines. I forgot how tired I was feeling and after shaking lots of hands, we all went out for a meal. I was expecting sheep's eyes and schwarma kebab, and was totally amazed at the actual foods available, some of the tastiest I've had anywhere. In the morning I looked out of my window across the flat-calm bay to see a still functioning, Phoenician built, dry-dock, the oldest in the world. Beyond that was the town of Byblos, the birthplace of modern alphabet. Also, the resorts entire surrounding landscape was carved into salt drying terraces, dating back to ancient times and beyond. Natural salt production has been the towns main industry for eons, hence the name of the resort Las Salinas. Lebanon is steeped in history and for an eternity was a hub for maritime traders. Shipwrecks lay in abundance up and down the coastline, from Amphora laden Greek vessels to, hopefully, the remains of HMS Victoria, currently exact-position unknown. We hoped to change that.

Christian had hoped to dive the remains of HMS Victoria on June 22nd 2004, to mark the 111th anniversary of her sinking. So much had needed to be done before this could have happened though. All the support divers and topside crew needed to be familiarised with procedures attached to divers performing the one hundred and sixty metre dives. Christian and I dived on other nearby shipwrecks in fairly standard equipment before concentrating on deeper diving afforded by the deep reef walls and even a nearby blue-hole. We spent a day inspecting and building our deep diving rigs and connected some large steel scuba tanks together with manifolds before diving shallow with them to see how they performed. The big dive cylinders had been recently cleaned at a local gas production company to remove any possible contaminants that could manifest problems on very deep dives. This company used Trichlo-ethylene liquid to clean the tanks as it is a powerful cleaner that evaporates after use. Popular in the past with clothing dry-cleaners, the 'Trike' liquid is as harmful to people as it is possible to be and banned from use nowadays throughout Europe and North America because of its effects on the ozone layer and carcinogenic properties. The tanks had been cleaned and then returned to the dive centre with the valves loosely in place. Christian's staff had tightened the valves up and then filled the cylinders with air. After adjusting a few components, Christian and I each bolted a set of tanks to our backs and went diving. I was using brand new breathing regulators and didn't immediately detect any unusual odours from the breathing air other than the stuff used to make the new equipment shine by the factory. However, by

40 metres depth I started to feel delirious and sick. Within seconds my head was pounding and I felt like unconsciousness was looming. I signalled over to Christian and pointed out that my head was seriously dizzy. He responded that he felt the same way. The seabed was in sight now, so we dropped the rest of the way to reorganise and head back up. By now I strongly suspected the tanks were contaminated with copious amounts of the 'Trike' chemical.

Diving to 50 metres with tanks awash with dry cleaning fluid was a bad move, the intense disorientation lasted the entire ascent to the surface and throughout the short decompression stops, even though we switched tanks to breathe 100 percent oxygen for the final stages. On the boat I felt like I had sniffed a gallon of glue, the nauseating effects lasted all that night and most of the next day. We were very lucky to escape a dizzy drowning that dive, and needed to take the next day off to recuperate. We set about re-cleaning the tanks properly the following day, disassembling the tanks revealed not merely a residue of the chemical, but still an inch or two of the actual liquid - we were lucky to be alive. Christian got some brand new steel tanks from his warehouse and I made sure that I got a set of those - my time here wasn't planned to include cleaning tanks or drowning at the hands of imbeciles.

I wanted to get as many practice deep dives in as possible, building up bottom time at each increment. Matching dive suits thickness to the constantly falling deep water temperature and getting comfortable with carrying all the decompression tanks would better prepare us for the planned fifteen minutes free swimming along Victoria on the seabed over one hundred and fifty metres down. The water was getting down to 12 degrees beyond one hundred and twenty metres, but from fifty metres up it stayed between 25 and 27 degrees centigrade, air temperatures in the high 30's made drysuit use very uncomfortable. Christians athletic 'Olympic rowers' frame and sensitive disposition favoured a 7mm wetsuit, whereas my winter coat supplemented by junk food and 'rufty-tufty' demeanour allowed up to four hours in a 3mm wetsuit and dive hood. All in all we completed twelve practice dives to one hundred and twenty metres and many others shallower, perfecting equipment configuration and technique. For most of the dives I supplemented the five scuba tanks with a bulky video camera system.

The weather was pretty much perfect, so we managed usually two dives per day. Evenings were spent filling tanks and then driving to the nearby town of Tripoli (the Lebanese one) for some local food. Haidar, one of the dive centres instructors, came from Tripoli and showed me round the old town and along its scenic promenades. 'Tripoli' translates to three poles, a term reflecting the three main thoroughfares that meet on its shores, just like its namesake in Libya. It's a very old city, steeped in history, still with some fantastic medieval architecture. Tripoli is very rundown and has had little of the renovation that Beirut received after the end of the countries long Civil war in 1991. 'Civil' War is a strange name for a conflict that brutally killed so many. Incredibly ornate old buildings are left standing in virtual ruins, as testimony to darker times. Some buildings have been reclaimed and revitalised but still show their pockmarked outer walls damaged by rocket fire or heavy machine gun rounds, all this adds a sort of macabre feeling to the town and maybe is an attempt to show that the old wounds have not yet fully healed up. Up to forty armed militia's ransacked the towns and Cities of Lebanon during the war, both Christian and Muslim, fighting each other and often themselves, for over fifteen years. Rabble armies commanded by self-serving warlords fought tit-for-tat battles, mostly against civilians thought to be unsympathetic to the cause of the day. Most combatants were fuelled by religious rage and greed, and supported in many cases by unknown western influences. Fought mostly at ground level with hand-to-hand and street-by-street guerrilla tactics, the troops rampaged to gain land and garner respect, i.e. the biggest gun, or the most kills, demands the most respect. The conspiracies get deeper as stories of subterfuge and destabilisation from western infidels are added to the mix.

The Lebanese war gave the world new weapons – the car and truck bombs. Aerial supremacy was afforded by the most highly elevated snipers, not so much fighter pilots but those situated in the tallest hotels or government buildings. Israeli and Syrian jets did have something to say loudly also, the predictably ironic message - 'Our bombs ensure your peace'. In 1991 a ceasefire agreement was made, but hinged around a contingent of 40,000 Syrian troops permanently garrisoned in Lebanon to police the accord. During my visit, discussions about the war were commonplace and always with someone actually present - it was also best that I just listened - my views on things tend to be a little black and white and therefore likely to get a reaction similar to putting water on a hot chip pan. I've noticed that logic doesn't apply to religious arguments...anywhere. Tensions and anger obviously still simmer, and not that far from the surface. Although so many armies fought the war, the battlefield was solely Lebanon, the reason, if there ever was just one, was religious intolerance. What is certain - Lebanon and its people with their myriad of faiths have been gravely affected by the conflict. It will take many generations to put the memories behind them, as with all conflicts that end without a clear winner.

North of Enfeh, up to Tripoli and beyond to the Syrian border is now 'Bin Laden' country. Osama Bin Laden's mother is reported to have come from the Tripoli area, and the family name still supports ideals that have an extensive following. Although Lebanon was once a vibrant holiday destination for the western socialite elite in the fifties and sixties - even the Orient Express Train tracks crossed the country - it's different now. Syrian secret police roam the city in telltale white Peugeot 504 cars, a reminder of the new guard that mistrusts the more liberal followers of Christianity with their decadent western influences. The luxury train tracks are now overgrown with weeds, or have been twisted beyond recognition by explosions. Music in public is limited to the loudspeakers of the minarets with their ubiquitously echoing call-to-prayer chants. There is no feeling of the Arab Riviera anywhere. Despite all this, I felt pretty safe wandering the streets by day or night there, way safer than any London suburb, obviously I didn't wear anything openly provocative, US or UK flags on clothing would simply be seen as possible targets for aggravation, both verbal and even ballistic. Lebanon has no hoodie's or chav scum to avoid, my only concern was surprisingly that, like Pattaya, Thailand, Tripoli is home to a large gay and transsexual contingent, aggressively servicing visiting men, this time from neighbouring Arab countries. Haidar joked that even if you dropped a one hundred dollar bill on the floor while in Tripoli, you should not bend over and pick it up! One of Haidar's dive students had a take-away shop near the main beach boulevard, or 'Corniche'. The Hot-Fish sandwiches he sold, amongst other things, were fantastic tasting and very popular. Several times a week we drove the short distance from Enfeh to Tripoli to stand in the street to eat these Garlic-supercharged spicy fish-paste sandwiches - they may sound grim but they taste great. Tripoli boasts some of the finest 'Halab' sweet makers in the world and the impressively flamboyant restaurant buildings that they are housed in can be very conspicuous in an otherwise run down neighbourhood. Almost all of the restaurant staff seemed honoured to give a tour of the kitchens to show off their pastry chefs' skills, and if you ate all of the free samples they offered, quickly enough, you wouldn't need to order a proper meal!

Luckily we were doing two dives most days, or we would never have fitted into our dive-suits. When Christian and I were happy that everybody on the dive-boat knew what they were doing after our extensive practice sessions, we headed out to the area where HMS Victoria was suspected to be lying undiscovered. We planned to make some short discovery dives to ensure the giant iron-clad warship was actually down there, and to check its orientation. Hours were spent trolling around the area and staring at the dive-boats echo sounder, although it revealed few clues. Occasionally the screen revealed an abundance of fish life, or maybe even a small debris field from the wreck, but the shallowest depth of these images was 156 metres. The fairly uniform depth only strengthened the idea that Victoria's heavy frame had settled far into the soft sediment far below. An occasional shadow on the bottom-scanning equipment revealed an unusual shape that resembled a fishing net floating upwards from the seabed. Maybe it was a large trawl that had been snagged in the past on the wreckage, only an actual dive could tell for sure. Christian had purchased a remote camera system capable of being lowered down to the seabed, but with the likely presence of large trawl nets at the wreck site, the risk of losing the camera was just too high. We headed back to the resort harbour to organise our equipment and arrange the next few days of deep diving. Travelling back along the Lebanese coast in perfect conditions, like we often had, you could easily see Syria to the north, stretching from north to south were the snow topped peaks of the Golan Heights mountain range that rises sharply from the sea, right up to 3000 metres altitude. Late afternoons would have the sun cast a vivid orange hue across the range, sometimes the snow would reflect the sunlight like a mirror.

The city of Tripoli is the closest mainland point to HMS Victoria's final resting place. Some reefs that break the surface lay between Victoria and Tripoli port, but even closer, to the south east lay Rabbit Island. This island is mentioned in the subsequent Victoria court marshal / enquiry papers. HMS Victoria, after being prematurely disengaged from the collision with HMS Camperdown, headed full steam towards Rabbit Island just a few miles away in the hope of beaching the mortally wounded vessel. Rabbit Island received its name from the fact that it resembles a giant sitting rabbit from a distance. I though it looked more like an oil tanker than a rabbit, but I guess as such craft had not been invented back then the rabbit connection was made instead. Closer inspection of the not-so-barren island reveals extensive fortifications and trenches. Used by the PLO and Hezbollah armies as a training camp during the Lebanese conflict, it serves as tourist destination now and a grim reminder of the recent past. That afternoon in June 1893, a wholly different tragedy played out as Admiral Tryon ordered his stricken ship to head towards this closest landfall. The range and bearing from Rabbit Island were accurately stated in the court documents, and this gave Christian a starting point from which to base the search. At the dive centre we had some late lunch before tank filling commenced - Pita bread, Houmous and Fool dip, washed down with a cup of Herbal Mate tea, completed the menu. Traditional foods could sometimes look a little unusual, but is generally much healthier and the ingredients easier to distinguish than western grub. It's funny how squeamish the English can get with food made without frying, or camouflaged by a pastry crust or batter.

Replete, we set to work. Unfortunately, by the time we finished pumping our dive tanks with the expensive Trimix breathing gases to dive, the weather decided that the sea should keep its secrets a little longer. A squall had blown in from nowhere and looked to be now taking root. Sadly, my visa was expiring in the next couple of days - before the weather was forecast to improve. We managed no dives to the wreck during this first trip. I agreed to come back in two weeks time as the weather never stays bad for long in the Mediterranean Sea.

I retraced my journey back to Thailand. Pattaya hadn't changed while I was away, but the stories in the local paper had got ever more incredible. An Italian holidaymaker had apparently jumped out of a small sightseeing aeroplane, naked, clutching plastic sacks full of cash. The Thai pilot said that he was as surprised as anyone when the man stripped off before leaping out the door. The lifeless suicide jumper was found a few days later, his money surprisingly wasn't. After a quick interrogation, the pilot said the man could jump from the aeroplane if he left the bags of money behind. The pilot couldn't remember what happened to the money after he went to a beer bar to console himself. The story may have had an element of truth in it though, as many times recently the newspaper had reported western men stripping naked before jumping from the roofs of their own bars in final acts of desperation. My beer buddies and I pondered that jumping from aircraft would be more preferable to sitting sober in a Thai mental hospital with broken ankles. My two weeks in Thailand flew by. Soon I was back in a taxi headed for Bangkok airport, and onwards to Dubai for my connecting flight to Beirut, to find HMS Victoria with Christian. Dubai International airport is a glitzy place, with lots of shops and distractions to while away a stop-over. I had nine hours to waste this trip, airlines are magicians when it comes to wringing extra cash from the pockets of travellers. I could have had a two hour stop-over for only an extra $200. Diving Instructors generally don't earn $30 per hour, I took the long wait option and counted the cash in my pocket. Actually, I spent most of the money in Starbucks. There is a nice hotel in the airport, the Dubai International - showers are just 22 Dirham (three quid) and this allows you to lurk in the lobby, lounging on their leather-look Chesterfields and reading semi up-to-date foreign newspapers…pure luxury.

Arriving in Beirut airport is a different kettle of fish, there are some shops on the Departures side, but on the Arrivals there are only aggressive cab-drivers clamouring to help you spend money. The public toilets in the arrivals lounge are typical of a place were the machine-gun toting guards openly smoke underneath a no-smoking sign. As in all Arab countries, it is customary to actually stand on top of the toilet when using it - so as not to touch it with anything but your dirty shoes. If the toilet seat is still in enough pieces, it again would be expected to stand on top of this, to smash it into smaller pieces to make it less comfortable for western users not familiar with this type of tight-rope walking. Then there is the ubiquitous 'Bum Gun' – a sort of 'Bidet' in a hose pipe. Toilet paper is strictly outlawed because it is apparently 'filthy', it is okay though, to spray others accidentally-on-purpose with the 'Bum Gun', inadvertently, while you use it. It is a lot funnier to be standing, waiting outside non-Arab cubicles when occupiers not used to standing on such flimsy and slippery 'infidel' sit-down toilet seats, slip, and fall into the bowl. Where was I? Christian turned up two hours late to collect me from the airport.

We drove up to the resort and planned the next couple of weeks. I had a customer I knew from Thailand contact me, wanting to do a Trimix course. He was willing to come to Lebanon to complete the training at my promise of some interesting wreck diving opportunities. Paul is a Major in the British army - stationed in Borneo. Currently he was holidaying in Egypt and would travel over-land to Beirut via Jordan…rather him than me. A couple of days of travelling later he did arrive, mostly in one piece. Christian, Paul and I did some Trimix dives to some wrecks and down a couple of walls for a few days to complete Paul's course. Paul agreed to act as a deep support diver for the upcoming Victoria dives, and this swelled the number of sensible support divers on the team to one. On August 22nd, we left the harbour to find and dive the position of the wreck HMS Victoria. With Christian's two fishermen friends as skipper and wreck finders, two additional support-logistics-consultants or deck-swabs, plus us three divers, as a team, we couldn't fail! We looked for signs of the wreck for hours, during what must have been the hottest day of the year. Tempers were running as hot as the deck temperature, as the boat danced around in the choppy seas that also adversely affected the sonar equipment. The fishermen said that 'this was the spot', a dozen times, while we drifted around aimlessly. These 'exact' positions had been handed down for generations, from Grandfather to Father to Son, the sonar equipment continually stared downwards, bathing the seabed with its electronic chirps and clicks, but never agreed with anyone's inherited knowledge. The large 'floating' fishing-net image showed up a couple of times and we threw the anchor in here eventually to at least have a starting position. Three more hours elapsed and a mutiny was starting to kick in. I struggled hard to keep my toys in my pram, I hate dithering. I wanted to dive on the position of the strange net-anomaly just to see what it was and rule it out, but also to cool down. This is what we did.

Christian, Paul and I went over the side of the boat with four scuba tanks each. Back-mounted tanks of Trimix 10/60 gas were supplemented by side slung cylinders of Nitrox 50 and 100 percent oxygen. We followed the thin white line downwards. The visibility was excellent. The original idea was to drop down to one hundred and twenty metres and simply look downwards while swimming around for fifteen minutes. Even by ninety metres the ambient light level was superb, glancing back up to the surface I could easily still see the dive-boat slamming up and down on the choppy sea above. By just past one hundred metres we paused to group-up closer together and drop the next twenty metres no more than a metre or so apart. Approaching the maximum depth, it was obvious that all that was viewable beneath us were simply hues of grey and black. The water had chilled to about 17 degrees centigrade at this depth, and within our wetsuits it felt like we were walking naked during a blizzard. I was lowest on the line and stopped first. Paul was just behind me and I looked closely into his mask to make sure he was still in charge of his bus. He knew what I was doing and gave an expression that reassured me that all was good. Christian and I had dived to this depth many times before without incident - if he said he was fine, it was likely he was. Looking back to Paul, I saw a stream of bubbles coming from his ear as he tried to 'pop' his ears again down here. This could only be a perforated eardrum, I pointed and used a hand signal to ask if his ear was okay. He said he would live. Hanging around on the line wouldn't achieve much as the scene below was that of utter darkness. We had an idea of dropping magnesium flares to the seabed after activating them in deep water. This always looked cool in underwater movies, but the flares available outside of Hollywood only burned for thirty seconds. Unless they were heavily weighted they would extinguish themselves before even reaching their target.

I stared below in earnest, scanning from side to side. Eyesight could take 4 or 5 minutes to fully adjust to the twilight at this depth. We kept our dive-lights turned off to avoid further compromising our low-light vision...still nothing. I looked back up to the surface to see the anchor rope snaking upwards, but as my gaze moved back towards the seabed I saw a distinct shadow...in mid-water. It was very faint and almost on the edge of the visibility. I pointed it out to the other two, who were also looking that way now. I couldn't think what it could be, other than maybe the giant fishing net we originally thought on the boat. I indicated that we should swim over to it and investigate. Although there was no current, the boat above was being pushed by the wind and waves at the surface, this had a stretching effect on the anchor line we held onto. As we swam pulling the line behind us, it was like trying to pull an enormous bow-string. The anchor below was stuck fast in the sediment of the seabed, and the dive-boat above was being pushed sufficiently hard enough to make the descent line taut like a guitar string. As we approached the 'stain' in the water, it became obvious to me that this was no net, but was highly likely HMS Victoria standing vertically like its own tombstone. The limited slack in the line was finished and the effort spent in pulling it towards the wreck was getting tiresome. If even one of us stopped finning continuously, the pull on the line was enough to drag us away again as it resisted our efforts to reach our goal. Letting go of the line altogether the swim became easy, but the anchor line predictably sprang away – completely out of sight. As we swam closer it became obvious that this was an enormous battleship, but from our current depth and angle, we could only see one giant propeller and the outline of the hull. I was mindful of the lost anchor rope and intended to tie my reel line to the wreck to mark its position forever and aid our two hours of decompression stops that we had obligated ourselves to do. Heading upwards before our planned dive-time had elapsed would give us longer to gaze at the wreck from shallower water.

The three of us swam directly to the visible propeller as if caught by a tractor beam. As we neared, an identical four bladed propeller slowly came into view, like a solar eclipse and with exactly the same impact. We touched down onto the starboard propeller, and as I looked around at Christian and Paul they were shaking their heads - visibly affected by the magnitude of our discovery. Several divers had apparently looked for HMS Victoria unsuccessfully in the past. Without a definite position or confirmation from the surface from sonar electronics, compounded by the thought of one hundred and sixty metre dives, all previous explorers had baulked at the undertaking. We had dared and we had won. Our reward was locating one of the most fascinating shipwrecks ever found. The icing on the cake was that by actually preparing and then going deep diving, the wreck was found lying uniquely vertical with the shallowest part in just seventy-seven metres, instead of being buried up to its funnels, its story lost in the sediment.

Our dive-time was running out, yet there was so much to see. From our vantage point on top of a stern walkway we could stare down eighty metres of hull, only imagining what kind of balancing act was going on at the point where the wreck met the seabed. Swimming forwards over the deck, the 10 inch barrel of a deck gun looked skywards, still pristine considering it had been waiting for duty submerged for the last one hundred and eleven years. Huge Tuna fish swam round and round our position, possibly the largest living sentries to view the wreck up until today. The fish life all around the deck areas was very impressive and definitely not shy of divers. Coral growth was sparse because of the depth and gloomy light levels, red paint was still visible in patches in areas intended to be below the water line. Time was up, I had improvised an extended bottom time to take into account our time spent shallower than planned. Not leaving in the next few minutes could mean running out of breathing mixture later. I tied my reel line to the wreck and sent up a surface marker buoy. When the bag hit the surface it would join the past with the future and mark HMS Victoria's position exactly. As we ascended just a few metres away from the wreck, unequivocal confirmation of the ships identity came into view. Under the stern balcony, above what looked like a blanked torpedo tube opening, was the name – in twelve inch raised letters…VICTORIA. We were elated. We shook hands and headed up.

When HMS Victoria was lost, British Naval supremacy was cast into doubt. Rumours cast aspersions over its low design with the 'top heavy' pendulum effect afforded by its monstrous foredeck guns. This rumour was quashed as so many other British ships of the time had a similar design, recalling and redesigning of the fleet would be a costly exercise, both monetarily and reputability. Far cheaper would be to blame those involved. In charge of Victoria was Admiral George Tryon. Commanding the Flagship was a meteoric responsibility. George Tryon had risen to the top of his profession with unprecedented speed; his taciturn practical style ran roughshod over the sensitivities of many of his peers with their 'inherited' leadership skills, honed to a blunt edge by years of non-combative study. Tryon strove to overhaul the entire Navy with his insightful abilities in seamanship, and in particular, inter-ship communication. Time and again during

Naval manoeuvres Tryon had embarrassed his more inept subordinates as they blustered and bluffed their way through the training exercises. He wanted officers to take more responsibility for their actions and spend more time practicing for war, trimming the fat from out-dated Navy doctrine. On the day of the sinking, Tryon was aboard the flagship, leading the first column of ships through a complex set of course changes as they headed for their moorings off Tripoli. Leading the second column of ships was Admiral Markham aboard HMS Camperdown.

Markham was the less able of the two Admirals, and in past exercises they had crossed swords many times, as Tryon demonstrated aggressive leadership and Markham came second with his 'tried and tested in peacetime' predictably-textbook responses. Admiral Tryon was famed for his 'TA' system of 'follow-my-leader' fleet handling that flummoxed Markham again and again, as he was more adept at following the ubiquitous flag-signal system in use since time immemorial. Tryon sent memos throughout the Navy bestowing the virtues of his almost 'wireless' communication system, and also promoted the notion that officers must not blindly follow orders that may have less than desirable consequences. What is for sure is that on that fateful afternoon, 358 officers and men were sent to their graves – the result of a deadly game being played. Admiral Tryon gave an order that would bring two ships on a collision course. The leadership on both battleships saw the error almost immediately. No one did anything to avert the collision - Admiral Tryon had too much faith in his subordinates, they had too little esteem to question an order, and definitely not query the great man himself.

The result, a terrible loss of life and massive numbers of casualties, plus the unimaginable sinking of the flagship itself. HMS Victoria capsized in a little over ten minutes - the largely non-swimming crew stood no chance, most were resting below decks. They all had a proud, seemingly-blind faith in their commanding officers' abilities, but these chain-of-command principles definitely weighed heavily around the necks of those that couldn't even tread water. Many non-swimmers attempted to climb the upturned hull rather than enter the water, but instead met their fate against the still rapidly-turning ships screws. Lifeboats from nearby ships were short-sightedly ordered by Admiral Tryon to stay away from Victoria - even as she listed heavily, such was his belief that the great ship would not go down, or maybe he was of the opinion that to seek assistance in this way would be seen as weakness.

Many changes to Navy doctrine came from Victoria's sinking, most notably the way that command orders were issued and followed. The number of drowned sailors also prompted the Admiralty to issue compulsory swim tests for all new inductees. As the vessel sank in such deep water the wreck has never been visited, not even by the authorities. The British Navy would much rather forget the entire episode as soon as possible. The unknown position, compounded by almost six hundred feet of water, helped dampen all curiosities at the time and since. Christian became interested in the plight of HMS Victoria in 1994. Scouring through archive materials, from newspapers to transcripts of the court marshal, threw up lots of questions. Only a dive to Victoria could answer some of them, Christian wanted to be the first to do this.

Part of the court marshal notes mentioned the order for water-tight doors to be secured to prevent inter-compartment flooding. The general vein running through the officers recollections was one of 'causal amnesia', but that it was definitely 'someone's fault'. In fact two high ranking witnesses stated that Admiral Tryon repeated the phrase "It's all MY fault" as he prepared to stay with his sinking ship. During our first dive, it was obvious that stern-side external doors and portholes had all been left in an open position, quite predictably during that scorching afternoon off Lebanon. Now the wreck was found, so tantalizingly close to the surface, we could delve deeper and deeper below the waves, to confirm whether door-closing orders were either given or followed. Because of the importance of the find, the authorities were informed and permission sought to continue the exploration and obtain video footage of HMS Victoria. A 'fisherman and diver' exclusion order was also discussed and subsequently granted, in order to preserve the wreck from further dynamiting and/or bad anchoring technique that could topple the ship, causing it to be lost forever. Before all this happened, we celebrated.

We dived the wreck a further seven times in the following 10 days. Each time I took the video camera to record the amazing scenes. HMS Victoria is almost completely free from silt and the only damage to the hull is now encased in the seabed far from view. The sheer scale of Victoria is fully appreciable because of the excellent visibility in the area and the cross-section viewing style afforded by its orientation. Large distances of decking and superstructure can be covered without exerting any effort, simply by falling downwards. The upper decking of the iron-clad warship was constructed of wooden planking and this has almost vanished completely, allowing the below-deck areas to be viewed without penetration. Victoria was a heavily armed battleship and just by dropping from 80 metres depth to 120 metres, over twenty assorted cannons poke through hatchways to complement the dozen or so early machine gun placements every few yards. Enormous ships compasses still sit in place on their binnacles, and from the detailed ships plans Christian obtained from the Maritime museum at Greenwich it is possible to navigate from stern to bows with pinpoint accuracy. Most of the video footage recorded was taken at close range so as to build up a more complete picture of the wreck, and especially any areas showing metal fatigue. 10,000 ton ships were never designed to stand on their bows and maritime engineers might be interested to see how the hull was standing-up considering its unusual inclination. Christian and I spent some time looking for evidence of vertical movement in Victoria, but even in the roughest sea conditions the shock of the swell doesn't reach to these depths and the wreck appears rock solid…for now.

After taking nearly 3 hours of camera footage down to 120 metres depth, it was time for us to dive to the seabed to see what was keeping the majestic ship upright. We planned a dive to 156 metres on the deck side of the hull, another dive would be carried out to check the keel area as it sliced into the sediment. During this dive it would be necessary to wear five scuba tanks each and to place two more decompression tanks at prearranged depths on the anchor line. The lack of current in the area made this a viable proposition and with the excellent water clarity it made sense not to wear the additional tanks. I am always loathe to clip necessary decompression tanks on an anchor line - as tidal movement and Murphy's law often contrive to make the tanks vanish. Floating directly above Victoria, if the tanks fell they would likely hit us on our heads. Another thing here was that support divers seemed less available or reliable than quality knots. We planned to spend 8 minutes on the bottom after arriving there. Because it was pleasant diving, I didn't mind diving down there several times to harvest video images. The other option was going for the Full-Monty twenty minutes on a single dive, but without support divers I didn't fancy the odds of complete success. We filled our dive-tanks as per usual the night before and hit the hay early to prepare for the big day.

Something I found amazing was that each time we returned to the wreck, the same Evian bottle tied to mono-filament fishing line was still bobbing, marking the position, as it had for nearly ten days. I'm sure the Mediterranean could be rough if it wanted to be, but the rise and fall of the tide was never much beyond thirty centimetres. This contrasted heavily with my Channel Island experiences when we sometimes dived when the water would move twelve metres between high and low tide. We clipped our extra deco tanks to pre-measured lengths of rope attached to large floats before kitting up and going over the side. Like previous times, the enormous propellers of Victoria came into view from fifty metres or so down. Christian and I would follow the line down to Admiral Tryon's stern cabin doorway, unclip two of the deep water decompression tanks and simply meander down across the decking to where ship met mud. Slipping past the big stern gun, Christian traced a finger down the barrel as I videotaped the gun with him in the picture to give size perspective. Dropping below the gun placement we headed past the enormous anchor capstan at

105 metres. I drifted outwards to follow the swell of the gunwale as Christian swam over a hump in the super structure. The water dropped several degrees which I definitely noticed in my 3mm wetsuit. By 140 metres I started slowing down as I was getting snagged on fishing hooks attached to some long lines broken off in rigging. Christian joined me closely as we looked downwards to search for a clear path and good landing spot. I panned the camera upwards to capture a striking silhouette of Victoria's almost entire length as she basked in the eerie turquoise gloom of deep water. Whilst looking upwards I didn't notice my trajectory downwards through some rigging. I was a little irritated to see that I was now behind a virtual spiders web of Victorian lines and more modern fishing net. I looked outwards to Christian, who had stopped now, hovering on top of a huge pinnacle of debris that had fallen from the wreck as she fell all those years ago.

There were boats, masts, port holes, smashed compasses and a myriad of boxes all jumbled into a sort of 'divers honey trap'. I recorded as many of the debris-jumble images as I could. In our back tanks was Trimix 10/60, the helium percentage was tailored to give us the same feeling as if we were at fifty metres depth breathing normal air. It felt a lot deeper than this now, and I noticed a definite complacency in my predicament and a worrying sense of well-being. Although lines were all around my exit route, I decided to swim further inwards underneath some towering superstructure. I was at 150 metres, but clearly thought the wreck was penetrable even below the seabed, and this drew me further inwards. The narcosis I was experiencing masked the fact that half of the camera lighting was now flooded and useless. I only noticed the darkness when I looked at the damaged video lights to check they were on. Alarm bells rang in my head, but instead of being shrill these particular bells sounded like the deep air Wah-Wah effect. I turned around and could still see the hole I had swum in through - Christians light was shining from outside and it illuminated the way out. Despite feeling fine, my memory was blank. I noticed that I couldn't remember that last few minutes actions and this was just the shaking my head needed to wake up. Swimming into clearer water I saw Christian, still swimming around outside of the ropes and lines, we signalled simultaneously to head-up. Just a few metres from the bottom I noticed I was stuck, pain in my finger followed soon after. Looking down at my hand through the video camera lens was surreal, fluid was leaking from hand and only then I noticed a huge shiny fish hook stuck between my thumb and forefinger. The cold water had sedated my gloveless hands as effectively as something in the breathing gases I was breathing earlier had overcome my mental faculties. The slow-motion pain sharpened my mind though, and I dropped the camera down on its safety lanyard. I squealed through my regulator over to Christian, who could obviously see the hook glinting through my hand. I couldn't cut the line with my knife one-handed and had no trauma scissors with me, so just clenched my teeth and pulled the barbed hook free from my hand. Now I was free of the entanglement and fully awake. We headed up, Christian looked happy to be leaving and I certainly was. I had felt very relaxed down there - overly so, and it crossed my mind that I was maybe breathing the tail-end of dry cleaning fluid residue again.

HMS Victoria is one of the few wrecks in the world where it is possible to ascend most of the way to the surface and still be within the ship itself. I felt a lot clearer headed passing 120 metres. I paused to check my ascent rate and check my progress against the decompression plan's run-time. All was in order so I stuck the video camera back against my mask and continued filming. The deep water decompression stops were uneventful; my hand had stopped bleeding even before we left the wreck at 77 metres. Christian was three metres ahead of me throughout the deeper deco stops, until the longer pauses had us side by side. Long decompressions give plenty of time for reflection, some divers daydream as the minutes boringly tick by - personally I am never complacent or sleepy but become invigorated, constantly doing mild exercises and checking the stop timings all the way to the surface. We surfaced to calm seas and a jubilant boat crew. After nearly four hours of waiting underwater to off-gas the excesses of helium and nitrogen from our bodies before the seemingly final act of surfacing, we were exhausted. Even after climbing aboard the boat, deep divers have to avoid all forms of exertion and have to endure several more hours of calm before a sigh of all clear can be released. Christian and I lay on the sunbathing mattress on the back of his boat, slowly recharging as Haidar and Edmund drove the boat home.

Long showers followed the rinsing and packing away of our diving equipment. Like most evenings, we then sat back with a beer to watch the footage taken during the day's dive. Today's deeper images were much gloomier compared to the shallower and therefore brighter scenes recorded during previous visits. The silhouetted image of HMS Victoria standing vertically like a tombstone, taken at the bottom, came out fine and captured the sombre atmosphere at this depth perfectly. Apart from the hole in my hand, we were both very pleased with the days filming spoils. This trip was coming to an end in a couple of day's time for me, as visa's expired and flights were already booked. After such a deep dive we needed at least two days to recover, so that would be my last dive to HMS Victoria. Christian organised a big press conference for the following weekend, to present the discovery of HMS Victoria to the world's media. I would be in Thailand by then. I checked my e-mail the next day and saw a group of customers from Russia would like me to join them in Dahab, Egypt, two days after the press conference. I arrived in Bangkok at 9pm and booked a ticket back to Beirut leaving at 7.30am the next morning. Although a little tired, I attended the press conference with Christian, giving a presentation to newspaper, television and radio reporters from around the world, attended by senior officials from both the Lebanese and English government, on how we discovered Victoria's Secret.

Teaching diving courses for a living is not a job that allows regular hours of employment. If the sun is shining, then Hay must be made. From Beirut I had to fly to Cairo the next day, and then travel by car across the desert to Dahab. I then took the group of Russian customer's crazy deep diving everyday for the next nine days, as deep as 145 metres with some of them. I had been at-it almost every day for a month, amazingly

I did not get the bends, but now I was exhausted. When this trip ended I stayed in my hotel room for two days to recover, but was out 'fun' diving soon after, to avoid drying-out completely.

All the travelling and diving sounds like fun, and it is - but after so many years of teaching scuba and moving from one place to the next, it's easy to get a little jaded and pessimistic with people and places. Perhaps you noticed during some of the chapters of this book, a caustic tone here or a sarcastic comment there, reflected by my mood at the time. Stuck in a hotel room somewhere, typing away, as my luggage had been stolen yet again or I had just been ripped of by another smiling government official.

Now the book is finished, I definitely feel a huge relief and am ready to get on with the next 'underwater adventure', whatever ocean it lies in. Life as a scuba instructor does have its ups and downs, but on the whole it's been so much more than just a 'pleasant waste of time' - as someone famous once said, no doubt after just a few minutes spent beneath the waves.

DIVE SAFE...X

****

Glossary of Terms and Slang

Caution: Sensitivity Warning – May Contain Sarcasm

A.

Air is what we breathe every day - it roughly comprises of 21% Oxygen and 79% Nitrogen. Air is the most commonly used divers' breathing mixture. It can be breathed as deep as 66 metres by the most experienced dare-devil users, or 30 metres and shallower for the average diver.

Algorithm is a term to cover a complex maths routine and rules system used in dive computers or software to calculate decompression stops. Algorithms can be less or more safe, depending on level of notoriety the designer seeks. Algorithms have traditionally been designed and validated around strict (expensive) testing protocols. However, more recent decompression software titles, especially bubble-model based versions, strangely use a 'trial and error' approach to decompression modelling, typically on the customer base. Historically, bubble models have evolved from being 'far too aggressive' (meaning: users get the bends), to 'okay' (meaning: that if used ultra conservatively they give tolerable results). Algorithms have been tested on users under the 'free-ware' software scheme for almost a decade. Modern algorithm designers prefer to turn a blind eye to competitors work lest the spotlight falls on them as well. The expressions 'Caveat Emptor' or 'Downloader Beware' take on a special meaning in technical diving circles.

Ascent Speeds used during scuba diving need careful consideration. Ascending too fast can cause decompression sickness (the bends). Technical divers should ascend at 10 metres per minute ideally. Recreational divers sometimes ascend at 18 metres per minute, but modern thinking suggests that this is too fast.

Ascent Ceiling: The depth at which decompression stops are performed is called the 'ascent ceiling'. Ideally the 'stop-depth' should be somewhat deeper than the 'ascent ceiling'. These 'ceilings' are advised by computer software, diver worn wrist computers, or pre-printed decompression tables.

B.

Bends describes Decompression Sickness or Illness (DCS/DCI). When a diver comes to the surface too quickly or without adequate decompression stops, bubbles may form within the blood and tissues causing a multitude of injuries.

BIB's stands for Built In Breathing System. Used inside recompression chambers, the Aviator style masks deliver the oxygen therapy gas, but also, and just as importantly, remove the patients' expired breaths. If the expired breath was not removed the oxygen concentration inside the chamber would rise to possibly combustible levels

Buoyancy control is an elusive skill all divers seek, a sort of underwater Holy Grail. Divers who lack buoyancy control usually get decompression sickness sooner or later. The state of Buoyancy changes with depth and needs continual diver input and practice.

Buoyancy Jacket or BCD or BC or Stab jacket is a jacket worn to firmly fix the scuba tank(s) to a divers' back. They are capable of being inflated with air to effectively make the diver feel weightless.

Bubble Model is a newer type of diving algorithm used by technical divers who frequent the World Wide Web. Bubble Models have been tested on unwitting divers by internet propagation. The offending programs bypass the cost-prohibitive but ethical testing protocols set up by the UHMS. Bubble Models are the antithesis of more traditional Dissolved Gas Models.

C.

Cable is a nautical unit of measurement. A Cable equals one hundred and eighty metres or 200 yards.

Caisson's Disease is the original name for the Bends or decompression sickness. A Caisson is a pressurised working environment used to keep workers safe when building underwater bridge supports etc. At the turn of the century, little was known about the effects of working under pressure. Caisson and Mine workers often developed decompression sickness after work, any symptoms would be dealt with by consuming large quantities of alcohol.

Cool is a state reached when people are envious of the appearance of your diving equipment. Divers who use rebreathers, or lack adequate safety equipment, are sometimes described as cool - until they are hurt or killed, then they are called idiots.

Counter-Diffusion affects extreme deep divers. Some breathing mixtures are incompatible with certain extreme decompression obligations and subsequently cause terrible injuries. Symptoms include nausea, vomiting and vertigo if occurring in deep water and lead to drowning. Pain in muscles or bones can occur in shallow water. Gas switches are the normal trigger of such injuries when combined with insufficient decompression and/or rapid ascents. Injuries often occur when ascent ceilings are violated by a jump in the relative equivalent narcosis depth, i.e. switching from helium to nitrox will make the diver feel theoretically deeper. The vestibular canals are a very fast tissue and are often damaged by switching from helium based breathing mixtures to those containing insufficient or no-helium mixes, for example Nitrox. Prudent deep divers will maintain nitrogen values in all breathing mixtures during deep and/or lengthy technical dives. Minor decompression dives don't trigger symptoms unless rapid ascents etc are present.

Cylinders or Bottles or Tanks are large metal containers filled with divers breathing mixtures to very high pressure. They come in various sizes with internal capacities from 3 litres to 20 litres. For deeper dives they are interconnected with a manifold.

D.

Decompression describes an act to help remove excess gases from the blood. As a diver breathes any gas underwater it becomes absorbed, much like the Fizzy bubbles in Pepsi. When a diver comes back to the surface, he must go either slowly upwards or actually stop (at a decompression ceiling) to let the blood circulation scoop up any excess gas so it can leave the body. If these excess gases are not removed then the Bends can occur.

Decompression or **Deco** stops are performed by stopping and waiting underwater at prearranged depths and times. They are not necessary if recreational diving. If mandatory deco stops are not performed then decompression sickness will occur. The depth at which decompression stops are performed is called the 'ascent ceiling'.

DecoChek is a software resource designed to reveal anomalies in decompression plans. Decochek is the first program to identify potential counter diffusing gas concerns. A very useful tool for all technical divers. Available at www.Decochek.com

Denial is a term used to describe a diver's *head stuck in sand* mindset, typically experienced after a fellow deep/cave/rebreather diver dies. Internet chat rooms can be similar to swimming in Egyptian rivers, in that it is possible to actually wade in *de nile* while viewing typical messages such as; "He did nothing wrong" or "He always did everything by the book". Only men experience denial, a woman has strangely never been killed on a rebreather unit to date

Deep Air is a style of diving where the diver intentionally dives deeper than 50 metres breathing regular air. With practice and luck it is possible to exceed 100 metres, but typically carries the same odds and outcome as Russian roulette. The deepest depth attained by a scuba diver descending alone, and returning unaided, while breathing normal air was 147 metres. A Deeper attempt led to unconsciousness and rescue. Trimix is better suited to dives deeper than 50 metres.

Deep Stops are decompression stops done below the mandatory ascent ceiling. Traditional ascent ceilings stop the diver from getting obvious bends symptoms in slow tissues. Deep stops better protect faster tissues. An older generation of deep divers ascended from deep water very rapidly (18-60 mpm) and noticed that by adding deep water pauses they felt *better* after surfacing. A fixed ascent rate of 10 metres per minute largely negates the need for deep stops. Most modern decompression software packages incorporate deep stops.

DIR means Doing It Right. Initially a mindset that strove for common sense equipment choices and procedures used in cave diving. Now DIR is simply a slogan for a Florida based technical training agency that also sells its own "Gotta-Have-It" equipment. DIR has become synonymous with cyber-pie fighting on the internet.

Dive computer is a wrist worn device that measures depth and time while underwater. It calculates decompression obligations using an algorithm and rules system

Dissolved Gas Model is an algorithm traditionally tested and empirically improved during the last century. An example of such a model is the Prof. Buelhman variant used extensively in personal dive computers

Drysuit is a divers' suit designed to keep the diver completely dry. It has rubber seals at the neck and wrists to keep the water out. Depending on the water temperature, the drysuit can be manufactured from thicker material. The thinnest drysuits offer no insulation themselves, so use a thick/warm undersuit. Thicker, winter drysuits may be dived without an undersuit. Because of the sealing nature of the drysuit, air must be added to 'equalise' the suit during the divers' descent as pressure increases. This 'equalised' added air must be vented carefully during the divers' ascent to avoid rapid or uncontrolled ascent speeds.

E.

Embolism is a pocket of air or gas in a body tissue that has erupted from the lungs in various fashions, all bad. Most easily caused by holding your breath whilst ascending. The most serious flavour of embolism is AGE, or arterial gas embolism, where the gas travels through the bloodstream from burst lungs to the brain, usually fatally. Divers must never hold their breath (when underwater…obviously)

Enriched Air is a term for a breathing mixture that has been modified by adding extra oxygen. Enriched Air is sometimes called Nitrox. The extra oxygen can help minimise decompression obligations. Adding oxygen to breathing tanks can make the enriched mixtures extremely dangerous if used by untrained individuals.

F.

Fathom: A nautical term used to measure depth. One fathom is equal to two yards, or six feet (depending on shoe size)

Fast Tissue: For the purposes of decompression calculations, the body has been divided into theoretical tissue groups. The better the blood supply to the tissue the 'faster' the tissue. The slower the blood supply the 'slower' the tissue. The relative speed of a tissue dictates its speed of 'on (or) off gassing' when calculating decompression obligations. Blood itself, followed by the brain and organs are said to be the fastest tissues. Bone, Fatty tissue and Tendons/Ligaments are typified as slow tissues. Decompression calculations are an extremely complicated, inexact science. The calculations themselves use an algorithm and rules system.

Fins or Flippers are plastic or rubber flattened shoes that divers use to move effectively underwater.

G.

Goggles were historically used by swimmers and divers. Mask is the preferred term for a scuba diver's ocular apparatus. Without a mask a diver cannot see properly, and will likely have a miserable time and/or get the bends.

Gradient Factors: Most ascent ceilings are derived from *empirically* calculated maximum surfacing values, each being optimised for the theoretical tissues in use by the algorithm. These maximum values are called M-values, and traditionally tend to be a little liberal. A more conservative approach would be to use less liberal M-values during the ascent calculations. The Gradient Factor method allows users to set more conservative M-values for both the depth of the deepest stop and also the length of the overall decompression. It has been likened to allowing car drivers to vary the elasticity of their car's seat belts. Unfortunately for divers, accidents underwater are far less predictable than on public roads. Users of the Gradient Factor system should only use the most conservative settings lest they unwittingly become more data points in the big 'decompression algorithm conspiracy' game.

H.

Heliair describes a breathing mixture that has been produced by mixing Air and Helium. Heliair simply abbreviates the blending process, it still contains oxygen, nitrogen and helium, although often at less ideal concentrations than specific Trimix's.

HPNS is High Pressure Nervous Syndrome. HPNS gives such symptoms as tremors and un-coordination. It occurs unpredictably during deep dives below 150 metres when breathing high helium concentrations, and especially where rapid descent speeds are present. A stop or slowing of descent can avoid / minimise symptoms

I.

Idiots (or worse) A term used 'expert' divers to describe other divers who get hurt, usually irrespective of the reason. Most self confessed 'experts' have completed just 20 dives. As a rule of thumb it is advisable to divide the number of dives stated by any 'expert' or instructor by 3 to get a more realistic number, much like their sexual conquests. Unusually, technical divers can hurt themselves simply by following this weeks 'best practise'.

Isobaric Counter Diffusion: A process that affects extreme deep divers. Some breathing mixtures are incompatible with certain extreme decompression obligations and can cause terrible injuries. Symptoms include nausea, vomiting, vertigo and drowning if occurring in deep water, or pain in muscles or bones if occurring in shallow water. Gas switches are the normal trigger of such injuries when combined with insufficient decompression and/or rapid ascents. Deep water decompression stops are necessary to avoid fast tissue bends. The fast tissues are found in the organs and brain. The vestibular canals are a very fast tissue and are often damaged by switching from helium based breathing mixtures to those containing insufficient or no-helium mixes, for example Nitrox or Air. Minor decompression dives (< 80 metres) don't trigger serious symptoms unless rapid ascents etc are present.

Isolator Valve is a simple on and off valve that sometimes sits in the middle of the manifold which connects two tanks. If the valve is in the open position then two tanks become one. If the valve is closed then the tanks become independent again. Isolators can be used to minimise gas loss due to manifold malfunction.
K.

Karst: A geological term used to describe limestone terrain that is full of sinkholes and cave systems.

L.

Lady-boy: A gay man masquerading, usually convincingly, as a woman. Beware - there is a very sizeable Lady-boy population in Thailand. Usually resembling the footballer Kevin Keegan, yet clad in a flimsy stained dress. Lady-boy's or Chicks with Dicks, Cocks in Frocks typically have very feminine names such as Kate or Keith and have apparently 'surprised' many drunken suitors, with their unusual and un-ladylike appendage. If a Thai woman has no 'stretch marks' on her abdomen and is publicly drinking alcohol or talking to a western man, they should be considered to be men thus avoiding any between the sheets embarrassment. Worryingly large hands and feet, or small scars around the 'Adams-apple' area on over-friendly females are give-aways also.

M.

Manifold is a metal bar that connects two scuba tanks effectively making one large one. Some more complicated manifolds have an Isolator valve that can separate the tanks again if necessary.

Muppet: An inexperienced scuba diver, or one displaying bad buoyancy skills

N.

NAUI: A scuba diver training agency.

Nitrogen Narcosis is typically felt when a diver descends beyond 30metres depth breathing air. Nitrogen, and to a lesser extent oxygen, have properties that suppress the central nervous system in much the same way as anaesthesia or alcohol. Symptoms include cognitive, reasoning and memory deficiencies. Experience and repetition can minimise

effects to some extent. Adding Helium to breathing mixes can lessen the severity of some narcosis symptoms.

Nitrox is another term for Enriched Air, a popular breathing mixture for advanced divers, widely used to minimise decompression obligations.

No-Deco or recreational diving is simply staying within time and depth guidelines generally accepted as safe.

Noddy or Numpty: An inexperienced scuba diver, or one displaying bad buoyancy skills. Dive-sites can have good visibility underwater until 'The Noddy's kick it up'

O.

Ouch is often repeated by divers when they get a mild case of the bends.

Or Worse: the meaning of this will depend on the relative severity of the idiotic antics measured against the actual outcome.

Oxygen Toxicity is the serious negative aspect of using enriched air or Nitrox cavalierly. Breathing high oxygen concentrations at increased ambient pressure (particularly underwater) causes central nervous system disruption and lung damage if breathed outside of established limits.

P.

PADI: A scuba diving training agency.

PO2 or pressure of oxygen is the dose measurement of oxygen toxicity. The dose is calculated by multiplying the fraction of oxygen in the planned breathing mixture by the ambient pressure. For example: 50% oxygen used at 22 metres yields a pO_2 of $0.5 \times 3.1 = 1.6$ pO_2.

R.

Recompression Chamber is a medical facility used to treat cases of decompression sickness. The chamber is filled with pressurised air to simulate depth while occupants breathe pure oxygen to minimise their bends symptoms. Entrance requirements are divers displaying poor buoyancy control and an insurance policy necessary to pay for treatment sessions.

Recreational scuba diving is classified as diving within the no-decompression stop limits imposed by breathing air. Recreational divers are sometimes called Scooby Doers. Dives that include planned decompression stops, or those that utilise enriched air can be classified as mild technical or *tech-reational* diving. Tradition states that recreational divers don't dive below 40 metres.

Regulator or Reg's or Breathing Regulator is a term for the equipment that reduces/regulates the pressure of divers' breathing mixtures. They have a FIRST stage that attaches directly to the scuba tank and a SECOND stage that the diver breathes from. In between the two stages are rubber hoses that transport the breathing mixtures. Using an internal spring and balance mechanism, regulators very reliably supply gas at a comfortable rate. When a diver exhales, the bubbles simply float to the surface and are wasted.

Rebreather is a term for a device that supplies a breathing mixture much the same way as a scuba regulator, but instead of letting the exhaled bubbles vent into the water, hoses recycle the expired breaths. Chemicals inside the unit remove carbon dioxide and return this *scrubbed* mixture back to the diver. This recycling ability makes rebreathers very gas-efficient. Rebreathers were invented for clandestine military use because they do not send bubbles to the surface that could give a divers position away. Rebreathers have been extensively developed recently as expensive diver gadgets that look cool. They can be extremely complicated, the complacent are usually rewarded with death. Rebreathers have the reputation of being *Boxes of Death* due to the number of recreational divers tragically killed while juggling with them each year. Ironically, the waiting list for the more ruthless brand of units only increases with its notoriety.

RGBM is a type of algorithm used to calculate decompression obligations, it is typified as a bubble model.

S.

Safety Stops are similar to decompression stops but are not mandatory. Typically a safety stop means waiting at 5 metres depth for 3 minutes before continuing to the surface. Their purpose is to slow the fast ascents often done by recreational divers. Fast ascent speeds and also dehydration are leading causes for divers suffering the bends.

Scubee Do-er: An inexperienced scuba diver, or one displaying bad buoyancy skills.

Slow Tissue: For the purposes of decompression calculations, the body has been divided into theoretical tissue groups. The better the blood supply to the tissue the 'faster' the tissue. The slower the blood supply the 'slower' the tissue. The relative speed of a tissue dictates its speed of 'on (or) off gassing' used when calculating decompression obligations. Blood itself, followed by the brain and organs are said to be the fastest tissues. Bone, Fatty tissue and Tendons/Ligaments are typified as slow tissues. Decompression calculations are an extremely complicated, inexact science. The results of the calculations use not only an algorithm but also a rules system.

Solo or Jesus diving is going scuba diving without a dive buddy. It could be argued that Jesus is always watching, but this will not satisfy an insurance company if the deceased was not certified or equipped to dive alone. Ending a dive alone does not make the diver a solo diver. Diving in pairs or buddy teams is the preferred method for scuba divers.

SMB or Surface Marker Buoy is a device made up of a reel of line and a lift bag or similar brightly coloured surface signalling aid. The SMB is filled with air by the underwater diver and it is allowed to float to the surface. The attached line ensures that the diver remains in contact with the balloon at the surface. This arrangement allows people at the surface to see a diver's approximate position underwater.

Stroke is a term used by DIR divers for those who are not in the gang. A stroke is someone who pleases themselves in the non-biblical sense.

T.

Tanks or Cylinders or Bottles are large metal containers filled with divers breathing mixtures to very high pressure. They come in various sizes with internal capacities ranging from 3 litres to 20 litres. For deeper dives they are often interconnected with a manifold.

Technical or Tech diving means diving outside recreational limits in terms of depth or time, and/or using rebreather equipment. Tech divers typically carry out formal decompression stops, use breathing gases other than air, and (should) have extensive dive-plans. They generally know everything, or will at least have an opinion on it. Technical divers only wear black coloured equipment, in an attempt to reduce contrast and camouflage gross ineptitude when underwater.

Trimix is a breathing gas containing oxygen, nitrogen and helium. Limitations imposed by breathing oxygen and nitrogen can be minimised by adding specific quantities of helium. Helium unfortunately complicates decompressions and is usually expensive. Trimix is used to minimise nitrogen narcosis and oxygen toxicity, mainly during dives below 50 metres.

U.

UHMS or Underwater Hyperbaric Medical Society is an internationally staffed think-tank advising on general diving topics. The UHMS have instigated and (used to) promote, ethical testing protocols for new decompression algorithms (amongst other things...I'm sure)

V.

VPM is a type of algorithm used to calculate decompression obligations, typified as a bubble model.

W.

Wetsuit is a suit either covering the whole body or just the torso. Wetsuits are made of Neoprene, a rubber based product infused with nitrogen bubbles. The thicker the wet suit, generally, the better its insulating properties will be. Wetsuits should fit snugly, but should never be tight.

X.Y.Z.

ZZZZ...A continual noise made by Dive instructors/Burmese boat captains as they sleep in hammocks while supposedly working. Usually found sleeping with one eye open in case immigration officials board dive-vessels checking for work visas.